Beyond
the Last Oasis

BEYOND
THE LAST OASIS
A Solo Walk in the Western Sahara

Ted Edwards

JOHN MURRAY

LONDON

TO THOSE FREE SOULS
*to whom the quality of life
is of infinitely greater importance than its quantity,
and to those who will not allow the word 'impossible'
to inhabit their vocabularies,
this book is most respectfully dedicated.*

© Ted Edwards 1985

First published 1985
by John Murray (Publishers) Ltd, 50 Albemarle Street, London WIX 4BD

Typeset by Inforum Ltd, Portsmouth
Printed and bound in Great Britain by the Pitman Press, Bath

British Library CIP Data
Edwards, Ted
Beyond the last oasis : a solo walk in the Western Sahara.
1. Mauritania—Description and travel
2. Sahara—Description and travel   3. Mali
—Description and travel   I. Title
916.6'1045   DT554.27
ISBN 0-7195-4205-7

Contents

Illustrations

Taken by Alistair Macdonald: 9, 11, 12. Taken and copyright by
Alistair Macdonald: 5, 14, 15, 24. Taken and copyright by Errol J.
Heywood: 26

Foreword

The conversations recorded in this book have been translated as near as possible into English. For the most part I cannot recall the actual language or languages spoken; indeed I have always found a common language to be a barrier to understanding, attempting, as it so often does, to define the indefinable.

Since it is difficult to write Arabic place names using the Roman alphabet I have tried to use the French spellings to give some uniformity, though these themselves often vary. The continental Centigrade scale I have abrogated in favour of Fahrenheit.

As to the problems of linear measurement, all my navigation was done in *kilometres* since this was more convenient on French-made maps, and converted into *miles* for conceptual purposes. Distances are thus set down in the text. I have no understanding whatsoever of the strange measurement known as the *metre*, or of its derivatives. I have therefore used the good old British *yard*, the fine upstanding *foot*, and the homely *inch* whenever appropriate.

T.E.

Acknowledgements

To the countless numbers of friends, acquaintances and total strangers whose encouragement made possible both the expedition and this book I would like to extend my heart-felt gratitude.

Special thanks are due to Pauline Andreou for correcting my outlandish spellings, to Lynda Byrom for her excellent cartography, to Karrimor for the supply of equipment, and to Alistair Macdonald for taking the cover photograph, thinking of the title, permission to use some of his photographs, his practical assistance and for the confidence he showed in me both in and out of Africa which in no small way contributed to the project's success.

Finally to the Thesigers, the Moorhouses, the Cailliés and the Lawrences of this world, for in order that a midget may see his goal he must stand upon the shoulders of giants.

T.E.

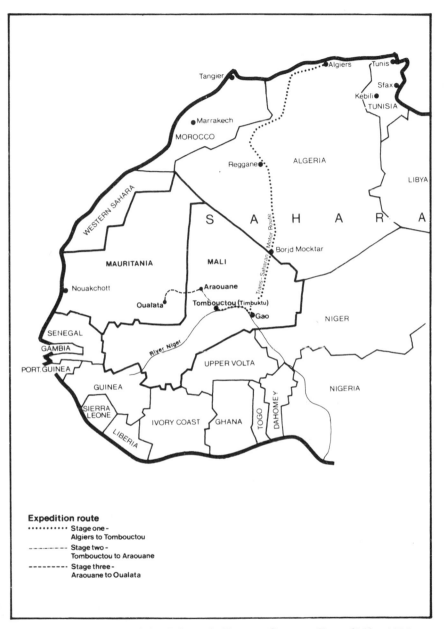

The three stages of the Edwards Empty Quarter Expedition 1983

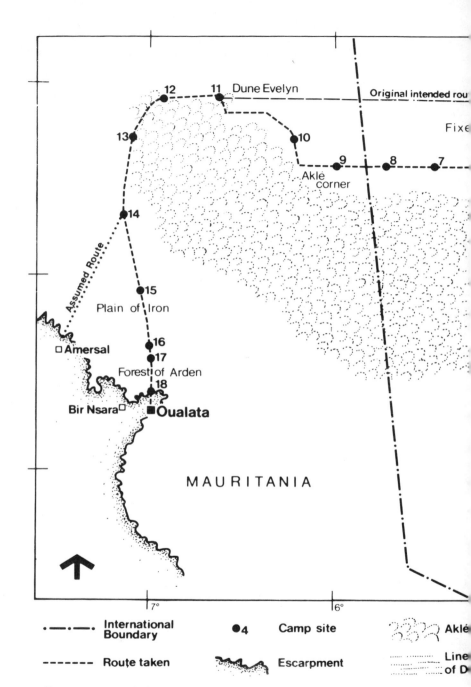

Stages two and three of the Expedition

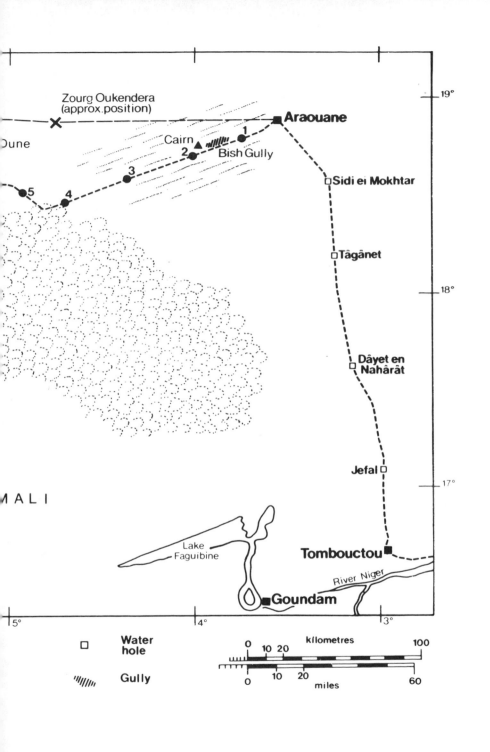

Zourg Oukendera
(approx.position)

Dune

Araouane

Cairn

Bish Gully

1

2

3

4

5

Sidi ei Mokhtar

Tâgânet

Dâyet en
Nahârât

Jefal

MALI

Lake
Faguibine

Tombouctou

River Niger

Goundam

19°

18°

17°

5°   4°   3°

☐   Water
     hole

⫽⫽⫽⫽   Gully

kilometres

0   10 20   100

0   10   20   60
        miles

Enjoy the smooth. Enjoy the rough.
The best is all that's good enough,
And quantity can over-stuff
The quality of life.

TED EDWARDS 1983

Part One

GENESIS

1   The Shaping

It was a cold March afternoon and my father lay his eighth year in his grave. From my pocket I took a small bag of sand and let it run through my fingers onto his covering of earth. Some was whipped away by the chilled wind, but most of the dry, yellow powder fell onto the wet Lancashire soil and took on some of its wetness.

The gesture was as old as mankind. I was sharing an important part of my life with the one who had given me life. The sand was from the Saharan Empty Quarter where, two weeks previously, I had battled for the preservation of that life. Memories came and built upon each other. Thoughts of a gentle man who smiled much; sadness that he could not share this thing more fully.

I walked down the path, along the wall of Hindley cemetery, and ran my eye over a section of pointing. It still looked new. Was it really almost thirty years since, as a young apprentice bricklayer, I'd clumsily filled in the gaps in the stonework whilst Ron Brown, with great dexterity of trowel, smoothed and cut and shaped the cement?

Near the cemetery gate was a familiar school yard, the school having been lately demolished. Its concrete slabs still seemed to echo the clattering of small, gleaming clogs. Further afield, unseen but sensed, were the slag heaps of ancient coal mine and iron works where innumerable Everests had been climbed, complete with base camp, sherpas and borrowed washing line. This was where my craving for adventure had had its birth, in the childhood imagination and the spirit of 'I DARE YOU!', for the fear of ridicule was far more fearsome than the fear of the act.

I was born just before Hitler's war, the only child of a truck-driver and a factory weaver who were soon to part. I was brought up in the ancestral terraced house, two up and one down, owned by the Co-op, with grandparents, an aunt, mother and a succession of cats. Life was far from luxurious but I lacked nothing, though, as is the way of children, I did not realise this. My early memories are peppered with air-raid sirens at the sound of which I was drilled to crouch in a cupboard, or, as I grew in stature, under the great, solid, kitchen table, proof against all that the Luftwaffe could throw against a defiant Castle Hill Road. Grandmother, meanwhile, would go down the yard for a bucket of coal, determined that the might of the Fatherland should not impinge upon her life one iota more than was absolutely essential.

At the age of four and a half I was taken to school to see the great sage known as *The Teacher*, who, I had been led to believe, was the repository of all knowledge. I was not impressed. She was the first adult I had ever met who did not know my name, or my address, or even who my mother was. If she lacked this basic information, what chance was there that she would open for me the great portals of wisdom? When I reported this to my mother she was, for some reason, amused. Ever after I would take the word of adults, and particularly educators, with varying quantities of salt.

At the school I discovered prayers, which were a way of talking to an old man called God, who was like Father Christmas in reverse. He it was who frowned upon any kind of fun, especially on Sundays. I hated Sundays.

The day of victory in Europe was a day of parties, and of a bonfire. We six-year-olds had never seen a bonfire and were thoroughly entranced as backyard gate after backyard gate was sacrificed to the occasion. Flags flew from clothes-props sticking out of bedroom windows. Now we all prepared to settle down to something called Peace, which seemed to me something of an anti-climax after a lifetime of war and hate.

Victory over Japan came and out stuck the clothes-props once more. Owing to a shortage of backyard gates several outside toilet doors were utilised, which caused considerable embarrassment. The celebrations were subdued. They lacked the spontaneity of the ending of the German war, and there was much talk amongst adults of a bomb.

Some days after VJ Day my mother took me to the Rex cinema. I have no recollection of the feature film, but the newsreel is indelibly printed upon my mind. The camera was in an aeroplane and far below was a harbour with several warships anchored in the still waters a couple of miles offshore. There was a great flash of light momentarily blotting out all vision. When it cleared the harbour was a mass of smoke. A shockwave was very slowly creeping out across the water towards the ships, a distinct line of death inexorably and quietly approaching the sailors on board. I knew that they were Japanese, but in that moment they became people. I willed those ships to turn away, to run from the death line, to live – to live!

The line, impersonally, crossed the ships and continued out to sea as a mushroom cloud rose above Hiroshima.

The newsreel ended and the lights came on. Where normally there would be the loud hum of conversation there were now whispers, as in a church. I will never forget those fearful whispers the day the Atomic Age came to Hindley. That day was to colour my relationship with all other races and cultures for the rest of my life. I went into that cinema a child of nationalism, but I came out a dedicated internationalist.

Shortly after this I received a present of Bible Stories in comic book form. This was the first time I had ever encountered camels, or deserts. Camels appeared to be incredibly noble beasts and I made up my mind that some day I would own a camel and travel the wilderness. This seemed to be an excellent way to spend my life for did I not enjoy building sand castles at Blackpool? The thought of all that sand sent me into raptures. I even announced that one day I would ride a camel up Castle Hill.

There was one other long-lasting effect of my picture Bible. I began to doubt. 'If Adam and Eve were the only people in the world and Cain and Abel were their sons and Cain married another woman then where did she come from?' I demanded to know. Predictably the adults lacked this knowledge.

My first recollection of actually challenging death was in about my eighth year. I was staying with an aunt in Blackpool and at bed-time I was shown a broken electrical socket in my room. If I touched those bare contacts, it was announced with gravity, I would instantly die.

Seconds after being left alone I was out of bed and staring with great interest at this death-dealing device. Here was a great dilemma. Adults were usually wrong, but not always. There was only one way to find out. Maybe if I just touched the metal quickly I would be all right. Excitement tingled as the adrenaline surged and my mouth dried. Slowly my fingers came closer to the yellow gleam, and then a quick jab. Instantly I was shocked, but I lay on the rug grinning. I was alive and the adults were wrong again.

About a year later I again met the Angel of Death, or Old Baldie as I came to know him, face to face. It was Sunday afternoon and and a number of others were 'wagging it' from Sunday school. Around Hindley were ancient pit shafts, some capped and others filled in. There were yet others which had a ten-foot wall around them topped by rusted barbed wire, a half-hearted attempt by the powers that be to keep out the local children. It didn't, of course, and periodically some child would fall to death.

We had all climbed these walls and peered into the bottomless green-bricked gloom, delighting in our fears. Ten feet down, on the inside of one, was a grass-speckled brick ledge that sloped for about three feet at a forty-five-degree angle before dropping down into the horrendous gate of Hell. We sat on its rusty wire and stared at this inaccessible area. Inevitably, 'I dare you' was shouted by one who dared not and I found myself carefully climbing down the crumbling brickwork towards the ledge, seemingly so far below.

After an age I set foot on the ledge, slimy with moss. I turned my back to the wall and there, a spit away, was the great gaping maw. My feet began to slide on the moss as the pit seemed to suck at me. I froze with fear. My muscles seized solid. My knuckles were white around clumps of grass growing from spaces between the bricks. The trembling of sheer terror began in my legs and spread through my body, and my hands ached with the power of it.

Time passed; how much time I do not know, but it passed. The crows on the wall began to caw and announce their intended departure if I didn't hurry up and climb out. Still my hands grasped the grass. I knew that I would have to release it in order to climb. I ordered my hands to let go, but they refused to obey. Again the order and again the refusal. Again the cawing from the wall. The thought occurred to me that I should send the crows for help – but who could trust crows? In any case I ought to be in Sunday school and I'd be in TROUBLE. No, I had got myself into this, and I would have to get myself out. The hand holds existed for had I not used them coming down?

This thought helped me to relax enough to release first one grass clump, then the other. I clasped solid brick. Slowly, very slowly, I turned my back on the pit and eased myself to a stand. The hand and foot holds were there, plain and beckoning. The crows were silent as their surrogate began to climb. I concentrated on each hold, testing it, and approving it before trusting it with my weight. Gradually I moved upwards. Some bricks crumbled under my sweaty fingers but I carried on upwards, each course of bricks moving down in turn.

Suddenly I was at the top and scrambling quickly down the outside, a grin splitting my face. I had done it! Old Baldie departed, minus gruntles.

Almost all my life seemed to be taken up by school at this time. My opinion that adults knew little inevitably showed itself in my school work. It was the cause of great consternation to all therefore when, at the end of the list of names of those having passed the eleven-plus exam, my headmaster orated '. . . and, strange though it may seem, Edwards!' I entered the portals of Hindley and Abram Grammar School. This was not a happy association, made somewhat unhappier by the constant application of the cane. My ideas and those of my tormentors differed at a basic level over what constituted education. Mathematics was to me an arcane subject, and why people insisted that I, in the company of others, should chase over a freezing field in order to get a ball between two poles, was beyond my ken.

It was at the age of thirteen or so that I met the first adult who, I felt, actually knew what he was talking about, and what was more, talked about things that interested me. Ron Brown was a scoutmaster and ex-commando who had fought the hordes of Nippon and, as a result, saw the futility of war. He was a hero. He knew about the woods, wild life, camping, tracking, climbing, survival, first-aid, hiking and living.

Life took on a new meaning. I threw myself body and soul into the Scout Movement. Every evening saw me at some scouty task. Weekends were for taking to the hills. My first rucksack was an old naval kitbag with mackintosh belts for straps. Each Friday I would turn up at school with this stuffed with blankets, hitch to Wales all night, climb all Saturday and Sunday, hitch back all night and sleep through every class on Monday. This was the cause of much worry to my maternal parent.

The school just gave up on me. I was allowed to draw cartoons in French classes, probably the only useful thing the place ever did for me since I later took it up professionally. The real business of life continued. With the expert guidance of Ron I became a Master of outdoor activities. I could tell the age, breed and time of passing of a dog from a single paw print. From scant evidence I would discern the menu and time of lunch of a tawny owl and leap over miles of mountain accurately plotting my course with map and compass.

Wild Snowdonia was my stamping ground. Crib Goch, Tryfan and the Lliwedds I came to know rock by rock. My heroes were climbers. Mallory and Irving were gods; 1953 was not for me the year of the coronation, but the year Tenzing climbed Everest. Always it was the little Sherpa who held my imagination, not Hunt or Hillary. He had spent his life dedicated to the task, and had finally conquered. And there were other, remoter heroes. I had not forgotten the far-away sand seas and names like Lawrence and Thesiger were familiar to me. But the deserts were as distant as other planets. Mountains there were aplenty on my island.

On one occasion when I was about fifteen I was walking towards Capel Curig. I had just descended Snowdon on top of which I had attempted to see in the New Year. The time would have been about five a.m. as I passed the shuttered Pen-y-Gwryd Hotel and the freezing sleet was being blown hard into my face. I was soaked to the skin, waterproof cagouls not having been invented. Fatigue was heavy on me and the soft, white snow looked so comfortable. I wanted to lie in it, just for a while, to rest. The feeling was very strong and I almost gave in but something kept telling me to keep going. So I kept going, ploughing numb limbs through the slush and bending into the wind. Miraculously I was picked up by a car and warmed to life. Years later, after the invention of hypothermia, I recognised my closeness to death on that occasion, but at the time I was just cold. Poor Old Baldie had missed me again.

Always on these trips I went alone. At an early age I had discovered that to wait for someone to hold my hand was to wait for ever.

Another lone trek was continuing throughout this period, the trek through the mazes of religion. I had long since discounted the opinion of the hosts of the Galilean that they were the sole custodians of Truth. My gaze had gone east to the smiling face of Buddha and to the Hindu pantheon. I was pleased to discover the concept of allegory and thus solved my earlier problem of Adam's daughter-in-law.

This was the Great Search. God was no longer the miserable Sunday-Man but a massive enigma. I was seeking and finding, and as I knocked doors began to open. I took great joy in it. I lost reverence for the things of dogma and transferred that reverence to Truth, wherever it should be found and no matter how unwelcome. It was a great step forward.

At sixteen the school and I bade each other a grateful farewell, I clutching a single O level in art. I embarked on a short-lived career as a bricklayer's apprentice, the firm boasting a boss who, trowel in hand, sang grand opera at various walls. The rest of the firm consisted of Ron Brown and myself. I was allowed to keep my first week's wages solely for my own use, so with hours of overtime I managed to amass the grand sum of four pounds. With this I purchased my first real rucksack and a pair of commando soled boots from the local Army and Navy Stores. Thus equipped I branched out to the mountains of Derbyshire, the Lake District and the Scottish Highlands.

Six months after I joined it the firm folded. There followed a succession of short-lived jobs during which time I burned a considerable quantity of midnight oil as a freelance cartoonist. I spent a year or so with the local Council as a general labourer when I worked with a number of old men crippled in the First World War on the fields of Flanders, and others, younger, who had fought Hitler's gang. To a man they hated war, its pointlessness, its hardships, the wounds, the losing of mates; all these things they hated. They would reiterate and reiterate the lack of glory on the field of battle.

But always they would speak of it. Always it was on their minds and it was obvious that they gloried in it.

Looking at their normal mundane existence I concluded that their war had been the only time in their lives when they had really lived, when their closeness to death had made the adrenaline flow, when the blotting out of life was imminent and each second had to be lived to the full.

Came the time when Her Majesty required me to be prepared to defend our sceptred isle. I applied for the Lancashire Fuseliers; I was made a Gunner in the Royal Artillery, told to report to Oswestry, and marched before an Officer Selection Board. The interview was very short.

'Ah, Edwards. What school did you gew tu?'

' 'indley and Abram Grammar School, Sir.'

'Ew. Whea's thet?'

'Wiggin, Sir.'

'Ew. Ay see. Well thenk yu, Edwards. You may gew.'

I was seconded to the Army Air Corps and sent to RAF Wildenrath, Germany, as a signaller for 12th Independent Flight. After almost a year of national service I signed on as a regular soldier for three years. In my spare time I travelled throughout Belgium, France, Germany and Holland.

In Holland, there is a town called Nijmegen where an annual event of enormous proportions takes place. Upwards of 16,000 masochists, military and civilian, from most parts of the globe, assemble in order to spend four days walking and getting incredibly drunk in each other's company. The military walk thirty-one miles per day and the civilians, who are usually fitter, walk thirty-five. The rewards are a great comradeship, a medal and an enormous feeling of achievement. I entered this event as a civilian, but anything which led to the glory of 12th Flight was fine by my Glorious Leader. I received time off for training and ate steak.

That walk was the hardest thing I had ever done. Thirty-five miles in a day on hard roads is pretty punishing. To have to get up for a further three days at four-thirty a.m., stiff as a board and hurting in places I'd forgotten about, borders on self-immolation. But I was as fit as a butcher's dog and on one day led the entire field for most of the way to be pipped at the post by a Dutchman who passed whilst I was drinking some free milk. The whole thing was such a magnificent event of international togetherness and friendly rivalry that I was to do it on seven consecutive occasions.

Nijmegen was where I learned about pain and the conquering of it. It was a crucible in which base metal was refined. I learned to ignore pain and to disassociate myself entirely from it. When one stopped, even for a few seconds, the pain upon beginning again was incredible. There were several tricks of the trade. One was to stamp one's feet with all one's might onto the hard road, blisters and all, shouting like a karate expert breaking a paving stone. Another was to run a short distance to unlock the leg muscles. These were designed to fill the brain with such a surge of pain that it couldn't handle it and gave up receiving the pain signals. It worked.

Another method, no less drastic, was to call in at every pub on the way. This had marvellous anaesthetic effects, but tended to slow the pace somewhat. As a result of using this method I and a German once staggered to the finishing post in darkness, the last to report in.

Back with my unit in Germany I learned various ways to kill my fellow man. As my three-year stint as a regular soldier wore on I became less content with my lot. There had been time to think and when it finally dawned upon me that basically I was not a signaller, but a hit-man for a government of which I wasn't entirely in favour, I began to look forward to my release.

At some stage in my military career I had been put in charge of the signals store and my final week at Wildenrath was spent in stock-taking so that I could sign the lot over to some other poor sod. There were thousands of pieces of equipment. Eventually all was accounted for save one item which rejoiced in the meaningless title of Min. Amp. Watt. Var. 10/237/B. No one had a clue what it was, what it looked like, or what it did. Two things I was sure of. The previous incumbent had managed to get me to sign for it, and I didn't have it.

This was drastic. The thing could be a large piece of equipment costing thousands. It could take all my demob pay and more to pay for it. Worse, it might even delay my demob. Then light dawned. If no one knew what it was, what it looked like or what it did, then it couldn't be recognised other than by its number. I took a small tin box, fitted it with a couple of old meters, some knobs and a pair of wires with crocodile clips. This I painted green and carefully, on its side, etched the designation 10/237/B.

I was promoted to the rank of Mister and left Wildenrath, my home for almost four years, not without some sadness. For the first time in my life I experienced real freedom. I was without responsibilities and subject to no orders. The world was mine for the taking and I took it. The nineteen-sixties were idyllic years for the free soul. Travel was unrestricted in a friendly Europe, and should one require a little money this was easily come by.

I saw Europe and poked my nose into Asia and Africa – Istanbul and Tangier, those magical mysterious cities, I came to know, in turn, as home. Greece I took to my heart and the Alps felt the tread of my boots.

I began to think of the Sahara, and of Timbuktu, that other magic name. There was a German, an ex French Foreign Legionaire, whom I met in Spain. We half-arranged to cross the Sahara from North to South on motorbikes: it hadn't been done. He backed out. It was ever so. A couple of years later someone else did it.

Sometimes I would return to England to work for a grub-stake. On one such occasion I worked in the kitchens of a hotel in Grasmere amid the English lakes. Days off were spent climbing. One day my mate Ringo and I were leaping around the Langdale Valley. I was leading a climb up a crag. Hand holds were sparse and the whole pitch, slightly overhung, seemed to be built upside down. There was nowhere to put a protective piton or chock and I found myself forty feet above the deck with the rope hanging free from my waist to the rocks below.

All the holds seemed to have petered out and I clung like a crab onto some very dubious anchors. My left foot had the tip of the toe jammed into a minute flake of rock. The right boot was as flat as I could get it on some discoloration of the stone. My left hand had a fingernail clawed into a crevice and my right hand was busy searching for somewhere to go. There was nowhere.

Hand and eye searched in vain for several minutes. My strength was beginning to ebb. There came a point when I realised that I was in trouble. I had little strength left in my left hand and my legs, at awkward angles, were beginning to stiffen. There was no way up and I didn't think I had the strength left to go down. Old Baldie was grinning at my back.

I froze, just as I had in the pit shaft those many years ago. My knees began to quiver as fear took over my body.

'I'm coming off, Ringo,' I shouted.

Then a curious thing happened. I knew that I was about to fall and die. The fear left me and was replaced by a great calm. Death was not an unwanted visitor, but a welcome friend. How long I experienced this I do not know.

I found myself in mid-air and slowly, impossibly slowly, falling past the rock. I was working on an entirely different time scale. Calmly I thought about my life. How had I done? There were things of pride and things of shame, but on the whole I seemed to have come through with the good side in credit. At the Last Judgement I had been acquitted.

The ground hit me incredibly hard in the middle of my back. I bounced and came to rest on my side. I was conscious! I was alive!

All the air had been knocked out of my lungs. Breathing would not come automatically. I instructed my lungs to expand and, reluctantly, they did. Air moaned down my windpipe and then out again. I had to fight for every breath against Old Baldie, who had overstayed his welcome. My whole body was seized solid from the shock of impact. Ringo jumped around with concern. I managed, after one agonising breath, to gasp out instructions to get help. He ran off to the Old Dungeon Ghyll pub. I knew that I was seriously damaged and gradually the initial numbness gave way to pain, but Old Baldie had gone.

The rescue bell clanged across the valley and eventually the team arrived, lifted me with hard but gentle hands onto the stretcher, and carried me to the waiting ambulance where they filled me with morphine.

At Lancaster Hospital an X-ray revealed a smashed vertebra and some broken ribs, but miraculously the spinal cord was undamaged. During or just after the examination I heard someone say, through my morphine euphoria, 'He won't walk again.' My torso was encased in a plaster shell and a week later I walked to the toilet under my own steam.

I was transferred to Kendal and, some weeks later, was

discharged complete with plaster and rucksack. Homeless and broke, I spent a whole day extracting one pound sterling out of Social Security, the first time I had ever asked for such help in my life. It was Catch 22. I had no address, therefore I could have no money. I had no money, therefore I could have no address. I had flown the nest and pride would not allow me to return to it.

Finally, after filling in numerous forms, I was reluctantly handed the pound note as if it were the crown jewels by a magistrate-type lady who obviously considered me to be the scum of the Earth. Fish and chips and a couple of greatly needed pints later I was broke again. I hitched to Grasmere and managed to land a job washing up, just for my keep.

For six months I was supposed to inhabit the world as a tortoise inside my body shell. After four months I decided that enough was enough. A power saw was acquired from the tool shed and plugged in. Ringo looked upon this with some trepidation, declared that he would have nothing to do with it, and departed. I forced a broom handle up my carapace to gain some clearance and started to cut from the crotch upwards. The room was filled with white dust as the saw bit through the plaster. When I had cut up to my chest I happened to catch my thumb on the blade. It bled profusely all over the cut in the plaster. At this point Ringo entered, concerned as to my welfare. A look of utter horror spread over his visage as he regarded the blood-splattered gash across my stomach. He yelled, which brought in a chambermaid, who promptly fainted.

It took about eight years for my back to sort itself out fully. I was to spend my life an inch shorter, not a terrible prospect since I had already spent much time standing on the ends of group photographs. By the time I was physically capable of climbing again the entire thing had become a sport, pursued by shipyard fitters with enough ironware to build the Titanic. One didn't go climbing any more; one did 'a few routes'. Gone was the raw challenge. It was now merely an exercise in technical expertise. I wanted no part of it, or the 'crag-rats'.

Since, owing to my injuries, I couldn't take to the hills my spare time took other directions. I discovered an ability to write songs and poems. These I would sing and recite in the public bar for the odd pint.

Later, when my back was somewhat improved, I managed to bluff my way through an NCB medical and became a coal miner. My home was a Ford Popular which was immobile and spent its days gradually rotting into the car park of Bickershaw Colliery, Leigh.

Early one morning, returning from a visit to my girlfriend in Liverpool, I arrived at the car park to find my home absent. To find one's home gone is somewhat annoying, especially at three o'clock on a cold wet morning. I finally ran it to earth up a back alley.

The following morning I ceased to be a collier amid a loud string of adjectives in the personnel office. I became a steel worker at Irlam near Manchester. This was a job not unlike working in Hell, with molten metal, slag and sulphur fumes everywhere. The job was Hell, but the money was reasonable, so I was able to obtain a small flat in Eccles.

I had continued my study of comparative religion during these years, much of it in libraries owing to my nomadic state. Now I had somewhere to store my own books so the study could really begin in earnest. I made many discoveries and a very important personal breakthrough, as a result of which I began to study the life of the Galilean from a new angle. This in turn led me to many years' work on a religio/philosophical novel based on the 'hidden' period of his life and entitled 'Parable'.

On the day before Passover 1969 I descended a gangway on the docks at Haifa and caught the bus to Jerusalem. It was my wish to experience this land of parable at first hand.

Entering the old city of Jerusalem was like passing through a time warp. Suddenly it was two thousand years ago. Bearded men in flowing robes led inconceivably overladen donkeys down narrow alleys. Water skins and spices were for sale. Whole camels, skinned and grinning horribly, hung from high on butchers' frontages. Everywhere was the fruit of Palestine, oranges, grapefruit, bananas and lemons. From a thousand mouths came the sounds of barter. This was the Arab city, taken by Israel in the Six-Day War two years previously, when another chapter of history was burned into this ancient capital.

Galilee in spring must be one of the most breathtaking places on Earth. Exotic flowers vie with each other to bloom. The Sea of Galilee changes colour a hundred times a day. Wild life abounds and the air is filled with the shouting of birds and the rasping of crickets, not to mention the croaking of frogs.

One reason I was in Israel was to experience a desert, alone, in order to gain some understanding of what time spent in the wilderness was really like, the better to write of it. The desert I had decided upon was the Judaean Desert, a strip of baked earth merely twenty miles or so wide between the Hebron road and the Dead Sea. There was an archaeological dig in En Gedi on the sea's western shore which I wished to visit, so I decided to cross to there from Hebron. Up until the Six-Day War this entire region, with the exception of En Gedi itself, had been part of Jordan and was still populated by Bedu hostile to the Israelis.

I was offered a firearm by a worried Israeli Army Major. I took advantage of practice with an Uzzi submachine-gun and a captured AK47 assault rifle, but decided not to take either, my reasoning being that if I entered their territory armed then the inhabitants had every right to assume me to be an enemy and take appropriate action. In any case, I had no quarrel with the Arabs. It wasn't my war. I would rely on the fabled hospitality of desert peoples, a large Union Jack sewn onto the flap of my rucksack, and an Arab *kafia*, the indigenous tablecloth head-dress held on by a black rope-ring, which kept the sun from my head and would, I hoped, prevent the most militant Bedu from taking potshots at me. I considered that when a potential antagonist was close enough to conclude that I wasn't Arab, then I could convince him that I wasn't Israeli either.

The Major was very concerned about my safety. It was impossible to cross the Judaean Desert alone and unarmed, he said. I looked at him closely. He was an adult!

So it was that one evening I left the outskirts of Hebron and set out east towards the Dead Sea. My only map was a tourist map which merely showed the position of my start and finishing points. I had with me a compass and a gallon of water.

As I entered my first desert I was somewhat worried about the things that Hollywood, books and the media had told me of deserts. There were quicksands and lethal snakes and scorpions.

Packs of wolves were not unknown, and there was a war on. An artillery duel was in progress many miles to the North, the crump of shells muffled by distance as the perpetual Semitic war continued to continue.

The ground was hilly with short scrub grass covering hard grey clay, cracked like the moon. There was no path so I simply headed cross country towards the distant salt lake, keeping a sharp eye open for anything moving in the greenery.

Night drops quickly in the desert. I had barely gone five miles when the short dusk became night. It was such a night as I had never seen before. Through the dry desert air the sky was a mass of light. The stars which I had known of old were multiplied a millionfold, each of a different colour and no two alike in magnitude. It seemed that I could tell this was a dim red star which was close by, in the cosmic sense, whilst that one was a brilliant sapphire blue remoter than remote. There was a gibbous moon, its craters visible even on the dark side. Obviously it was a near-by sphere. It could not possibly be imagined to be anything else. I understood how the Arabs had known so much about astronomy before the invention of the telescope. As I lay down to sleep beneath the jewel-bedecked Orion my small worries about scorpions seemed very unimportant compared to this vast storm of stars.

The morning was briefly cold, as is the way of deserts. I was stiff from the hard ground. My rucksack was quickly packed and I ate biscuits, washing them down with water. It was still hilly as I continued east, my back still giving me an occasional reminder of its ills. Twice I topped a rise to see the black tents of a Bedu camp beyond. I managed to duck down without being seen. It was not my wish to tempt fate any more than I already was doing.

Again I topped a rise and saw two black tents in the hollow beyond. A scrawny mongrel saw me and roused the camp with its yapping. It rushed at me in a frenzy and snapped at my heels. An Arab flew out of the nearest tent brandishing a large stick which he waved through the air as he charged towards me yelling what I assumed to be Arabic war cries. I was about to defend myself when he began to beat the unhappy hound.

'SMILE!' I told myself.

'*Salaam al laikum,*' said the Arab, obviously wary of the white stranger, but being ritually friendly as custom demanded, 'Peace be upon you.'

'*Al laikum el salaam* – And upon you be peace,' I replied.

We touched our foreheads, lips and breasts to signify that each would think no evil, speak no evil and harbour no evil in his heart for the other. Then we shook hands in the manner of the West.

He was dressed in the long white nightshirt-type garment of the Bedu over which was a grey worsted lounge suit jacket and on his head the perpetual *kafia*. Sandals completed the ensemble. He was a man of about forty, hardened by the desert, beardless but with a black, pencil moustache. Still he was wary, but he motioned me to his tent, spread out a mattress and proceeded to make tea. This had to be done before he could decently ask what I was about.

The ritual, age-old, continued automatically. First green tea, then water from a *guerba*, a goatskin, was poured into the small enamel teapot, which was then boiled over a charcoal fire. After a while its colour was tested by pouring it in a long stream from as high as possible unerringly into a small glass. When the shade was satisfactory a large lump of sugar was added to the pot and it was boiled once more. Finally it was again poured from a height into a glass, tested by the host, pronounced acceptable and dispensed to the assembled men in half-full glasses.

We had been joined by an older man with whom the greeting had to be repeated. Three times the tea was made and drunk with loud slurps at the demand of etiquette. Then we were free to speak.

We had no common language, I having just exhausted my entire Arabic vocabulary in the greeting. This is seldom a major problem, however, as I had discovered during my European journeys. I explained that I was English and pointed to the Union Jack on my rucksack.

They positively beamed.

'*Ingilis!*' they both shouted and, grasping my hand in turn, tried to shake it off. They invoked Allenby and El Orance (Lawrence) and it was as if I were a long-lost brother returned from the dead.

My host was Sheik Moustapha beni Hazim, as near as I could get it, and the other man his brother, or cousin, Absolem.

Moustapha had two wives, two children and some daughters.

At his insistence I stayed for several days and there became a bond between us. He showed me his desert, of which he was immensely proud. Here lived the tortoises, and here the jereboa. Amid his sparse cornfield, for nomads have time to plant and reap, he revealed a bird's nest with three young. Often on our walks he would simply stand atop a hill and gaze out at the vista, taking it all in with a sweep of his arms. No amount of poetry could better convey what he meant.

One day a friend of Moustapha lent us two camels. I was amazed at the size of these beasts, and the power of their spindly legs. The stench from both ends was phenomenal.

Moustapha made gurgling sounds and the camels folded themselves up onto the ground. The Arabian camel is the one-humped dromedary and these Bedu used no saddle; they simply tied a blanket around the hump and sat on it over the withers, crossing the legs over the left shoulder of the animal.

I removed my boots, for a camel will not accept footwear upon its neck, and holding the single head rope, gingerly put my foot on the back of its neck and swung myself aboard. Immediately the camel gave a roar, reared onto its knees, then raised its backside yards into the air. I came to rest some distance in front of it, much to the amusement of Moustapha and the camel's owner, and doubtless the camel. I programmed myself to expect this movement and the second time managed to stay aloft, with much flailing of limbs. The motion of a walking camel is quite pleasant, once one gets used to letting one's body move to and fro with the camel and keeping one's head steady.

We rode for perhaps an hour along deep wadis, the steep clay sides eroded by the rains, then sadly I had to dismount owing to pain in my back. The camel's walking gait is about two and a half mph, slightly slower than my normal walking pace, so that the trip back was taken at a stroll. There was no hurry and a pleasant cool breeze blew the little tufts of grass, making them quiver at us as we passed. The desert was awakening to spring and poppies spotted the hillsides redly.

The camels' owner gave us tea, boiled eggs and sheets of unleavened bread, the staple diet of this part of the Arab world. He had a broken transistor radio which I managed to fix for him and when we left he was gleefully listening to the propaganda of Radio Damascus. All propaganda has the sound of a machine-gun, no matter what language is being spoken. It was a sound that would destroy his way of life, did he but know it, subjugating a free man to the will of others.

Each night Moustapha would unroll two mattresses in the guest half of the tent and sleep on the one nearest to the entrance, an ancient sword drawn at his side. This was more than a token gesture. I had heard many tales of guests being bloodily defended against all comers, even members of the host's own tribe.

In the mornings, after breakfast had been prepared, one of his wives would whisper from the other side of the dividing screen, 'Moustapha . . . Moustapha . . . Moustapha . . . Moustapha . . .', until he stirred and raised himself. Then he would pray to Allah, giving thanks for all that he had, and all that he was. He would pray for each of us in turn, we standing in line behind him as he prostrated himself towards Mecca in total submission to his God.

There was a young goat of that year's early brood that had its front legs deformed. Moustapha took it upon himself to feed it from a bottle since it could not reach its mother's udder. Sadly he would state, 'It is the will of Allah.'

All was the will of Allah; all the good and all the bad in the world. Golda Meir, Yasser Arafat, the genes of the kid's mother and this stranger from another world were all merely instruments of that will. The only hope for a future which one could mould for one's self seemed to lie in a glorious death in Jihad, the Holy War. To imagine this gentle man at war was impossible, yet somehow, from his submission came a magnificently powerful beauty, per-haps because of its absolute, honest totality.

En Gedi and the Dead Sea were waiting, so one morning, reluctantly, I said goodbye to Moustapha. We embraced and he told me, his hands on my shoulders, that he now had three sons. It was a moving occasion. I put on my rucksack and turned my face once more East. As I breasted a rise Moustapha was waving with both hands. I never saw that good man again.

It was about an hour later that, walking across a rocky plain, I heard the unmistakable sound of a light aircraft engine. I knew the sound well after four years in the Army Air Corps. Looking around the clear blue sky I saw nothing. It was close from the sound of it. Then the sound changed and I knew it was in a dive. It came out of the brilliant sun and did a sideslip to my right at about two hundred feet. There was a glimpse of a Star of David on its fuselage, then, superimposed on the engine's screaming, was the distinctive fast rattle of an Uzzi submachine-gun. The rear observer was leaning from the back seat and firing at me. Stones and clay jumped around me and the plane was gone.

I stood dumbfounded as the pilot leaned the aircraft over for another sweep. There was no shelter and he was coming again. I thought impossible thoughts of throwing rocks. He came around low over the clay hills to the North. Then I remembered the Union Jack on my rucksack. I whipped the sack off and held it up towards the plane, ripping off my *kafia* and throwing it away.

He came on from my left just a few feet above the ground. I think it was a Piper Cub. I could see the rear observer leaning out with the Uzzi pointed at me. It occurred to me that I had done the same job, but I felt no affinity with this man who held a gun. I waited. I could do nothing but wait. The plane passed within twenty feet of me as I stood on the rocky plain like a matador, my eyes on the eyes of my assailant. He did not fire.

The plane gained height and banked steeply to its left to come around again. I put down my rucksack so that he could see my flag and waved in as friendly a fashion as I could muster. Past he came again. There was no Uzzi in the rear observer's hands. He waved back. The plane was gone, its sound gradually blending with the sigh of the desert wind. Old Baldie had to go back alone again.

For some minutes I stood watching the aircraft recede into the distance. I realised that my mouth was dry and bent to my rucksack for my water container. As I undid the strap my hands began to tremble. Shock was setting in. But at the time of the incident there had been no fear, just the simple operation of the preservation of life. Had I possessed a firearm I knew that I would have used it to try to take the lives of pilot and observer; not for reasons of hatred, or ideology, for this was not my conflict, but simply to stop them killing me. I wondered how many men had died in battle for similar reasons.

After a time the shaking stopped and my heart resumed its

normal pace. I continued East. An hour or so later the ground
simply dropped away and before me was a great canyon over a
thousand feet deep stretching to the shores of the misty green
sea five miles distant. Beyond were the dim grey hills of Jordan. It
was breathtaking.

Somehow I had to get down into this canyon. I walked South
and found a narrow track averaging eighteen inches wide which
descended into the depths, on my left a sheer wall of rock, on my
right a drop into space. Years before, as a cartoonist, I had drawn
many like it, but never expected to see one.

Down I went into the canyon, hugging the wall at first, but
gradually gaining confidence and bounding along happily. This
happiness was somewhat curtailed when a raven, anxious for
my demise, followed me down, gliding silently a few feet away.

Eventually I hit the canyon floor. A small stream trickled
towards the Dead Sea, which I followed until I was stopped by a
wall of green bamboo-like plants about ten feet tall. Drawing my
knife I hacked and squirmed my way through for a while and,
breaking through, was presented with the second breathtaking
view of the day. I was in a natural garden with rock pools and
exotic flowers and shrubs around the pools' edges. Bees and
brilliant dragonflies flitted here and there. Multi-coloured birds
eyed me with more curiosity than fear, and sang songs to me. I
stood and drank it in. For some reason I glanced at my watch. It
was not yet ten a.m.

It seemed to me that I had earned this view of Shangri-la and I
was pleased that one had to 'attain' it. The pools looked inviting
so I stripped off my dusty clothes, washed them and spread
them around to dry. I lay naked in a pool's coolness and simply
enjoyed being there.

Then from downstream came an Israeli soldier leading a party
of garishly clad and camera-bedecked Americans.

'Gee whiz Elmer, this is real nice. Wait'll I tell the folks back
home.'

'C'mon Eleanor, you're holding up the party.'

'Well God-dammit, would you look at that.'

'Oh shee-it, that water's cold!'

Somehow some of the beauty of the day seemed to trickle away
down the stream.

The time came when I returned home, though my beloved Greece held me for some months. I had only meant to go there for a day or so in order to avoid Bulgaria, but Greece is like that.

I resumed my labours at the steel works and much of the rest of my time was spent writing 'Parable' in another Eccles flat. Two years later it was ready, but there were no takers.

Meanwhile my song-writing had gained some popularity and I had begun to perform in folk clubs throughout the North-West. In 1974 the steel works closed and I decided to take up folk-singing professionally. Moderate success was my reward, but those were good days, travelling the country in an old Post Office van and dossing on strange floors.

A jobbing folk-singer has much time on his hands. My thoughts went in the direction of education and I enrolled as a student teacher at Didsbury College of Education to study art. There I discovered drama, loved it, and became, four years later, a qualified teacher in it.

In 1979, possessing a good honours degree, I went in search of employment. There were thirteen thousand teachers on the dole. Owing to my studies I had let my singing slip so that it was imperative I obtained employment forthwith. My bank manager agreed. The rest of the world did not! I lacked experience in my chosen profession and was too soft-handed and over-qualified for a return to manual work, even if there was any, which there wasn't.

The future looked bleak.

2   The Idea

I encountered a book entitled *The Fearful Void* by Geoffrey Moorhouse. This excellent work is Mr Moorhouse's account of a remarkable journey he undertook by camel from the west coast of Africa across the Sahara heading for the Nile in the east. This first attempt at crossing the Sahara from west to east was unfortunately unsuccessful, but must be one of the most magnificent failures of history.

I was inspired by this book and all my old desert ambitions came once more to the fore. There was one section of the book that really excited me. Moorhouse was speaking with Theodore Monod, the Grand Old Frenchman of Saharan exploration. Monod pointed out the towns of Oualata in Mauritania and Araouane in Mali and suggested that he include them in his route, if he really wanted adventure, as the country between was unexplored.

I read the words several times, found the two towns on the map, and sat back dumbfounded. In 1972 there had been a part of the Sahara Desert that was still unexplored. It was amazing. I had assumed that all of Africa was now well traversed and charted, but here was solid gold. Here was a bit that was left, for Moorhouse had declined the challenge and I had heard of no-one having picked up the gauntlet.

It was the chance of a lifetime, actually to tread where man had never before trodden, not just white men, but any man, for there was one well only between the two towns, Zourg Oukendera, the position of which was uncertain but was about seventy miles west of Araouane. The Arabs would have no reason to continue from there to Oualata since to do so would probably mean losing camels which are much more valuable than anything they could carry. A far more commercial route was available via Timbuktu which, though longer, had water throughout at regular intervals. I expected a hundred miles or so around the towns to have been explored, but the remaining hundred miles in the middle was, it seemed, untrodden. My head reeled at the thought.

Eagerly I snatched up the gauntlet and held it tightly. I did not know how I would set about this journey. I was out of work with an overdraft and had very limited desert experience; the problems seemed enormous. But I had accepted the challenge and was determined to see it through. Many years previously I had come to the conclusion that if one wanted something enough, then one would get it. Both consciously and subconsciously one would work towards the goal until it was achieved. If one did not achieve it, then the wanting had not been enough. I knew that I wanted this thing though.

For months, since leaving college, I had been becoming more and more despondent as application after application was rejected. It seemed that my society considered me to be utterly useless and had stuck me on a shelf labelled NOT REQUIRED. Now my life had a purpose. I was ecstatic! I mentioned my thoughts to no-one, for the whole thing was so enormous that I knew I would have to live amongst ridicule. Quietly and in secret I began my research.

The area in question was about two thousand five hundred miles south of Manchester, in the South-Western Sahara. To reach it I would somehow have to cross Europe and the Mediterranean Sea to North Africa, then cross the Sahara Desert, the biggest desert in the world, to the River Niger. Then I needed to go up the Niger until I arrived at Timbuktu. Araouane lay one hundred and fifty miles to the north of Timbuktu and Oualata was three hundred miles in a westerly direction.

How was I going to cross this three hundred miles of unexplored wilderness? A Land Rover was rejected both for reasons of cost and the strong possibility of mechanical failure over such an expanse of rough country. Camels seemed ideal, but I would need at least two and the going price was about £300 a time. I tried to imagine the reaction of the long-suffering guardian of my overdraft if I asked for a bank loan in order to buy two camels in Timbuktu.

The only other way was to walk. Three hundred miles of walking did not dismay me as I had recently done the Pennine Way over a similar distance in twelve and a half days. The problem was that I would require upwards of six pints of water per day, and there was no known water for the entire distance. I had to assume that the well at Zourg Oukendera was dry.

I pondered this problem long and hard, but no solution appeared for some time. Meanwhile I was reading everything I could lay my hands on concerning deserts in general and the Timbuktu area in particular. There wasn't much.

The history of the search for Timbuktu in the early nineteenth century made exciting reading. The whole area had been known as the white man's grave and few came out alive, being ravaged by disease and marauding tribesmen. Timbuktu had been known to Europe since the fourteenth century as a fabulous city whose roofs were made of gold. It was a centre of great learning and of commerce, so the Arabs said. The gold, slave and spice trades of West Africa were conducted here and it was the object of many expeditions from Europe to locate it and set up trading relations.

The Scottish Doctor Mungo Park passed it during his search for the mouth of the Niger in 1805, from which neither he nor a single one of his forty-four European companions returned. In 1825 Major Alexander Gordon-Laing suffered incredible hardship crossing the Sahara from North Africa, to have his party massacred and himself severely wounded almost unto death by twenty-four sword cuts. He managed, despite his condition, to arrive in Timbuktu where he was allowed time to recover to some degree. However, when he left on his way to Araouane he was treacherously murdered by his escort and decapitated.

But the one who fired my imagination above all was a little Frenchman, the orphaned son of a baker who died in prison, his mother dying shortly after, when he was seven. René Caillié, at the age of sixteen, boarded a boat for Senegal in 1816 with the sole object of locating Timbuktu. He taught himself Arabic and, years later, dressed as an Arab with a story about having been sold into slavery as a child and wishing to return to his native Egypt, joined caravans going inland. He arrived in Timbuktu after severe hardships and illnesses, and eventually returned to France after crossing the Sahara from the south to the north with a slave caravan. His experiences weakened him so much that he never enjoyed good health again and in 1838 he died aged thirty-eight, but he had achieved his ambition; he had wanted it enough.

I needed maps of the area. After a great deal of searching I finally managed two maps of a scale of 1:1,000,000 or one centimetre to one kilometre. These were made by the Institut Géographique National in Paris. Larger-scale maps would possibly be available at their Paris shop, but these were the best I could get in Britain. They had been drawn from aerial photographs and were not very informative, simply showing the extent of aklé dunes, the big crescent dunes beloved of Hollywood. To see this great expanse of nothing was a worrying experience, even on paper. I wrote in my dairy:

'I received my maps today. For the first time I was afraid.'

During my reading I often encountered something called a 'solar still'. This was invented by Barnes Wallace for the use of fliers crashed in the desert, its purpose being to extract water from the sand. One dug a hole in the sand about two or three feet deep, placed a receptacle in the bottom, covered the hole with a plastic sheet weighted down at the edges and placed a stone or a handful of sand in the centre of the plastic.

The principle was simple. The sun would heat up the air beneath the plastic, which would evaporate any moisture in the sand. This would then condense out on the plastic and run down into the receptacle. Estimates of yield varied considerably from a quarter of a pint to over a pint in twenty-four hours. An ex 'V' bomber pilot friend had obtained a quarter of a pint by this method in North Africa. This, then, was my key to unlock the desert. If I took sufficient plastic and cups to obtain from six to eight pints of water per day then I could, in theory, cross any expanse of waterless desert.

I didn't know when the best time for collecting would be. Opinions of self-appointed experts varied. Some said day and others said night. It seemed to me that if I started walking around midnight and continued until mid-day then I could set up my stills having sufficient time left in the day to heat up the air and soil, and when the temperature dropped at night, advantage could be taken of the cooler plastic which would assist in the condensation process.

But all this was theory. The only way to ascertain the facts was to experiment near Timbuktu. Nowhere else would do as

conditions could not be the same. I made a bargain with myself;
a solemn pact. I would go to Timbuktu and try out the stills. If,
after experiments, the journey seemed feasible, then I would
continue. If experiments showed that it was not feasible then I
would simply turn round and come home. If I carried a reservoir
of two gallons of water, in two one-gallon containers, side by side
to cut down on the sloshing about, then put out sixteen stills, this
should yield sufficient to keep me going indefinitely if the one
pint in twenty-four hours theory was correct. I ordered my
plastic and obtained a quantity of small dispensable plastic
bowls which weighed nothing.

The average monthly temperature in Timbuktu for December
and January was 56°F at night rising to 90°F during the day. This
rapidly rose in March to 72°F at night and a daytime temperature
averaging 106°F. Clearly I needed to be in Timbuktu before
Christmas if at all possible.

Navigation was another problem. All my previous navigation
had been by map and compass, simply walking on a bearing and
estimating the distance walked. In Britain and Europe there was
never any problem with this method as, even if massive error
occurred, within a very few miles one would encounter a recognisable feature, or a road which would lead to habitation. In the
desert this would not be so. The desert is indeed a sea of sand and
according to my map the only features recognisable throughout
the three hundred miles were the two-hundred-mile escarpment
on which stood Oualata and a line representing the start of aklé
dunes. I had never seen aklé so I didn't know if it was a distinct
line, as portrayed by the map, or a gradual change.

The problem with map and compass, or 'dead reckoning' as it
is known, is that there is always error, either in distance or
direction. Each time one sets off the error is therefore com-
pounded. I did not think that it was a sufficiently accurate
method to use over three hundred miles of virtually featureless
desert.

The only other practical method was astro-navigation, navigation by the stars, involving the use of a sextant and an un-
fathomable publication known as *Sight Reduction Tables for Marine
Navigation* Volume 2; *Latitudes 15° – 30°*. A normal marine sextant
was useless since it required a distinct horizon, something rarely

available in any kind of rough terrain. The instrument I required was a bubble sextant used formerly by RAF navigators, which incorporates an artificial horizon and was now in extremely short supply.

After much advertising and letter-writing I finally ran one to earth, and located instructions for its use in an ancient dusty tome by Sir Francis Chichester which was housed in Manchester's Central Reference Library. Since the book was for reference only it was necessary to take the sextant to the library in order to gain enlightenment. I duly gained knowledge of the use of the various knobs and dials amid curious sideways glances by the other seekers after truth.

Part of the instrument was a large clockwork device which, when wound up and triggered by a lever, would whirr and tick alarmingly. Its purpose was to average out a number of sightings. As I was leaving the building with the sextant in my rucksack the security officer, alerted by several bomb scares in the area, demanded to see the contents of my bag. His hands vanished into the depths and emerged clutching this strange, black, bedialled and beknobbed article. I had inadvertently left the averaging mechanism wound up and as he inspected the contraption he touched the trigger. The motor began to whirr and tick in his hands as a digital display spun around ominously. He went white, gripped the machine for a second more, then dropped it.

I caught it before it hit the ground and explained to the municipal guardian what it was and what it did. When I left the building he was just beginning to shake as shock took over.

Several parts of the instrument, including the clockwork mechanism, were of no use to me, so I removed them, thus reducing the weight from over six pounds to less than three.

Meanwhile I had been reading books about astro-navigation, trying to figure out what to do with the information the sextant gave me. Every book seemed to assume that I already knew. Not a single one managed to explain to me, a layman, in simple terms how to navigate using a sextant.

Around September disaster struck. It was my habit to wear Lancashire clogs, excellent footwear, hand crafted in natural materials, which keep the feet warm and dry in winter and, with the leather and brass nails gleaming, are a cause of pride. They

are also cheap and I could repair them myself for coppers.
When renewing a sole I would place the clog between my knees
and drive in the nails with a small hammer. This resulted in some
jarring of the knees but had never caused me hurt and was the
accepted method of generations. One day after accomplishing
this, I was seized by excruciating pain in my left knee, so that I
could hardly walk. The pain stayed with me for several days
before it settled into a sort of pattern. My knee would be fine until
I had walked for about a mile, then the pain would return with a
vengeance. This was not constant; I would go for perhaps a
week or so in a painless condition, then back it would come
again.

My doctor could not help so after much insistence I saw a
specialist in hospital, who couldn't help either. I placed painkillers high on my list of equipment.

It was coming close to Christmas and plans were far advanced,
but as yet I had no money, nor did prospects of obtaining any
seem good. Still I continued my preparations, having implicit
confidence that my desire to succeed would somehow bring forth
the wherewithal.

I corresponded with NASA and the Department of Industry
(Space Branch) about food, with various agencies about learning
Arabic (abortive), with the Malian and Moroccan Embassies in
Paris about visas, with the Algerian and Moroccan Embassies
about travel, with equipment manufacturers and the press about
sponsorship (refused in every case) and with a pedometer
manufacturer about a pedometer that was less than perfect. I
sent for anti-snake venom serum, ordered spare spectacles and
bought a nautical emergency rations pack. For money I sold
some possessions and went without food. Because I had been
long a student my wardrobe was ragged and my tailor's name
was OXFAM.

By now the project had leaked out and my sanity was debated
at length by friends and acquaintances. Many put it down to
what was becoming a common complaint in the North-West,
Dole Blues. One elderly gentleman summed up the general
feeling succinctly: 'The man's nuts!'

People would ask the inevitable question, 'Why do you want
to do it?' These were mostly adults. The children understood.

There were two stock replies. To the less discerning I would launch into long tirades about how the economy of the country forced a man to risk his life in order to write a book and make a crust. They went away nodding with understanding. To the rest I would reiterate Louis Armstrong's reply when asked 'What is Jazz?': 'Man! If you's gotta ask, you'll never know!'

I struggled on with astro-navigation but made no headway whatsoever. The principles I understood perfectly, but since I hadn't acquired one iota of mathematical ability beyond long division throughout my years of schooling, I was at a loss. My one remembrance of the times tables, drummed into us with such tenacity, was the tune.

My knee continued to trouble me so I added more painkillers to my equipment list.

I received a letter from the *Sunday Times*, to whom I had applied for sponsorship, which contained the following words: 'I should also say, candidly, that as outlined your trek looks suicidal. And we would think very hard before encouraging someone to undertake such a venture. (Have you read Geoffrey Moorhouse's *The Fearful Void?*)' They also suggested that I approach the *Geographical Magazine* who, they said, sometimes sponsored projects like mine.

I did. They didn't.

Not all was discouragement, however. An engineer friend manufactured for me a small lightweight shovel which was ideal for digging the stills. Bob Millard, an expeditioner with Karakorum and Chitral experience, gave encouragement and useful advice.

My equipment was beginning to amass in a large cardboard box in my room. An ancient ex-army sleeping-bag which I had bought second-hand some twenty years previously, the zip of which had broken the first time out, was ritually washed in lukewarm water. I purchased a heavy duty space blanket which was to keep me warm and dry when wrapped around the sleeping-bag, and would also serve as a shelter from the mid-day sun which mad dogs and Englishmen were prone to encounter.

I had no tent, being long of the opinion that such an article has but three basic functions:

1. It enables wardens, farmers and such to know one's whereabouts so that they can charge exorbitant fees for the privilege of occupying their grass.
2. It makes tent-manufacturers rich.
3. It traps a small quantity of air and impregnates it with the smell of stale sweat and slightly off bacon.

Though I had learned that wood was generally available in the desert for cooking purposes I decided to take a solid fuel stove just in case I did find myself without. Also a plentiful supply of matches as foreign ones tend to be pretty useless. Plastic bags galore of all shapes and sizes I obtained. Into these went medical supplies, tea-bags, maps, writing materials, in fact anything with bulky packaging, requiring protection or in need of being kept together. Since I would probably be walking mostly at night I had opted for the normal Western dress of jeans and tee-shirt with stout hiking boots on my feet.

Most of my food would be freeze-dried meals which could be reconstituted by adding boiling water. I experimented with the various brands available in camping shops and ploughed my way through some pretty revolting messes. One in particular called itself 'Liver and Onions with Gravy'. The liver had the taste and consistency of an old fag packet, the onions were like a slimy mass of frogspawn and the gravy was reminiscent of the water that used to leak from the radiator of my late-lamented Post Office van.

I did, however, find a brand, 'Raven', that was excellent, and stocked up on these. A couple of tins of corned beef and salmon I included as a special treat. All the food I was taking with me was for the actual expedition, not for the trip down to Timbuktu. For this I would eat locally and hope that the malady known variously as Delhi Belly, Gyppie Tummy, Turkey Trots, Mali Marauder, Aztec Two-step and Franco's Revenge would remain at bay.

The trip down was a problem. Even if I managed to hitch through Europe I would still need a fair amount of cash for the Channel and Mediterranean crossings, both ways, for public transport through North Africa, and for my passage by truck, the normal way of travel, across the Sahara and along the Niger to Timbuktu. I would also need to eat for between two and three months.

At the end of January 1980, out of the blue, I was offered a temporary teaching post to fill in for a sick teacher during several weeks' absence. There was to be one week off in the middle for half-term, but this I would fill working as an extra for the film *Reds* with Warren Beatty (I'd answered a local ad). Also several singing engagements materialised including a broadcast for local radio. I would have the money.

Things now began to move quickly. Replies from various correspondents rolled in. It would be necessary to go to Paris for my Malian and Mauritanian visas. This suited me fine as I wished to visit the Institut Géographique National's shop there to see if I could obtain larger scale maps.

I booked a cheap bus ticket to Paris. It was a strange feeling having that ticket in my pocket, as if the whole thing had ceased to be a game and was now a reality.

The astro-navigation I gave up, being of the opinion that even if I cracked the code my knowledge of it would be superficial and liable to go haywire under stress. Dead reckoning was to be my method, with all its inherent faults. I needed a decent sighting compass for the greatest accuracy, and a wrist compass for constant reference. The best were made by Silva so I bought these. Navigation was absolutely crucial and only the best would do.

Gerard Morgan-Grenville, the author of a Saharan traveller's handbook, warned me of the presence of iron ore in the Southern Sahara. I took this warning seriously and resolved to make a large intentional error to the west as I approached the escarpment. This warning, and my subsequent action, were eventually to save my life.

There were periods of doubt as the time for departure drew near. The journey to Timbuktu was itself no mean feat. Then to mount the last major exploration of the Sahara, alone in a strange land, had indeed aspects of madness about it. I made sure that the trip was known of amongst all my friends so that to back down would mean an enormous loss of face. Sometimes, when in a doubting mood, I would drink too much. My friends noticed the tension building up. I must have been very difficult company during this period.

Whilst obtaining an international driving permit from the Automobile Association's office in Manchester I spotted a copy of Michelin's sheet 153, the best road map available for North-West Africa. This map was legendary and as scarce as hen's teeth; it had inexplicably been out of print for three years. I descended upon it like a ravenous vulture and left the office clutching it to my breast, cackling horribly.

I began to think about things like honour and being British, things I hadn't thought of since my scouting days. Always I had taken pride in my nationality, but Lancashire and the North were more important than the strange, voracious country of the South. Now the Union Jack seemed to hold within itself the essences of our many freedoms and the monarch herself seemed less remote.

About death I pondered a great deal. It seemed to me that as birth was a capital offence then the interim might as well be used to the full. Since the universe in all its physical aspects did not appear to be wasteful, never destroying but simply transmuting, then it seemed reasonable to assume that the knowledge acquired in life would, in some form or other, continue to exist. Whether this would be housed in a continued individuality or simply be absorbed into the great corporate universal oneness I knew not, neither did it seem important. If the former were the case it would be a pleasant surprise, but if the latter, then I simply wouldn't know about it. Either way I couldn't lose. It occurred to me that considering the vastness of the universe in both time and space, life was an extremely unnatural state.

I knew from my climbing accident that the transfer from life to death was not an unpleasant experience in itself, though there might be associated unpleasantnesses. There was a worry about dying slowly of thirst, should things go very wrong. It seemed that a quick death was preferable to this, so I resolved to dispatch myself swiftly using my sheath knife, inherited from my father and always referred to as 'my father's sword'. If all hope was gone, with a broken leg, pelvis or back, then I would simply insert it into the heart. We of the North are of Viking blood and must die with sword in hand.

I made a will, the occasion of some morbidity as I distributed goods and chattels to those who would best appreciate them. There was the constant feeling that this time I had bitten off more than I could chew.

There were various inoculations to have, making me proof against just about everything microbic. Anti-malaria tablets were a necessity before I reached a malarial area. Teeth had to be serviced. Once, in Asian Turkey, I had developed a maddening tooth-ache. Asking for a dentist I was taken before a grubby individual on the market who had a pair of electrician's pliers in the mouth of a terrified victim; his molar was extracted with much grunting, twisting and bleeding, and threaded onto a huge string of teeth around his neck. My tooth ceased to ache at that precise moment and has never ached since. He was undoubtedly the finest dentist I have ever encountered. Apparently the normal method in Mali is to drive a red-hot nail into the cavity to kill the nerve, whilst the patient is held down by several friends. I considered that it would be less trouble for all concerned if I did what was necessary in England.

My rucksack wasn't big enough to contain all my gear so I borrowed a larger one from a friend, a massive affair with ample space and a light frame. This I packed, complete with two one-gallon containers filled with water, and carried several miles as an exercise. It weighed a ton in spite of my being absolutely ruthless with the editing.

On the day before my departure I held a wake. Since if I did not return my body would not be present at the subsequent wake then I considered it necessary to hold one whilst the said body was available. In any case I enjoy a good wake. Cards were delivered in sympathy for my impending demise. The afore-mentioned body entered into the spirit of the thing by being in extremely poor condition upon the following morning.

I had time for the consumption of a large hairy dog before I boarded the train for Manchester. There was no emotion left. Bob, my old comrade whose rucksack I was wearing, and which he later told me he didn't expect to see again, waved and went for another pint. Together with the afternoon shift on the train I was off to work.

3 The Try

Paris in the spring is like Paris at any other time once one has seen all the sights. This I had accomplished many years previously so I simply went about my business through the dirty, people-ridden streets. It was hot when I came out of the Metro on the Champs-Elysées not far from the Arc de Triomphe. The Institut Géographique National's shop was on rue Boétie, so there I went. They were very helpful and patient with my awful French and I came out gleefully holding three 1:200,000 (1 cm: 2 km or about 3 miles to the inch) maps covering the Mali half of the journey. Unfortunately the Mauritanian half would have to be done on the smaller scale 1:1,000,000 maps.

I spoke to one of their important people who told me that there were police restrictions in the Araouane area and that it was a garrison town with little there but soldiers. Where he obtained this information I know not. It turned out to be completely erroneous, but I didn't know this at the time and considered the possibility of leaving the Timbuktu to Araouane track before I actually reached the town. There didn't seem to be any way that the authorities could police an area such as this. It was one more problem to deal with when the occasion arose.

My next job was to obtain Malian and Mauritanian visas and for this I needed to cross the city. The Paris Metro is an excellent way of doing this, once one gets the hang of it. It was about eleven o'clock when I arrived at the Malian Embassy in the rue du Cherche-Midi, Paris 6.

An officious black African told me to return at twelve. This I did. He looked at my passport and I filled in a form. I was told to return at three. For three hours I sat in a café waiting whilst the Embassy officials drank great quantities of alcohol all around me. Three o'clock arrived and I filled in another form. They demanded fifty francs and told me to depart for a further hour, which I did. At four, after much stamping and mumbling, I was handed back my passport containing a visa for one week, renewable in Mali weekly, doubtless for another fifty francs.

I have, over the years, formulated a theory which I call 'the Edwards Theory of Latitudinal Bureaucracy', which clearly states: 'Paperwork increases in direct proportion to the decrease in latitude.' The Embassy on the rue du Cherche-Midi testifies to the truth of this theory.

Since the Mauritanian Embassy was in another part of the city and would be closed by the time I reached it I would have to spend a night in Paris. This I was loath to do as it would cost me money. It seemed to me that since there would be no border post where I would cross into Mauritania, then they would either have to grant me a visa in Oualata or have me deported. Either course of action suited me fine. I decided to try hitching south.

France was always a bad country for the hitch-hiker. I remember on one previous occasion a fellow Hindleyite and myself walked most of the way from Orange to Lyon, a distance of about one hundred and twenty miles, without obtaining a lift. Indeed the French hatred of the hitch-hiker is such that drivers will make serious attempts to run one down.

I arrived in Dijon at about two o'clock on a freezing cold morning and found the railway station where I slept. Four hours later I was being kicked to death by an ageing madame who looked as if she could knit, in front of whose magazine stall I had happened to lay my head.

Coffee and croissants for breakfast in the station café and I tried to hitch out of town. Hours later I gave this up and, with a painful knee, returned to the station. I bought a ticket for Marseille and drank more coffee. The French equivalent of a British Rail pork pie is a boiled ham roll. Several of these later and I was on the train speeding south once more.

Proprietors of transport systems the world over seem to have the insane idea that passengers will always appreciate having their ears battered by loud music-like sounds. This is common in buses and coaches but the French railways have reached new heights of sensual flagellation by introducing into their cars video screens constantly belting out an inane load of pap and advertisements. The vision in my car was faulty and the programme repeated every half-hour. I retreated to the bar. The French are a morose people who are at their most morose when drinking: this possibly stems from the condition of French beer. I was almost pleased to watch the bar close. When I found my seat again the video had mercifully switched itself off and I was able to slumber on down the dark Rhône valley.

It was a warm night when the train pulled into Marseille. I had a meal and slept on the harbour wall. The following morning saw me at the ticket office seeking passage to Algeria. It was Wednesday and the next ship for Oran, my preferred destination, was on Saturday. There was, however, a vessel for Algiers the following day on which I booked a single ticket. My rucksack I put in the left-luggage office, and I was free to wander for the rest of the day.

The yachting harbour was a fine sight with expensive schooners and many smaller craft bobbing on the water. Trips could be made around the Château d'If, its island visible outside the harbour. Fresh fish was for sale and tourists photographed each other in rows.

There is a place not a stone's throw from the fine yachting area and the glittering shops, entered by one of several alleys, where many of the locals live. It is a place of multi-centuries-old high tenements, of narrow, open-sewered streets and ragged, wide-eyed children; of smells both interesting and nauseous, of toiling old/young women and hanging washed rags. It is a place where the tourist does not go, lest he feel, perhaps, something he does not like. I have seen many such throughout the world. And if the President of France were to come here would he find revolt festering, or perhaps just sullen, cowed eyes; or would they wave joyous flags that the Great Man had deigned to visit them? I think, sadly, the latter.

I watched the sun set magnificently behind the Château d'If and ate spaghetti in a restaurant.

All perimeter fences have holes in them and the one around the French Foreign Legion grounds was no exception. Since they owned the only bit of grass around I slept on it.

In the morning there were hundreds of Algerians in the harbour reception area, all carrying huge parcels of goods not available at home. On the passenger deck these cluttered up the aisles, spilled over into all other places and generally hampered passage throughout the vessel. The trip was to take about twenty-fours hours, a whole day amongst this teeming mass of refugees from Europe. As always Europeans drifted together, if for no other reason than that a common language can usually be found. The contingent on this boat consisted of a young Dutch couple, Kees and Wilma, a Canadian named Gary and myself. The language was English.

Kees and Wilma were doing a general wander over the face of the Earth but Gary was interested in Timbuktu, which I had now come to think of by its French spelling of Tombouctou so I will use this spelling for the rest of the book. Gary could be useful as, though I usually travel alone, from time to time in the more notorious parts of the world it was handy that those of like mind should band together for mutual protection. Algiers seemed to be such a part.

Spirits were for sale on board at about three pounds a bottle and Ricard was available in quantity. At the sight of a bottle of Ricard strange things happen to me. My mouth begins to drool. Shakings commence in my body. My hands start an involuntary clutching motion and a silly grin appears upon my face. I am rather partial to Ricard.

A bottle or two was purchased, cups produced, water for mixing obtained and we set about the business of fending off the boredom of a day-long voyage. Beer appeared, and a number of Algerians who did not adhere strictly to the guidance of the Prophet. Soon quite a sizeable party was in progress. Songs were sung. Arabic songs, Dutch songs, French songs, Canadian songs and Lancastrian songs rang through the throbbing of the engines. There were songs of joy at going home, and sad songs at leaving home beyond the ship's wake. Pop songs there were, and folk songs; songs sung well and songs sung not so well.

At one point I was informing a bleary-eyed son of Ishmael about my glorious Viking warrior ancestry. He was not impressed, but handed me a bottle from which I took a good slug. I wished that I had looked at the label. It was Scotch. Now Scotch has an inevitable and immediate effect upon my innards. The effect erupted straightway upon the gentleman's trousers. This appeared to impress him greatly. A chain reaction began as Arab after Arab displayed the weakness of his stomach. Those who made it to the toilet found it flooded to a depth of four inches in water, toilet paper, urine and carrots. This prompted some-one to start a rumour that we were sinking, which caused masses of children and ladies to weep, and wail, and gnash their teeth. Bedlam reigned for some time before everyone eventually sub-sided into a twitching, quivering, nasal mass.

There was a heavy sea the following morning as woebegone individuals jostled for a place on the downwind rail.

Algiers is a filthy combination of the worst of French colonial and Arabic architecture. To walk alone through its littered streets is to invite trouble. It is to cities the world over that the scum of humanity comes to fester. From now on I wore my father's sword beneath my shirt, under my left armpit.

Conmen were rife, trying to entice us down alleyways, attempting to change our money on the black market, demand-ing gifts. Gary and I said farewell to Wilma and Kees and, as Gary required a visa, we climbed the hill behind the city to where the Malian Embassy was situated. The architecture became more high-class and modern with huge apartment buildings and small parks lined with palm trees. It was a very hot day and when we finally located the Embassy it was early evening. There we were told that nothing could be done until Tuesday as the Ambassador was away. It was then Friday. We slept in a pleasant little park, hidden beneath the palms.

Since I was already much further into the year than I wished to be (it was the twenty-seventh of March and the desert would be getting hotter), I decided that I would have to go on alone, so next morning I wished good luck to Gary and set about find-ing a way to Tombouctou. First I checked out the possibilities of flying. The best I could do was a bus to Tamenrasset and a plane to Tombouctou. This flight would have cost seventy-five pounds plus airport tax etc, etc, much more than I wished to spend, so it would have to be overland via Bechar, Reggane, the Tanezrouft and Gao. I purchased a rail ticket for Bechar, the end of the line south, and waited for the train to leave at around six. By now I was beginning to reek a bit and was badly in need of a good clean.

At eleven p.m. the train, a modern affair, arrived at Moham-madia station, a whistle-stop where I was to change trains in the morning. There were several people trying to sleep on the floor, but when I attempted to follow suit the Station-Master would have none of it. He ushered me to his office and insisted that I sleep there on his floor. Though I was wary the man seemed genuine enough so I complied. At four o'clock he woke me up and tried to change money. Everyone in Algeria is in the black-market money-changing racket; cash, however, is tightly controlled and all money-changing must be done in banks, where they stamp a sheet of paper which one must produce upon leaving the country. Penalties are high and I had enough problems on this trip without running foul of the authorities. I declined the Station-Master's generous offer, so he kicked me out of his office.

I went exploring. There was an all-night café just down the street which served glasses of coffee that tasted of ashtrays. Several of these later and it was time to return to the station. Dawn was just breaking as I sat watching a moth being chased by a swift which was in turn being chased by a bat. All three were of comparable size and gave a magnificent display of aerobatics. I never found out the outcome for they flew out of sight as a stork flapped purposefully over the station.

Then I saw the tap. It was sticking out of a wall at the end of the station building. I approached it with joy, gently turned it on and clear water gushed forth in abundance. There is great happiness in a clean body. My water bottle was filled and purified with halozone tablets. That was the last tap I saw north of the Sahara.

And so I sat, awaiting the train that would take me over the Atlas Mountains, a seven-hundred-mile journey with a thousand miles of desert beyond. There was no feeling of adventure, just thoughts of a long, weary journey. Half a lifetime previously it would have had me wide-eyed; the yashmaked women, the Arabic station sign, the muezzin calling the faithful to the mosque.

'Allah is most great.
I bear witness that there is no god but Allah.
I bear witness that Muhammad is the Prophet of Allah.
Come to prayer. Prayer is better than sleep.'
Now it was all part of a long pilgrimage to a stretch of sand

with no one who knew me, or spoke my language, anywhere ahead.

Thus was my mood when I was ushered to my train. Then I was sent deeper into depression for the sleek new train I had expected had become a narrow-gauge, broken-windowed, paint-peeling, wooden-slat-seated museum piece. When it moved off, pulled by a small diesel engine, I discovered that the tracks were corrugated and the coaches lacked any kind of suspension. Seven hundred miles of this? Things couldn't get much worse.

Things got worse. I was buttonholed into a conversation by a leave-bound Algerian soldier whose only interests in life were Manchester United and Blondie, two subjects about which the sparsity of my knowledge was absolutely phenomenal. All this I had to discuss in French. After several hours I feigned sleep.

The soldier lost interest in the slumbering foreigner and went to badger another repository of superficial knowledge. Now I could look at the scenery. We had mounted the High Plateau and flat red sand with clumps of scrub grass stretched as far as the horizon. Occasionally there would be the black tent of nomads with goats and sheep close by, and waving children. Now and then a camel or two would raise their heads from the grass and look, chewing casually, in our direction.

Every hour or so we would reach a village where the train would stop. The driver wired up a field telephone to a couple of terminals and informed his superiors of his position. Almost all the station buildings had been blown up during the Independence War and never repaired. Bullet holes were everywhere. At each stop local children sold boiled eggs, bread and oranges, the staple diet of the traveller. Passengers leaped off and filled bottles with water from stand pipes or plastic hoses vanishing into the buildings. The driver tooted his whistle and moved off slowly whilst a hundred or so passengers emerged from the village and jumped on board.

There was only a single track but at one point there was a loop line. We waited for about half an hour for the northbound train to appear. At regular intervals the driver wound up his telephone and shouted to some remote controller, then he and the guard hurled invective at each other, waving their arms like windmills.

Eventually we heard the other train's whistle and it came onto the loop. The driver sprang out and, throwing his arms around our driver, kissed and cuddled him and generally treated him like a long-lost brother, our driver reciprocating in like manner. Doubtless they were congratulating each other on their arrival unscathed.

Eventually the waggons rolled once more. As the sun went down we reached the slag-grey Atlas and a chill wind began to blow. There was a full moon, a silver ball of light on the black velvet sky. The train trundled, clattered, rattled and banged on.

We arrived in Béchar at midnight. I found a road towards the edge of town and went down it looking for somewhere to lay a very weary head. Eventually I found a reasonable hollow in some clay dunes near an army barracks and decided that this would do. It was hard on the bones, but I hadn't had a good night's sleep for days. Soon I slipped into oblivion.

The sound of a pair of boots crunching clay shook me fully awake. I kept my body still and opened my lower eye a little. Whoever it was must think me still asleep. That way I had a certain advantage. Such precautions come as second-nature to the seasoned traveller.

Dawn had lately broken and a soldier was approaching me, cautiously, about thirty feet away. He drew a small automatic from its holster and pointed it at me. Old Baldie seemed to be around somewhere. I needed to stand quickly to lessen his new advantage. Slowly, one always moves slowly under a gun, I moved, yawned and stretched, pretended to see him for the first time, and rose to my feet casually.

'Good morning,' I said in French, smiling.

The soldier, a corporal, glared at me in stony silence. He stood three feet away, scrutinising me, his pistol pointed at my chest. About thirty years old, obviously a regular soldier, with the thick nose and the wide-apart eyes of a peasant. I knew that I could take him if I had to, but that would be as a last resort. It would probably have meant the end of the trip.

'Papers!' he demanded, also in French, and held out his hand.

I handed him my passport which he opened upside-down, recognising his mistake only when he saw my photograph. He scowled at me for seeing his error.

'Empty your pockets!'

I complied, there being nothing in them that shouldn't be. He viewed all and understood nothing. There were only a few pounds' worth of Algerian dinars in my pockets and this did not satisfy him.

'Where is your money?'

It was in a pouch which I carried around my neck, beneath my shirt, over four hundred pounds, mostly in twenty-pound stirling notes. I debated whether to deny its existence, or produce it, deciding on the latter as his knuckles were going white around the pistol grip. I was not moving fast enough for him. He knocked my hand away to one side and plunged his left hand into the pouch, withdrawing it clutching a great wad of notes. His eyes bulged. I doubt if he had ever seen so much money before. He thought for a while, staring at the cash, dragged his brain to a decision, stuck about two hundred pounds into his teeth and handed the rest back to me. So that was the way of it. Robbery!

It seemed that I was going to have to fight. Without that money the trip was finished anyway. My army training was going to come in handy. I would disarm him, retrieve my money and steal his bullets. I had done a similar thing to a hotelier in Istanbul some years previously. Then I would probably immobilise him and find a phone quickly to contact the British Consulate in Algiers.

He was busy stuffing my money into his breast pocket, I was equally busy working out moves. Then I decided on a try at psychology.

'My money!' I demanded with every bit of military authority I could put into it. Military authority sounds the same in any language. The military mind has been brainwashed into thoughtless obedience. He hesitated buttoning up his pocket.

'Quickly!' I rasped, thrusting out my hand for it.

We glowered at each other, staring each other out. Obviously I was military of some kind. He began to regret the error of his ways. The barracks were just across the road. He dared not use his pistol, not even as a warning shot, and he knew that I knew it.

'We will go to your Commandante!' I stated, with the same authority. That did it. He capitulated completely, handed back the money, and as a face-saver ordered me to pack up and leave forthwith. Then he stalked away like some little deposed Hitler, ramming his pistol back into its holster. I took a couple of deep breaths, packed my gear quickly, and headed for the town centre.

Algeria is an expensive country. The only water I could find in Béchar was in a sort of supermarket-cum-casbah: it cost about thirty-five pence for a litre with forty pence deposit on the bottle. Clothing was incredibly costly.

The sun was very hot as I located the bus station and bought a ticket to Adrar, my next destination over four hundred miles south. Then it was a case of drinking more ashtray coffee and being stared at by the locals.

This staring business is difficult for a European to come to terms with. We are taught from birth never to stare, and never, never to touch. Our lives are very private, closeted behind fences, walls, hedges and curtains. We eat from separate plates, drink from separate cups and generally ignore each other's idiosyncrasies. It is not like that in most of the world. Honest curiosity is the order of the day, which to us in our private little worlds can cause quite a traumatic culture shock.

I boarded the bus around noon and managed a window seat. The topography was changing, becoming more barren as we went further south. Undulating hills gave way to undulating dunes of red sand, and camels were a regular sight on the road. There were blinds on the windows to keep out the glare of the sun. Occasionally we would slow down to negotiate sand which had drifted onto the good metalled road. An occasional green-palmed oasis drifted by, and erosion-sculpted rocks stood sentinel. At five in the hot afternoon we entered a narrow valley and came through palms to the small oasis village of Kerzaz where we stopped for ashtray coffee. As I got off the bus I was aghast at the sight confronting me.

Beyond the end of the street was a sand dune. I judged its pointed summit to be about two miles distant. This being so it was a pile of soft sand something like a thousand feet from base to apex.

'Aklé!' said a travelling companion.

So this was what aklé looked like. There were other dunes of comparable size beyond the foremost one, and they just went on, and on, and on.

I wrote in my diary:

'I have just seen my desert . . . OH GOD . . . What have I let myself in for?? If what I have seen is not Aklé dune of the worst possible kind then the trip is *absolutely* impossible!!

'I am in shock. Dunes over a thousand feet high . . . I have just photographed one . . . It towers way above the tall houses two hundred yards away.

'When David said he would fight Goliath, had he seen Goliath? . . . And yet . . . he won.'

It was dark when we arrived in Adrar, a frontier-like town in a state of renewal. Everywhere there was building in progress. I was acquired by a building worker from the north who supplied me with a bed for a few American cigarettes and wanted to know all about Manchester United and Blondie. There was a bus for Reggane at six in the morning which, after ashtray coffee, I boarded.

Reggane was a real, one-storey desert town of mud bricks perched on the edge of the desert itself. Here the metalled road came to an abrupt halt just beyond the police checkpoint. Past the warning notice from which the writing had long been blasted by sun and sand was the Tanezrouft, the most barren and the oldest part of the world's biggest desert. It was four hundred miles across the Tanezrouft to the Malian border at Borjd Mocktar. From there the desert continued until the banks of the River Niger at Gao, a further four hundred miles.

A sandstorm was blowing as the bus disgorged us at a café. I drank the contents of two ashtrays before deciding to brave the elements. First I had to report to the police checkpoint. Everyone was checked into and out of the desert for reasons of safety. I enquired the whereabouts of the police post and picked my way through the drifts of sand down the appropriate street. There were three Peugeot 504 saloons parked at the post with a Frenchman driving each, the backs filled with jerricans of water and petrol, boxes of food and various other articles. I asked about the possibility of a lift and, after a short discussion, they agreed that they could use an extra pair of hands. I checked in with the police and we were off.

We followed an Arab truck for a few kilometres until we reached the 'piste'. The piste, on my Michelin map, was marked as a pink line going all the way to Gao. It was, in fact, a myth perpetrated by cartographers on bonus. It did not exist. All that did exist was a string of oil drums, one every couple of miles or so, a few carcases of animals and vehicles, a two-mile-wide criss-cross of vehicle tracks, and the Sahara. It was the first of April 1980.

Mostly the terrain was flat sand and gravel which was good to drive on, but occasionally we would hit soft sand where one or two of the cars would get bogged down. Then it was a matter of all hands to the task, digging, laying metal sand tracks, and pushing. We travelled strung out at an angle so as to keep out of each other's sand plume. Every hour or so we would stop and lift up the bonnets to cool the engines. The temperature was over 120°F and the car bodies were hot enough to burn naked flesh. My new companions were taking the cars to Mali or Niger in order to sell them at a substantial profit, a more or less legal procedure.

Sometime in the afternoon we saw a truck bogged down in a particularly large patch of soft sand. Rule number one in the desert is to help your fellow traveller, so when we had successfully negotiated the soft patch we walked back loaded with shovels and sand tracks. As we were pushing it out I found myself lying in the sand with no idea of how I got there. I must have fainted momentarily from the heat and exertion. It dawned on me that because of the heat of the last few days I had eaten very little, and I was probably dehydrated and desalinated as well. At the first opportunity I drank a quantity of water and took some salt tablets.

Later, when we stopped to rest, there were only two cars present. One was missing. We waited a while, eyes searching the horizon for any movement. The two Frenchmen decided to go back to look for him, leaving me with one of the cars. They vanished over the northern horizon and all was quiet. Even the wind had stopped. The only time I had ever experienced such silence was in the Judaean Desert eleven years previously. For a time there were clicks from the engine as it cooled, then the only sound was the pumping of blood through my veins.

I waited, then I waited some more. The sun was dipping to the west and dimly visible because of the sand in the air, whipped up by the morning's sandstorm. I heard an engine, but it was a diesel, and from the south. A large Mercedes truck appeared in the distance and veered in my direction. It came close and the Arab driver asked if I was OK. I said that I was, but asked him to keep an eye open for the other cars. A cheery wave and he was gone. Again the silence.

It would soon be dark. After sunset the Frenchmen would need a light to guide them to me. I checked the lights. They worked, but the car was parked sideways on to the piste. The lights needed to point north but they had taken the keys and the steering lock was on. There was nothing for it but to release the handbrake and push it in a great arc through 270°. A Peugeot is a heavy vehicle when unladen, but this one was loaded up to the gunnels. For perhaps an hour I toiled at the task, having frequent rests. When it was finally pointing north the sun had gone down completely and I was alone, in the dark, in the middle of the Sahara.

I checked the lights again, and the dipper. They were fine, sending out good strong beams into the night. I switched off to preserve the batteries. Next I checked for sustenance. There was ample food and water on board. It was just a matter of sitting it out until I saw headlights to the north.

About two hours later I spotted a flash to the north-west, and then another. I flashed the headlights three times on full beam and the lights veered towards me. At regular intervals I repeated the signal. After a few minutes I noticed that there was only one set of headlights.

It took them about half an hour to reach me. Both cars were there but one had the front end smashed in. It had gone over a small dune and nose-dived into the ground. The radiator had been pushed back and the fan was fouled by the water hoses. This was no great problem since the fan was smashed. The fan belt was broken and the generator was inoperative, which explained why the lights were out. All power from the battery was needed for the spark plugs.

We ate and slept where we were. The temperature was so high that I didn't need my sleeping-bag. At five in the morning we were on our way again so as to cover as much ground as possible before the heat of the day. We went in line abreast, close to each other, the two good cars with headlights blazing either side of the darkened lame duck. Periodically we would swap batteries to recharge the depleted one.

Even here, on the Sahara's most barren part, there was life. Moths flew in through the windows and once, in the headlight's beam, a flock of heron flew up in front of us, disturbed in their rest as they flew north. We had to change a wheel a couple of times and, as the sun came up, there was more digging, and more pushing, and more laying of tracks, and more digging, and more pushing. One car developed trouble with the hydraulic clutch which required adjusting and topping-up occasionally.

After much more of this we finally limped into Borjd Mocktar. We were finished with the Tanezrouft. Here we had to wait whilst the police and the customs approved our papers. For hours we waited, through the heat of the day. We tried every way to repair the broken fan belt, assisted by other waiting drivers. It was no use.

Finally we were released, the authorities once again having given weight to the Edwards Theory of Latitudinal Bureaucracy. On we went into Mali. The terrain had changed from sand to baked earth with vegetation, even trees, all about. The piste had now become a dirt road and was much more difficult to drive over. We were heading for Tessalit, the Malian border post a hundred miles south, where we would spend the night.

More wheels had to be changed, but thanks be to Allah, little more digging and pushing. The road was so bad that much of the time we drove parallel to it through the bush. We removed the silencers to give more clearance and increased tyre pressures, reduced previously for grip on the sand. Just before dark, dusty and weary, we pulled into Tessalit and reported to the authorities.

In a bar we ate *cous-cous*, split millet cooked in steam and covered with meat, vegetables, juice and sand. Beer was about two pounds a can but we figured that we had earned one each. There were other Frenchmen in the bar. One of them swatted a mosquito about an inch and a half long. Everyone gathered around, myself included, and looked on with interest as he systematically burned the stunned creature with his gaslighter.

Two weeks previously I would have been horrified at the spectacle and would have done something about it, but now it seemed interesting. Had I changed so much so soon? Is our western civilisation such a thin cloak over the man?

I slept in front of the bar, on the ground. In the morning we left for Aguel-Hok, a hundred miles or so further south. The journey was much the same as before and we arrived late in the morning. More bureaucracy of course, so we repaired to the Restaurant Desert. There was much commercial activity within. Various tools and accessories were vended by the Frenchmen and I sold my cagoule, sweater and, sadly, my ancient sleeping-bag with its memories of Wales, of sleeping out in thirty below on Mount Ararat, so many memories. Now it was just excess weight.

A buyer was found for the damaged car. The transaction took several hours so we drank much tea, which had taken over from ashtray coffee as the staple drink.

This was black Africa. I found the Malians to be a beautiful, open-faced people, but nobody's fools. Long ago I had discounted the idea that because a man lived in primitive conditions he was therefore stupid and lacking in education, a seemingly prevalent opinion in the so-called civilised countries. The Malians are in fact the most astute businessmen I have ever met, and are perfectly educated to cope with their environment. They may not have heard of Shakespeare, but could the immortal bard have tracked, stalked, killed, skinned, gutted, butchered and cooked a gazelle? They have their own poetry and music which can be every bit as sophisticated as the best of our own; the average national income in Mali is about thirty pounds a year, it is one of the poorest countries on the face of the Earth; yet its inhabitants eat, and laugh, and learn, and in the way of poverty the world over they help those in greater need.

There were many Touaregh in this area, the strange people of the desert who are neither negroid nor Arab. Theirs is a matriarchal society with the women ruling household and tribe. Touaregh women are the most consistently beautiful women I have ever seen, with high cheek-bones, open inquisitive eyes and white teeth shining in contrast with their dark brown skin. These are a proud race of women who require no liberation. Many have forsaken the desert and intermarried with the black

Africans. It is a proud thing to have a Touaregh wife and the Restaurant Desert's proprietor was justly boastful of his.

It was late afternoon when we left Aguel-Hok in the two remaining cars with a Touaregh guide who wished to return to his camp. He had never travelled so fast before and the driver terrified him with his skill at the wheel. Several minor repairs later we arrived at his camp. There we doctored the populace, relieving all manner of ills, the worst being a badly gashed Touaregh foot, the owner of which could well have lost his leg and very likely his life had we not happened by. I cleaned and dressed it and a Frenchman supplied antibiotics.

These desert Touaregh contrasted greatly with their urban fellows. The one-time proud warriors who fought and beat the French now had grandchildren who cringed and whined and wheedled. They had become a nation of beggars without pride. Open up a bag and they would simply hold out an open, drooping palm for any scraps that might come their way; nothing specific, just anything. There had been a great drought in the area for many years, but this alone could not account for what had happened to them. Somehow it seemed that the clash of cultures, theirs and ours, was responsible. The mighty Touaregh would raid no more. It was, in many ways, a sad thing.

I declined my driver's offer to sleep in the car. It was dangerous, he said, to sleep on the ground, for here there were scorpions. The sky was magnificent. I had forgotten about the other two million stars in Orion.

A Touaregh wandered past in the dark on his camel, towering over me, the moon behind him.

'*Salaam al laikum*,' he said.

'*Al laikum el salaam*,' I replied.

It seemed the most natural thing in the world. I was becoming 'of the desert', whilst my French friends clung to their own culture for safety, cramped in their hot cars with their sweat and their western smells. I preferred the scorpions, the sky and the night greeting. Already I loved this desert. My depression of days before had left me. I was no longer being simply conveyed, but was an important part of a great adventure. I slept soundly that night, in comfort and at peace.

In the morning – more piste. I almost lost a finger changing a wheel. If that was the only injury I got this trip I would, I figured, be lucky. On south towards the River Niger past camel, and goat, and donkey, and child-festooned wells. Some of them were very deep and required a pulley and camel power to obtain water.

Finally, in the afternoon, we arrived in Gao. A lifetime ambition had been achieved. I had crossed the Sahara.

We booked into the Hotel d'Atlantide, described by an Englishman there as the best little hotel in West Africa. There we washed and changed into clean clothes. Sores had begun to appear on my legs. I washed all my clothes, then reported to the police. It was Friday, the Islamic sabbath, so nothing could be done until the next day. Even the bank was closed. The market was, however, open. I would have no Malian money until the bank opened so I just looked.

There were fruits, and vegetables, clothing both African and European, rush mats with which to thatch one's hut, two-litre empty oil containers with sacking insulation were purveyed as water carriers and bread stalls sold sticks of French bread, for Mali too had been a French colony. Small portable stalls everywhere sold cigarettes both French and Malian, together with sardines and soap.

It was in the market area that I first met Musa. He was a black of about eleven with a great pearly tombstone grin. One of his legs was withered and useless and he propelled himself along at a great rate by the use of a T-topped metal stick. Unlike so many other street children he did not beg for 'cadeaux'. Musa offered a service. He would guide me, and show me the best places to buy. Anything I desired he would arrange. As I was talking to Musa another youngster tried to sell me a short ornamental sword. It was a good sword and I could have got it cheap, but it would be excess baggage on the way in. Maybe, I explained, I would see him in six weeks or so on my return.

I arranged to meet Musa the next day and wandered around the sprawling city for a while. Most of the buildings were single-storey mud brick houses. Dust and sand blew down the streets. One or two cafés were in evidence. There was a Café Paris, a Café Gazelle, even a Café Blackpool. A café in this part of the world consists of a bare wooden table with wooden forms around it set in a yard beneath a rickety framework over which are spread rush mats to keep out the sun. Hens will run about freely, there will be a sheep or a goat tethered in a corner awaiting slaughter and from somewhere beyond a door will emerge the smells of cooking. The sign is usually badly painted on a piece of old board which is nailed or tied at a slant somewhere near the entrance.

After a while I turned towards the hotel and as I crossed the wide road before the steps I was spotted by a crowd of about twenty men. One of them pointed, and they all began to move rapidly in my direction waving swords. Wondering what great sacrilege I had committed upon the Sabbath I fled up the steps. Then I noticed that they were smiling. Word had got around that I might just be in the market for a sword and every sword-maker in Gao fancied his chances.

In the hotel bar two of my French friends were talking to a blind man who was interested in buying their cars. He was well dressed in flowing robes and was, I later discovered, the local financial wizard. I bought a beer from Madame, the hotel manageress, a statuesque Touareg lady in her late thirties.

That night a deal was set up in the Café Gazelle over chicken and *cous-cous* and a couple of beers. In the corner a sheep bleated constantly, doubtless aware of its fate. We ate it the next evening.

On Saturday morning I changed some money at the bank, then sorted out a re-entry visa for Mali in case I should require it. I had thoughts of flying from Néma, a town close to Oualata, to Tamanrasset in Algeria should I be able to afford it, but every contingency had to be taken care of.

I sent Musa for someone who could arrange a trip to Tombouctou for me. He returned with a tall black man in his thirties who drove a Land Rover and said he would be going to Tombouctou the following morning. He would not set a price there and then, but said he would sort it out upon the morrow. There was something about him I didn't like so I designated him 'Le Cochon'.

Afternoon saw the Frenchmen, myself and two African boys down by the Niger. The boys valeted the cars inside and out with river water whilst we sat in the shade of a Boabab tree drinking cool drinks. The Niger is a beautiful river, wide and gentle, but unfortunately, since the great drought, not very deep. The rains, when there were any, came in July and August. There had been practically nothing for ten years. Otherwise it would be just as it had been when Mungo Park passed down it.

It was Tuesday afternoon when Le Cochon finally decided to go. That is the way of Africa. The Spanish concept of *mañana* has too great an urgency for the peoples of the Dark Continent. There was no chance of any other transport for a week or so. Le Cochon knew it and charged me seventeen pounds for the two-hundred-mile journey. I had to pay.

There were seven of us in a short wheel-based Land Rover, together with about three tons of goods. It was cosy. We followed the piste along the Niger; the scenery was beautiful; thorn bushes with inch-long thorns were everywhere. At one point we passed a broken-down truck whose occupants waved for assistance. Le Cochon never so much as glanced at them, but drove on. That was the only time I have ever seen a request for assistance refused in a desert.

Le Cochon would drink his fill from my water-bottle which was the only insulated one on board, thus leaving no cold water for two or three other passengers. Later he was kneeling down, checking the tyres. He held out his hand and demanded water. I held the bottle out to him so that it was about three feet from his hand and looked him in the eye with a look that said, 'You're going to have to crawl for this, Cochon!' He looked, and understood, and finally, crawled.

It was four in the morning when we arrived in Tombouctou. I was dropped in the middle of town, close to the mosque. The streets were deserted as the muezzin was not due to call for an hour or so. For two or three days I had had almost no sleep, having moved out of the hotel to conserve cash. But the sooner I began my experiments with the stills the better, so I moved north towards the desert. Dawn was just breaking as I left the town, past low rush mat huts. Every time I topped a rise there would be another camp beyond. I needed privacy and no interference so I plodded on. The rucksack was far too heavy and I knew that much of the gear would have to be dumped if I was to continue after the experiments.

At about six o'clock I found what I considered to be a secluded hollow, unshipped my spade and started to dig. After two or three inches of soft sand I hit a hard crust. A foot below this the sand was damp and a further foot down it was positively wet. This seemed to promise much. I could feel my key beginning to turn the great lock.

In all I dug eight holes in a long line, all three feet or so wide, but ranging in depths from two feet to three feet. I placed my receptacles in the bottoms and covered the whole thing with a six-feet-wide strip of clear plastic, weighting it down around the edges and across the divisions between the holes. Some plastic I made tight, and some I allowed to go slack. A handful of sand in the centre of each completed the graft and I drew up time charts with all the details set down.

By then it was about eight-thirty and I was absolutely shattered. The sun was extremely hot and I had to have shelter. This I made from my space blanket using my spade and rucksack as poles. During all this time heads had begun to appear above the rim of the hollow. Now thirty or forty people were squatting inside the hollow close to the rim. I knew that very soon I would have to open up the surgery. It is a well known fact amongst Africans that all white men are doctors and carry the pills to cure all ills. I had anticipated this and brought with me much more medication than I could possibly need for my own use. Sure enough, within the hour some fifty men, women and children were gathered before my shelter so that the Nazrani, the Christian, could cure them. Mostly they were Touaregh, but with some black Africans. One young black spoke some English so he helped with translation.

Most of the problems were toothache, headaches, rheumatics and such for which I prescribed painkillers, and indigestion for which I doled out masses of minty tablets. Very soon the mint flavour was discovered and there was an epidemic of gut rot amongst the young.

They also came just to stare at the Nazrani and loudly discuss his trappings. My tatty old hiking boots created great interest, and my compass was beyond them until I explained that it was Allah's will that the needle should point always to my home in the north. I was, of course, a Frenchman. All the Nazrani were Frenchmen. They allowed that, of late, Nazrani had been seen from places called America, Germany, Australia and England, but were these not provinces of France? Did not Allah's needle itself point beyond the great sands to France? I was too tired to argue the point.

A Touaregh woman brought her son of about eleven to me. He had some sort of a growth, like an enormous wart, on the side of his knee. There was pus around it and blueness spreading from it, darkening his already dark skin. It stank and was obviously painful. I didn't, and still don't, know what it was. My medical knowledge is little greater than that of the average European but it seemed to me that whatever it was it needed to come out or he would lose his leg, and probably his life. I was on the spot. There was no one else. It was up to me. Rarely in my life have I wanted so much to be somewhere else.

I honed my father's sword on my leather belt, sterilised the blade in boiling water, made my hands and his knee area as clean as possible, and with several people holding him down, cut out the growth and the putrid area taking as much care as possible not to slice through tendon. It took perhaps five minutes. The brave boy was quiet throughout, but tears streamed down his face. There was blood. I put antiseptic cream and a field dressing on the wound, gave his mother antibiotics and lit up a cigarette. My hands were shaking.

Since then I have spoken to several medical people about the incident. Opinions vary as to the nature of the malady, but all are of the opinion that I did the right thing. I hope they are right.

Later his mother brought me water, that most precious of gifts, and I drank thirstily. It was impossible to say, 'Thank you, but wait a moment whilst I put these tablets in to make it fit for a Nazrani.'

Towards evening two Arabs entered my camp riding camels. I was asked if I would like to mount. I would! Taking off my boots I gingerly boarded one, as I had done those many years ago in Judaea. First the foot on the neck and swing over. The camel was wearing a bench-like Malian saddle with a high pommel in front and a high back. When I was seated comfortably I signalled the camel's owner. He slapped its backside and, after a brief display of aerobatics, I found myself staring up at the animal from the sand, with saddle and broken girth in close proximity. 'I've been here before,' I thought.

With the other camel I had better luck. It sported a Mauritanian saddle, a sort of leather bucket with wings either side. We rose together quite successfully and loped around the hollow. The Mauritanian saddle was far more comfortable than the Malian. I felt strangely at home in it.

Later, when I checked my stills, I found not a single drop of water in any of them. Maybe, I thought, it had been too hot for them to work. The temperature had been around 140°F and even the Touaregh called it hot. The sun had badly burned my face and arms and I didn't expect to sleep that night.

I decided to dig one more hole. This was a wondrous hole, an artist's hole made with all the loving care of a Henry Moore. It was three feet wide and four feet deep, as deep as was practical. The soft sand was scraped away to stop it running into the hole. At the bottom the sand was very wet indeed. This was my last chance. If this hole did not produce water by morning then my key to the desert did not work. I was very apprehensive as I lay down that night to await the dawn verdict.

Despite the sunburn I slept soundly, awakening just as the sun lightened the sky. Two large black scarab beetles, fully an inch and a half long, were struggling to climb the slippery plastic slope of my newest still. I pulled them out and they retreated rapidly over the sand.

There was a mist of condensation on the underside of the plastic, I scraped the sand from the edge of the sheet and raised it to look inside. The bowl was absolutely dry, as dry as the surface sand all around. I went to the other stills and checked each one in turn. The story was the same in every case, damp plastic and a dry bowl. It made no difference at all if the hole was deep or shallow, if the plastic was tight with a gentle slope or slack with a steep one. All that had been produced in twenty four hours was a large area of damp plastic. There was not even enough dampness to sponge off with a cloth and wring into a bowl. The stills were a failure, and so was I.

Six months' hopes and fears, six hundred pounds – all for a bit of damp plastic two miles north of Tombouctou. I have never felt such defeat and degradation as I did when I packed my bag and left the beggars to fight over the plastic whilst they laughed at the demented Nazrani shouting, 'Where is the water? Where is your miracle?' I was too far down to care, even to get angry. I just walked away from them across the desert to Tombouctou. I wanted to get away from there as soon as possible, to run for home, back to people I understood, and who understood me – back to cool rain, and food to enjoy, not just to eat.

Tombouctou was a dusty beggar city with nothing to recommend it to the tourist. Nowhere were there any signs of a past grandeur. The most magnificent piece of architecture in the whole place was a breeze-block market hall with a corrugated iron roof. I had thoughts of flying to Niamey in Niger and thence on to Tamanrasset in Algeria from where there was a bus to Algiers. To tackle the Tanezrouft again was more than I could bear. The Air Mali office wasn't open until the next day so I booked into the only hotel, the Hôtel Campement. There was neither bank nor post office in town.

That evening I sat in the lounge of what must be the worst hotel in West Africa and wrote these words.

THOUGHTS IN A TOMBOUCTOU BAR ON THE FAILURE OF AN EXPEDITION

Nobody likes failure, particularly he who fails. The first reaction is to blame someone else, and there's usually somebody about upon whom, with a bit of imagination, much, if not all, of the blame can be heaped. In my case there was no one.

The next place to look for a blamee is at things. Faulty equipment, freak conditions, illness etc. etc. My equipment did, for the most part, what it was designed to do. One or two things could have been better, but that was not the fault of the equipment, just my concept of what was required. Conditions were not particularly freakish, though the locals did say it was hotter than usual. There was no illness, unless you treat shock at the conditions as an illness – I do not.

So the blame must, inevitably, fall on me. I did something wrong – what was it?

Basically I think I tried to do too much too soon. One thing that stands out like a sore thumb is that if the stills had worked and I had set out in this heat, powered more by bravado than common-sense, I would have failed – and this failure would have resulted in death. It is the wrong time of year and that's that. I knew it in theory, but I just didn't realise the fact of it. If I can find another key then that's the first thing I shall correct. Since I had missed last winter I should have waited until next winter. I was in too much of a hurry.

Another result of this impatience was that I came down here the hard way because of lack of funds. The result was that, even if the stills had worked I am in no physical condition to tackle the problem . . . I am weak and uncomfortable in filthy clothes.

Has the trip been worth it? It most certainly has!! I have achieved two lifetime ambitions – I have crossed the Sahara, and I have been to Tombouctou. All this and I only left home seventeen days ago.

On top of this I have gained that most valuable of all things – experience.

What of the future? Shall I continue with thoughts of the crossing? I don't know at this stage. It is too much to think about right now. I do know that my experience on this trip will increase immeasurably my chances of success should I subsequently decide to try again, by whatever method. But such thoughts are for the future. Now I want to go home.

And what of the Desert? We have become acquainted, she and I. She is the biggest bitch I have ever encountered, and the most beautiful. She has taken me and shaken me like a terrier shakes a rat, and she has made me love her. Our acquaintance is not at an end.

Tombouctou described itself as the 'Town of Mystery'. The only real mystery was how to get out of it. It took five days to get a ride out, flying having proved too expensive. Meanwhile I checked out of the hotel, having cleaned myself up somewhat, and slept on the desert.

Thus began the worst journey of my life. Seventeen of us were crammed into the back of a small pick-up truck together with about two tons of luggage and commercial goods. The journey to Gao should have taken ten hours. It took twenty-seven. About three hours out I felt the symptoms of a very bad dose of the

revenge of one Franco. At dusk I was attending to this problem
when something hissed and slithered away towards a beautiful
River Niger Sunset. Had the snake, for snake it must have been,
known the purpose of my errand it might have been more
vituperative. That was the only time I have ever encountered a
snake in the desert.

When we arrived I was incapable of walking unaided and
would have slept in the street where I was dropped had not the
driver and another passenger practically carried me into the
Hotel d'Atlantide. There Madame administered pills and found
me a room next to the toilet, where I lay for two nights and a day,
making frequent trips next door and praying for a quick death.

When I was partly recovered Musa brought me a 'fixer', who
took me across town to a truck which was heading for Adrar. I
could only stagger very slowly, and had to get a couple of boys to
carry my rucksack; the frame had been broken in the back of the
pick-up. For about thirty pounds, including food, the driver
would take me to Adrar. We would be there in four days, he said.
Altogether it took eight, including stripping down the engine
three times. This was a commercial run consisting of buying
Touaregh sheep in the desert and shipping them north for sale
in Algeria.

There were on board, besides the driver, two Frenchmen, an
American from Hawaii, his Danish wife, the co-driver, a flock of
sheep and myself. We humans built a platform above the sheep
and made ourselves as comfortable as possible under a makeshift
awning. I was very thin by now with little flesh on my bones; the
word 'comfortable' was extremely relative. It was four days
before I could eat anything at all. I managed a couple of small
pieces of gazelle and a handful of *cous-cous*.

At this point my haemorrhoids burst. All my body was bruised
and erupting with sores, but the pain in my nether regions ruled
supreme. All hours were spent in working out new positions in
which to sit. There I was, going through the world's most magnificent desert, and all I could think of was my backside, and
where to put it, and how, and for how long; and then what?

One of the sheep died, so we ate it with macaroni and sand. At
first there was a spirit in the group, but some of us knew, and the

rest had a good idea, what the Tanezrouft was like, and it was coming closer. We all had doubts about the viability of the truck. There was no adventure any more; there was just hope, and the constant thought: Go north . . . Go north . . . Go north . . .

At Tessalit we spent a day taking the engine to pieces again. I went to the bar and bought the only can of beer for several hundred miles in any direction for about two pounds. Outside I found a piece of cardboard, half an old box which had contained canned foods of some kind. This was a great find and my companions were envious. Cardboard protects and insulates, wafts, shades, irons out minor irregularities in one's chosen sitting place, and generally gives one a sense of well-being. The possessor of cardboard is treated with deference and his views upon everything are sought. He is indeed an aristocrat amongst travellers. It was speculated that when news of my find spread, as spread it must, cardboard prospectors would begin to flood into Tessalit. Claims would be filed, and mines opened. The Great Tessalit Cardboard Rush would have begun!

Tessalit's other claim to fame was that it was said to be overrun with scorpions. A local child had spent all morning looking for one to play with. He let it run up his arm and when it reached his shoulder he would simply grab it, blow hard at it, and replace it near his wrist to repeat the process. Sometimes he would poke it with his finger until its tail, containing the sting, began to curl upwards. It was about two inches long and very docile.

The next several days were much the same as each other on the Tanezrouft. The temperature was around 140°F and we had to push-start the truck every time we moved off. There are no good batteries in West Africa other than those owned by the Nazrani. My maladies subsided a little, much to my delight. Somewhere near the Tropic of Cancer I encountered Gary, my Canadian friend, on a truck heading south. In Reggane the American had visa problems so we lost him and his wife. One of the Frenchmen went missing so only one Frenchman and myself arrived in Adrar on a Wednesday morning at two o'clock.

This Frenchman was a hypochondriac who saw himself as a fitness freak and was in a permanent state of panic. He was going home to northern France so we decided to travel together. We boarded a bus to Ghardaia and another to Algiers. It was necessary to spend two nights in Algiers before the boat left for Marseille. Unfortunately the second of these was my birthday. I did not wish to spend it in Algiers as it was a pretty dry city at the best of times. My birthday was, of course, on Friday when all but one of the few bars were closed. The Frenchman was, naturally, a tee-totaller. This was a pity because a good booze-up would subsequently have taught him what feeling rotten was all about. The solitary bar charged over a pound for a disgusting beer, and almost three pounds for a tot of Ricard. I went to bed stone cold sober on the forty-first anniversary of my advent.

Little else of note occurred on the trip. We caught the boat, and the Paris train. The Frenchman departed at Lyon. I had a day to wait for my coach in Paris so I went to the Louvre, the one place in Paris that gives me great joy. The curators were on strike. It was closed. For the first time in fifteen years I was in Paris with time on my hands and they had to pick that time to strike! I sought solace in Montmartre.

Later, as my bus sped north up the M6 towards Manchester I reflected on the trip. I was returning home penniless, emaciated, smelly and in rags. My skin was brown and shrivelled like an old man's. I had had to abort the main expedition, but with honour, because my key didn't fit. The expedition had not been successful.

But . . . If it had . . . Ah yes . . . If it had . . .

4 The Training

I had picked up Theodore Monod's gauntlet. There was therefore no question of quitting, though I must admit to one or two thoughts in that direction soon after my return. Mostly people understood about the failure, and advised me to stop whilst I still could. There were, however, one or two adults who pointed the finger of ridicule, and this made me determined to succeed.

The method was the first thing to sort out. There were only two remaining possibilities, motor vehicle or camel. I was determined to do the trip alone so this more or less ruled out motor vehicles. My reasoning was that since I could drive only one vehicle, this would leave me in a very poor position should I suffer a major breakdown. I could keep a vehicle going if the problems were minor, with the proverbial bit of wire and a pair of mole-grips, but any major problem would leave me completely stranded. There was the possibility of carrying a trials bike as a sort of lifeboat, but basically the total cost of equipping such an expedition was way beyond my means for the foreseeable future.

Therefore it had to be camels. I worked out that I could mount an expedition with two camels for as little as £1,000 if I travelled the same way as before, not a pleasant prospect. The next job therefore was to gain some camel knowledge, a commodity in which I was greatly lacking. I wrote to Geoffrey Moorhouse and asked several questions about the logistics of camels. He was helpful, and suggested that I read his book *The Fearful Void*, the book that had started the whole thing. I also wrote to Wilfred Thesiger, the doyen of desert travellers, who recommended that I contact Geoffrey Moorhouse and read *The Fearful Void*. Thesiger was horrified that I wished to travel alone, and asked me how I would find my camels in the mornings without a guide to do it for me. It seemed to me that if an Arab could track camels, then so could an Englishman versed in the ways of tracking.

Both of these bold travellers had covered great distances over desert with camels, Moorhouse in the Sahara and Thesiger in Arabia. Most of their problems seemed to stem from their relationships with their various companions. Also I am aware that it is very easy in a bad situation to place responsibility upon others. If one is alone then this cannot happen: one must at all times shoulder the burden of responsibility and sink or swim by one's own efforts.

My troublesome knee required further inspection and, after much insistence, two exploratory operations were conducted upon. it. They found nothing, but after weeks of hobbling around on crutches it seemed much improved.

It was obvious that I needed experience with camels so I decided that some of 1981 was going to be spent in Tunisia, my nearest bit of desert country, there to ride camels and test myself as a walker of deserts. I was loath to spend another year away from the main trip as I was convinced that someone would beat me to it if I didn't get a move on. However I knew that this training was essential for the ultimate success of the expedition. I had made the mistake of haste before. A temporary job working with the unemployed youth of Salford financed the trip and on the evening of Saturday the thirty-first of January 1981 I arrived at Tunis airport for a month's stay in Tunisia.

My budget was pretty tight so I caught a bus into town and headed for the Medina, the old Arab city within a city common throughout the Islamic world. There I found myself a night's lodging at a seedy doss-house calling itself the Hotel de Tunis for the grand sum of two dinars, the rate of exchange being roughly one dinar to the pound. The Restaurant Populaire looked suitably cheap so I entered its portals. *Cous-cous* was off, and *Haricot avec Poulet*, so I settled for *Sauce avec Poulet* and a lot of bread. I walked out full and about fifty pence poorer.

Cold morning came and I wandered around the Medina for a while. As usual it was one big market with vendors calling their wares down crowded, narrow streets. Breakfast was consumed in a stand-up café and consisted of sausage and chips, all on the cold side of lukewarm. The sausage had 'Salmonella' written all the way through. When travelling abroad I always make it a rule that I will eat anything, no matter how revolting it may seem.

Many interesting dishes have passed my lips because of this rule, but I couldn't handle those sausages.

I found the railway station and bought a ticket to Gabès. My ultimate destination was Douz, a small town at the northern edge of the Grand Erg Oriental, the Great Eastern Desert, where I hoped to hire camels and a guide. The train was far superior in design and comfort to anything that British Rail had ever offered me. Sunshine shone upon a typical North African scene with its mixture of wealth and poverty. It was the first of February and prickly pears and the first crop of oranges were ripening. There was all manner of cactus and palm. Olive trees and black goats abounded. People were sitting outside their houses in the fields thinking, just thinking. Even the least of them (whatever that means) must have acquired a pretty comprehensive personal cosmology. Another of the ways, it occurred to me, in which we are the poorer for TV.

When I finally alighted at Gabès it was midnight, and the rain was falling as if from some celestial hose-pipe. Happy as a wet cat I squelched off to find a hotel, preferably with a roof: in this I was successful. The following morning I was offered a lift by taxi to Douz by two oil men I had met.

In Douz we had a few beers in the Hôtel Saharienne, a reasonably high-class tourist hotel. We said our goodbyes and I went into town to give it the once-over. Douz was what we would call a village, but in this part of the world was classed as a major town. Tourism was becoming an important industry in Tunisia and Douz was where the tourists came to experience the Sahara. As a result prices for everything, though cheap by European standards, were about double what one would pay elsewhere.

As I was taking tea under the awned frontage of a café, wondering about my next move, I was approached by an official, card-carrying tourist guide who welcomed me to his country and, like the genii of legend, informed me that my wish was his command. As genii go he was a bit tatty around the edges, and something of a hustler, but he was *my* genie so I'd have to learn to live with him. His name was Amor and his card informed me that he spoke French, Arabic, German, Italian and English. During the entire time of our acquaintance I discovered but four words of English that he could speak, namely, 'Yes, I speak

English', though, I must admit, he spoke them reasonably well. We settled for German.

It was my wish, I informed Amor, to make a caravan to the desert with camels and guide. He had a friend (I rather thought he might) who would arrange this. I told him to set up a meeting. Also I required a *burnous*, a floor-length woollen cloak with a hood, very useful for keeping out the cold and as an extra blanket. Amor had a friend.

We went to his friend the *burnous*-maker, who showed me one of dubious quality for which he wanted forty dinars. I told him that this was unfit for even the lowest peasant. He brought out a russet-brown one of excellent material. I eyed it, fingered it, checked the stitching, and pulled a face.

'How much for this poor but barely acceptable mantle?'

'For this finest of all mantles, a paltry forty-five dinars.'

I looked shocked.

'Forty-five dinars for this rag?'

'Normally forty-five dinars for this beauteous, long-lasting garment, but to you my friend, a special price. Forty dinars.'

'Ridiculous!' I made a move for the door.

'Wait! Will you not take tea?'

This was the next ploy in the age-old drama of commerce. It was an insult to refuse, so I stayed for tea. The play took about an hour and involved his deep love for the English, my great respect for his several wives, children and ancestors, his and my abject poverty, the weather, the price of macaroni, and international politics. Finally I bought the good *burnous* for fifteen dinars, a reasonable price which made us both happy.

Amor's friend the camel factor was Zaid Ali Zaid, a man in his early thirties with a ready smile. I liked him instantly. We bargained and arrived at twenty-seven dinars for three days with a camel and a guide, taking a circular route of about fifty miles or so.

We travelled the fifteen miles to Nouil, the village where Zaid had his camp. This was a purely tourist set-up, now out of season, with several nomad tents erected in a palm grove, western-style toilet facilities, a sick bay, a kitchen and a dining tent. The staff was called Ahmed. There is always an Ahmed.

They treated me like a visiting prince, waiting upon me hand

and foot. For a residence I was given the sick bay, a palm frond hut which contained a bed with clean sheets. I changed into Arab dress and hammed it up. Ahmed told me to beware of serpents in the area. His own cousin had been killed by a serpent. Then he asked about Manchester United and Blondie. Being good Moslems they did not imbibe the fruit of the vine. Being a good Nazrani, I did. We discussed matters of moment, had a thoroughly good evening in each other's company, and when the wine bottle had been drained, I bade them good night.

Before I retired I went for a short walk into the desert. It was a bitterly cold night and the sky was as clear as a bell. The other billion or two stars were back in Orion. I had returned to the mighty desert. It felt like coming home.

In the morning I met my guide, Bashi, an Arab of about twenty summers. He had with him a magnificent white camel, a cow which was well padded with flesh and extremely hairy for the northern winters, quite a contrast to the short-haired, somewhat emaciated beasts of Mali. She was a gentle animal, most of the time. On her back was a peculiar combination of baggage and riding saddle. In Judaea and Mali the riding position is forward of the hump, but here the saddle sat both fore and aft of the hump with a space in the middle for it to poke through. There were baggage attachments in front from which hung two enormous baskets, and a flat platform behind upon which the locals rode in a kneeling position.

We set off with Bashi leading the camel by her head rope and me trying to stay on the swaying animal, to the amusement of the populace of Nouil. First I tried kneeling, but that proved impossible for my European knees so I adopted the tourist position, sitting with legs dangling either side. Within ten minutes my backside was beginning to get sore. We left the village and headed south-east towards the oasis of Ben Charoud of which Zaid had marked the rough position on my map. After a while we encountered a caravan of ten laden brown camels driven by friends of Bashi going in our direction. We tagged along.

Soon we hit low dune which the camels picked their way

through very carefully. I had only ridden on the flat before, and the uphill and downhill bits were somewhat hair-raising at first. The camels would mount nothing but the gentlest of slopes and when they had to go downhill all their joints seemed to disengage and click and jerk. Someone once described a camel as a horse designed by a committee. If so, then no one on that committee had ever seen a hill. The beasts made throat noises like gurgling drains and foamed at the mouth with about two feet of blue-streaked pink tongue hanging out of the side. The smell of one camel is quite phenomenal. The smell of eleven is downright horrific, but one can get used to anything.

At about half past eleven, under a blazing sun, we rounded a palm grove and there, before my eyes, was a football match in progress complete with goal posts and referee. I knew that the desert was unpredictable, but this completely threw me.

We left the caravan and took a different route through the trackless desert. Bashi obviously knew where he was going, but the whole desert looked pretty featureless to me. The terrain alternated between low rolling dune, as barren as the Arctic, and flat scrubby plain with an occasional rise of the ground. The sand was white and as fine as talcum powder. Several times I took the head rope from Bashi and tried to urge on the animal, but she would have none of it. She just turned to Bashi with a look of sadness in her eyes beneath their enormous eyelashes, as if to say, 'What have I done, o Master, to deserve this twit?'

After a couple of hours we stopped at a water-hole. The water was on the surface bubbling from a spring. We couched the camel and unloaded it, leaving the saddle in place. I watched closely as Bashi hobbled her front legs. First he untied the head rope from a loop of cord which was threaded through a hole in her right nostril. Then he wrapped the middle of it twice around a foreleg close to the foot. Next he twisted the two ends of the rope together, leaving enough of each to wrap around the other foreleg, and finished by passing a large knot at one end through a loop at the other. He slapped her backside and away she hobbled to some scrub for lunch.

Water covered some hundred square yards to a depth of a few inches. The spring itself was indicated by a distinct circle of sand, about a yard across, just below the surface. Bashi took a *guerba*, a goat-skin, waded out to the circle, filled it carefully through the neck using a small bowl, and tied the neck tight.

He spread out a blanket on the ground and bade me recline and eat biscuits whilst he prepared a meal. There was a definite master and servant relationship between us which I knew had to be broken down quickly. I wanted to work and learn, not be conveyed like a tourist. There were going to be problems as we had hardly a word of any language in common, but there had been a similar problem with Moustapha in Judaea and we had triumphed.

I was really tired and very sore. We ate something tasteless, macaroni I think, and after a couple of hours' rest to allow the sun to go down a little, we were off again. The stiffness in my back, after the inactivity, was enormous, and my backside reminded me constantly of its presence. My body wanted to walk, but I was here to educate mind and body in the way of camels. I knew how to walk.

Onward we went, and still onward. The scenery was much the same as before and the gentle rolling of the camel seemed to ease, temporarily, much of the pain in my back. Eventually we saw several tall palms ahead, as picturesque a sight as I have ever beheld. It was the archetypal Hollywood oasis.

'Ben Charoud?' I asked.

'Ben Charoud!' confirmed Bashi.

We stopped short of the palms and as I dismounted the pains from parts of my body I'd forgotten about began to rage. The camel had been designed, I decided, not by a committee, but by Allah the Unmerciful specifically to satisfy the masochistic streak of the Infidel. He designed it well.

Bashi made something he called *tay rote*, which sounded Germanic for red tea. One of us was colour-blind. It came out of the pot in a stream about a millimetre thick, and that stream was black, opaque and lumpy. It tasted revolting and I was in fear for my tooth enamel.

The night was bitterly cold, but it didn't rain. We were tucked up in bed by eight o'clock and up at about seven. Bashi made desert bread. First he made a flat cake of dough, raked away the fire, put the cake on the hot sand and raked the fire back in place. Twenty minutes later he dug it out, turned it over, and reburied it. Another twenty minutes or so and he dragged it out like a poor man's phoenix and beat it savagely with a towel to dislodge any sand or charcoal therein embedded. It was quite pleasant, reminiscent of the dampers I used to make as a Boy Scout. We ate it with fig jam washed down with thick coffee.

All our sleeping gear was soaked in condensation and had to be draped over bushes to dry in the dawn sun. It steamed all around us.

One thing was becoming clear. A great deal of time was being spent cooking by age-old methods. Very ethnic and all that, but on the big trip I resolved to use much more freeze-dried food than I had originally planned.

We loaded up the camels, I insisting on doing my share which worried Bashi at first. He was happy to be my obedient servant but I wanted him for a teacher. It was nine o'clock when we finally set out. We passed Ben Charoud and turned west towards the Huites Bir Belgasem which we hoped to reach before nightfall. The sun was fierce and the temperature was already over 70°F. I rode again, and devoutly wished that my posterior was someone else's. Mentally I composed lists of those to whom I would like to donate it. This seemed to ease the pain somewhat.

By now I'd got the hang of steering the beast. Just a gentle tug of the rope to right or left and a little foot pressure on the opposite side of the neck did the trick. A camel won't be forced, it must be persuaded, though sometimes the persuasion has to be less than gentle.

After half an hour we hit aklé dune. Not the big thousand-foot aklé but the small ten-foot variety. It was a new experience necessitating a meandering path taking in all points of the compass since the camel didn't like steep slopes. To advance a mile one had to travel three, a long way in soft sand.

At about ten o'clock the wind began to blow from the southwest whipping the sand into our faces. The camel didn't like it so I had to dismount and haul it along. By eleven the wind was quite strong and I had to wrap my *chèche*, my head cloth, around my nose and mouth to keep out the sand. It kept out some of it, but much time was spent spitting and snorting. The work was hard as the camel didn't really want to come.

There was a small water-hole about a yard wide which Bashi

led us unerringly to. Alongside was the skeleton of a long dead camel. Hollywood came to mind again, and poisoned water-holes with the skulls of long-horns scattered around. Bashi knelt and drank. The camel knelt and drank. I shrugged my shoulders, knelt and drank. Skeletons near water-holes were to be a common sight in the times to come. Beasts just liked to die there.

At noon we found a hillock to shelter behind. We unpacked the gear and I hobbled the camel under the strict supervision of Bashi. His only criticism was that I should always have my head behind the camel's legs as it was less likely to kick my head in. Bashi knew about deserts and camels, but the sum total of his culinary knowledge could have been recited by a stammering parrot in one second flat. Lunch consisted of potatoes, olive oil, peas, water and tomato purée all boiled/fried together in a pan until the potatoes were warmed throughout, and served garnished with sand.

The sky was clear and out of the wind it was very hot. Later, when the sun had sunk a little, the wind dropped and we set off once more. I was beginning to get on very well with the camel. Every time we stopped she would put her muzzle over my shoulder and belch in my ear, a sign of affection, so Bashi indicated by his facial expression. At half past four we came upon a shepherd's tent with a few week-old lambs inside, flop-eared black and white ones with wide eyes and plaintive bleats. The shepherd was away somewhere shepherding. I went solo on the hobbling, a successful operation, and we walked over towards the Huites Bir Belgasem, a grove of palms on a hill about a mile or so away.

On the way Bashi pushed up the speed, so I overtook him, ignoring the pain. He overtook me and we both broke into a headlong charge for the trees. I reached them just before Bashi and we both collapsed in their shade, panting and laughing with each other. The master/servant relationship was gone forever. We were friends.

It was cool in the grove and a couple of falcons were circling the dunes. We sat and watched them for a while, surveyed the desert and chatted. Mostly we spoke in signs and grunts, or had a stab at a Franco-Germanic-sounding word and construction which the other would recognise and elaborate on. We talked about the army. Bashi, too, had military experience as a conscript. He had a family, and a grandfather who had been killed by a serpent. Nouil was overrun by serpents.

The Arabic for bread, he taught me, was *hobsa*, and for camel, *zmal*.

Bashi climbed a palm tree to vindicate his racing defeat and shook down some very poor wild dates.

'*Por zmal?*' I asked.

He nodded, and grinned at his prowess as a teacher of language. The *zmal* appreciated them later.

We collected wood on our way back and the shepherd, an ancient hermit with long white beard, hook nose, and a face like a walnut, fed us on cold macaroni and garlic, the ingredients being roughly of equal proportions. Garlic I like, but not in that concentration. The pan it inhabited was passed from person to person and we ate with our right hands. In matters of eating the left hand does not exist since that is the hand concerned with toiletry. I managed to make a little look a lot and retired gracefully. Even the *tay rote* tasted good by comparison. At least it killed the taste of the garlic temporarily.

To the old man I gave matches. Bashi approved. They were a valuable present and would ensure that he had heat and cooked food for months to come. Before retiring I inspected my nether regions and discovered from whence came the pain. The skin was not broken, it was absent. My underwear was red with blood. I cleaned up the mess, dressed it, and went to bed sore. It was another freezing night.

After breakfast next morning I announced that I myself, Ted Edwards, would retrieve the camel. She was chewing grass about half a mile away. As I approached she lifted her great head and looked at me sadly, then resumed her chewing.

'*Salaam al laikum zmal,*' I said in my best Arabic.

The *zmal* took no notice.

I came in from her right, knelt down and, with my head behind her legs, untied the hobble. So far so good. Next I had to get the rope through the cord loop in her right nostril. She wasn't keen and every time I sneaked close to it she tried to bite my arm off. Being unhobbled now she was free to roam, so roam she did, I following in her wake making friendly noises. Eventually, as she was attempting to disarm me once more I managed to catch the loop. She roared her disapproval, but she was caught. Quickly I tied the rope in place and couched her down in order to ride her back to camp. I boarded and extricated myself from the bush into which she threw me. Second time lucky I mounted and rode back towards the smoke of our fire, proud of my achievement and feeling like Peter O'Toole.

I decided to walk, my injuries being too severe for further punishment. About mid-morning it started to rain and continued steadily for an hour or so. Bashi showed me a small growing thing like a cactus, about a couple of inches high. He dug around it and brought out a great root, like a parsnip about six inches long which he gave me to eat. It tasted bitter, but was cool and full of water, and could be a life-saver in emergency. The *zmal* enjoyed it. She had by now been entirely turned over to my charge and I proudly led her across the great sandy plain towards Nouil, dimly visible on the horizon. We both sang and the camel belched and farted happily. The sun shone, and it was four o'clock when I led the great caravan through Nouil and into the Campement Nomade. Amor was waiting with green tea.

Bashi departed with my combat jacket as a present, its pockets stuffed with boiled sweets for his brood and American cigarettes for himself. I was sorry to see him go.

Apart from my rear end, which was abominable, I was in good shape. The aforementioned part of my anatomy was subjectively in bad shape, and objectively an entirely different shape from what it had been on Tuesday morning. My bad knee had held out well and I was very pleased with the way things had gone.

That evening was spent over good food and reasonable wine. We were joined by a nomad and sang many songs. Zaid told me of his uncle who had been killed by a serpent.

In bed that night I reflected upon the situation as regarded camels. I was happy with my basic ability to handle a camel. Any polishing and local idiosyncrasies would have to be acquired in Mali, probably on the approach from Tombouctou to Araouane. Most of my problems had stemmed from the peculiar saddle preferred by the Tunisians. I must, I vowed, have a Mauritanian saddle, that great leather easy-chair of the desert.

The following morning I asked Zaid the name of his uncle whose demise had been occasioned by a serpent. He gave it. I asked Amor the name of Bashi's grandfather, who had suffered a similar fate. It was the same name. So was that of the cousin of Ahmed. It appeared that, far from an epidemic of serpents, one frail old man had been killed some years previously, and because of the insular nature of Nouil he was related to all.

I bade them goodbye and hitched back to Douz where I booked a room for the night at the Hôtel Gazelle, a cheap but clean hostel-type establishment, there to work out my next move. It seemed that walking through the desert carrying my own water and testing my navigation was the thing to do. To this end, the next day I moved fifteen miles north to the town of Kebili to establish a cheaper base. The Hôtel Petit on the main road gave me clean accommodation at less than a dinar per night. I ate well for about forty pence, found the local den of iniquity, the Hôtel Fort des Autruches, and the town drunk, Mehdi.

Mehdi worked part-time for the local Tourist Bureau, wore spectacles like bottle bottoms and spoke English. It was pleasant to speak English again. We drank a considerable quantity of cheap wine, for which I paid.

For a few days I allowed my injuries to heal, simply getting to know Kebili. I liked it. It was small, had all the necessities of life at cheap prices and was a good centre from which to do some walking. The people, whom I quickly got to know, were friendly, and the tourists only came in on a coach for an hour each morning. Mehdi showed me the old town, now overgrown, and I encountered the local palm-wine-tapper. I took several short walks into the desert both with and without equipment. On a couple of occasions I even tried out a solar still, with the usual result.

For a few days I just wandered the country, looking and tasting. Then, with ideas forming, I jumped on a train and headed south again to Kebili, where I was greeted like the Prodigal Son.

According to my inadequate map there was, forty miles or so south of Douz, a hill. On the way was the oasis of Ben Charoud, which I knew, and according to the map, two more water-holes. If I set out with my gallon container and my water-bottle full, a total of ten pints, I was sure that I could make it to the hill and back, replenishing my water at the water-holes, in about four days. It would be an excellent way to test my navigation and walking prowess. One of my main worries for the big trip was my capability of walking out of the desert should my camels die. Now was the time to find out.

At the Hôtel Fort des Autruches that night I talked to Mehdi about my intended trip. He was horrified, as were the others in the bar when he translated. It was impossible, they all agreed, to travel the desert alone carrying one's own water. No one had ever done it, therefore it couldn't be done!

The following morning I devoted to zeroing in my pedometer and checking my walking speed. I loaded myself up with the gear I would be taking and set off down the road. Since my navigation was to be by dead reckoning and I needed to know as accurately as possible how far along a bearing I had travelled it was necessary that I establish what was my average pace in normal conditions.

I walked five miles out through the desert, parallel to the road, then five miles back. My pace was consistent at five m.p.h., which was French Foreign Legion pace. My pedometer had taken quite a lot of zeroing in.

The weather turned nasty. During the night there was thunder and lightning, and the wind howled through the shutters. Torrents fell and gurgled down gutters all the day. I wasn't going anywhere in that!

It was two days later before the sky brightened enough to consider the walk to the hill, or Jebil as it said on the map. I had done a couple of local walks during respites from the downpour. Now it was time for Jebil. Douz was crowded as it was the day of the camel market. The main square was packed with stalls selling fruit and veg and old clothes. When a Tunisian buys a chicken he buys it fresh – it's still clucking. Just grab it by the wings and off home to the pot. All manner of livestock was going cheap. Some were going 'Baa', some 'Hee-haw,' 'Nyaa', 'Me-e-e-', and 'Cock-a-doodle-doo'. One young camel about three months old was going for people's arms.

I met Zaid in the market and informed him of my plans. 'It is impossible! You will die!' he said. It was not a speculation, but a statement of absolute fact. Zaid ran tourist caravans out to just beyond Jebil and back via the Huites Bir Belgasem, a slightly longer route. This trip, with camels, took ten days. To go to Jebil and back in four days was inconceivable.

I looked at Zaid afresh. For the first time I realised that he was an adult. We would, I told him, see.

At noon I ate, and set out at 12.30. My pack, including my gallon of water, weighed about twenty pounds. I was dressed in jeans and tee-shirt with a zip-front sweater, and my *chèche* on my head. My feet were clad in plimsolls and cotton socks. Thesiger had recommended plimsolls without socks, but I had my doubts about this.

The temperature was about 80°F as I left the town heading south for the position that Zaid had given me for Ben Charoud. First there was a little rolling dune, then low aklé. Sandpipers sandpiped and gigantic gerbils surveyed my passing, sitting bolt upright on dune crests. Navigation was a fulltime job. I kept a log of every move and every calculation for upon my accuracy in this department depended my life.

I would sight an object ahead with my sighting compass and go to it by whatever route I could, using my wrist compass to get me there. After an hour and a half in the heat I topped a dune and saw the palms of Ben Charoud about three miles away, not where Zaid said they were. Now that I knew definitely the position of Ben Charoud, and my own position, I plotted them on the map.

For a half hour I rested, then continued on through a huge palm plantation, arriving at Ben Charoud an hour later. Its hole was dry and collapsed. My pedometer was giving some very erratic readings, probably due to the soft sand and the peculiar gait one must adopt somewhat akin to the rolling motion of the old sailing ships. The pedometer requires a certain amount of impact to operate it. I decided to ignore its gaugings.

A cool breeze was blowing from the south-west. I rested and made out the log. According to the map there was a water-hole three miles away. I checked the bearing and scanned with my sighting compass. Sure enough there were two very tall palms smack on the nose. An hour later I arrived there and there was indeed a water-hole beneath the palms. There were in fact seven palms in two bunches leaning in opposite directions with their respective foliage intermingling in two green blobs in the sky. These I called The Twins. I replenished my water and a few minutes later continued on a bearing for the next water-hole six miles away. The ground was level and scrubby with bushes as high as ten feet. As the sun dipped the temperature did the same. At quarter to six, about half an hour before sunset, it was time to set up camp.

I found a sheltered spot out of the wind, dumped my gear and collected enough wood for supper and breakfast. From Kebili I had brought a whole cooked chicken and some bread and these I made a start on as the water heated for a cup of English tea.

In the desert a cup of English tea of an evening, with or without milk, takes on the proportions of communal wine. When taken with a cigarette in the fire glow, with all the heavens spread out above, the feeling of *rightness* with the universe is indescribable. It becomes obvious why the prophets and sages of old went to the wilderness.

I was almost a third of the way to Jebil. That night I slept contentedly.

An enormous night bird screeching a few feet above me dragged me from slumber just as the sky was beginning to lighten. It was very cold and cloudless with a slight breeze. For a while I lay collecting my thoughts, then, decisions made, I sprang to the tasks. Biscuits for breakfast, and a cuppa, then pack up camp, remove all evidence of occupation, and away again on the same bearing.

An hour and a half later I was where the water-hole should be, but I couldn't see it. There were a few camels around so it was probably in the vicinity, but not necessarily. There was much scrub around which would make it even more difficult to find. For an hour or so I had followed the two day-old tracks of five camels, a donkey and two men, but had lost them in the scrub.

I made a quick search but there was no desperation about it. Jebil was about four hours' hard walking away and I had five pints. There was no known water ahead so that meant that five pints would have to last me all the way there and back to The

Twins, which all being well I would reach on the evening of the next day. It was decision time. I was well hydrated and in no imminent danger. The temperature probably wouldn't get much higher than 80°F. I decided to go on a new bearing, directly towards Jebil, for two hours and review the situation again.

About half an hour later, topping a rise, I saw Jebil in the distance, a small bump on the horizon, grey but distinct, exactly where it should have been according to my calculations. Joy abounded.

Onward, ever onward I marched, humming marching tunes to myself and eating up the miles. At mid-day the sun was high and hot. I was very tired and Jebil was hidden by a ridge about three miles away. It was time for a good rest. According to my reckoning Jebil was about two hours away, perhaps a little more. I couldn't turn back at that stage when it was almost in my hand. The sand-filled wind was hot, which meant that it was over 90°F. I sheltered behind a dune and ate some more chicken. Scarab beetles appeared from nowhere to chew the bones, soon to be joined by blue-streaked lizards.

At three, when it was a little cooler, I set off again. The terrain was still mostly scrub. My shoulders were aching like mad and my feet hurt. Progress was much slower because of fatigue. I composed a marching tune in my head and called it 'Jebil'. It took my mind from the pain. Every half hour or so I had to stop to shake the sand from my plimsolls. My cotton socks disintegrated into rags so I threw them away. Thesiger had been right about plimsolls without socks.

After an hour and a quarter I encountered a dried-up lake with crystal deposits shining all over its flat surface. There was a danger, I had read, that flat areas such as this contained quicksand. I removed my rucksack and very carefully walked out over its surface to collect a few samples of these crystals, having first programmed my mind to lay me down should I begin to sink. The method of getting out of quicksand, which is simply sand and water mixed and is absolutely incapable of sucking one down, is to lie down and either swim out slowly or roll out.

There were no problems. The surface was solid. I collected my souvenirs and resumed my trek. Jebil was visible, but very reluctant to come closer. There was about an hour and a half of full daylight left. My body was desperately shouting to me to turn back, but I needed to be sure of my ability to survive in an emergency. This was the entire object of the exercise. Jebil was only a secondary goal. I just switched to automatic and went on walking.

Two hours later, the sun having vanished leaving a final glow, I was on the lower slopes of Jebil, about two miles from the summit. It was just three hundred feet or so above the surrounding desert, but it was the highest feature in sight with a gentle slope to my left and a steep rocky drop to my right. I couldn't walk another step. I just dropped where I was and laid out my sleeping-bag. There was no wood about, which made no difference as I hadn't the strength to collect it. Tea was brewed on my solid fuel stove and it brought some life back to me. I opened a can of peas, drank the juice and ate the peas cold.

My crotch was very chafed in spite of the administration of talcum powder, so I used a little of my precious water to wash it clean and spread red lotion on it to keep infection at bay. On my feet were a couple of blisters. These I ignored. Then I just piled into my sleeping-bag and dropped into unconsciousness.

I was up an hour before a freezing dawn, brewed up and ate some bread. My body felt better for the sleep; not good, but better. There were three pints of water left. The normal minimum consumption of water in these conditions was six pints per day, so I had read. Something had to be done about the weight of my rucksack. I went through it with a fine toothcomb dumping all manner of things not essential to my survival, including most of a roll of toilet paper, a bottle of red lotion, my plastic solar still sheet, the half of a paperback which I had read and which I particularly wanted to finish, and a loaf of French bread. My pack now weighed about ten pounds or so.

At six-fifty I set out for the summit. The sun poured out over the horizon as I was half way up the gentle slope and became a circle as I reached the highest point half an hour later.

I was ecstatic. I yelled and laughed in triumph. I laughed some more. Tenzing himself could not have felt better standing on Everest than I did atop my three-hundred-foot pile of stones and sand in the Great Eastern Desert. It was necessary, of course, to build a cairn to the gods of Jebil. There were many rocks about and half an hour later I stood my rucksack against the three-foot edifice for a photograph.

Then I set course for home. At the base of Jebil I turned to take a farewell photograph and the camera winder arm fell off, worn through by the sand.

Though my spirits were high I knew I was walking more slowly than normal. The wind was from behind me and the sky was mercifully clouding over. Periodically I would look back and watch Jebil shrinking lower and greyer in the distance. It took a long time before I could no longer make out my cairn, or at least so I imagined. After two hours of walking I rested, then walked for another hour. I was getting noticeably weaker and really had to force-march myself forward. It was almost two in the afternoon, and I had walked through the heat of the day, when I reached the position of the supposed water-hole, complete with camels. After fifteen minutes' rest I set out on the new bearing for The Twins. I still had about a pint of water left.

An hour and a half later I was hailed by a figure standing on a dune. We converged. It was an Arab who, with a companion, was chopping wood to pile on a donkey cart and take to Douz. He could not believe his eyes when he saw the lone Nazrani striding across the dunes out of nowhere.

The two men offered me a meal and a lift into Douz the following morning. I thanked them, but said no at the risk of giving offence. I was going well and had decided to try to make Douz that night. There were still almost three hours of daylight left. If I could reach Ben Charoud before nightfall then the lights of Douz should guide me home. Though I declined their kind offer, I did accept a pint of precious water and set out once more. The Twins were visible high above the scrub to the north-west.

It was quarter past five when I reached The Twins and took on more water. To be able to drink one's fill is a wonderful thing. After a twenty-minute rest I was off again and an hour later arrived at Ben Charoud. There was a beautiful golden watery sunset of which Turner would have been proud.

The water in the sunset began to fall as I trudged north from Ben Charoud. The sky was completely clouded over and it was difficult to pick my way in the almost absolute pitch-dark. There was a light six miles away, on the water tower of Douz, and that was my beacon. I had a torch which was operated by a hand-pumped generator. This ceased to operate at all after half an hour. I found a track and, more by instinct than sight, followed it towards Douz. More lights became visible, and the track became a metalled road.

Further down the road I passed a hotel, out of which came my genie, Amor, the German-speaking guide, who was somewhat surprised to see me. We went in for a beer. It was nine p.m. and Old Baldie didn't even know I was in Africa.

That night I slept at Amor's place. In the morning I was sore all over but fit enough to repeat the exercise, though the inducement would have had to be enormous. This pleased me greatly. In two and a half days I had walked eighty miles carrying my own water. That was about a quarter of the distance of the big one. My navigation had been perfect and I knew that, should my camels die on me, I was capable of walking home. Conditions had been comparable with those I expected in Mali, though the temperature would probably be a little higher. The desert held no further terrors for me. I knew I could handle it.

It was a great feeling.

I returned to Kebili and had a few days' holiday recovering from my exploit. The Tourist Bureau spent some time quizzing me about my trip. They were interested in taking tourists to Jebil and wanted to know if a Land Rover could make it. I said it could. It felt strange advising the Arabs about their own desert, but then how many Manchester people know their way around the Peak District? Lamentably few. The vast majority never set foot outside their own little community from cradle to grave. Arabs too are like that. Most have never seen a desert sunset, or ridden a camel over aklé. If they didn't want their heritage, then I was more than willing to take it off their hands.

One night, in the Hôtel Fort des Autruches, Mehdi and I were discussing comparative religion over about the third bottle of wine. We talked of the few differences and the many basic similarities of all creeds, and we spoke of the many names by which the Universal Spirit was known. We began to list Jehovah, Brahma, The Ancient of Days, Allah, Elohim, The Cosmic Principle, God, The Be All and End All, The Great White Goddess,

Ammon, Helios, Jupiter and many, many more. We ran out of names, slowly, and ground to a halt.

Mehdi filled our glass and passed it to me. 'The camel knows more,' he said.

'What do you mean?' I asked, taking a drink and passing back the glass.

'Well!' he continued, 'You know that a camel looks . . .' He searched for the word in English, gave up, and made a creditable imitation of a camel's holier-than-thou appearance.

'Haughty?' I prompted.

'Haughty!' he confirmed. 'A camel looks haughty. That is because he *knows* the thousandth name of Allah!'

Days later I flew home. I was ready for Mali and Mauritania and I could hardly wait for the next winter. All I needed was the money.

5 Moroccan Manoeuvres

Shortly after my return to England I was elected a Fellow of the Royal Geographical Society, the honour being the greater since my application was endorsed by Wilfred Thesiger. This, I thought, would help considerably towards the success of the expedition, for had the RGS not sent forth Scott, Hunt, Livingstone, Stanley, and Fuchs? They must have maps and information not available to the layman.

I took myself off to the Society's premises near the Albert Hall in London. It was a disappointing trip. The map room had nothing comparable with my own maps, and virtually no information was available about the area of my interest. I was indeed on my own, and doing pioneering work for the foremost British exploratory body.

From the RGS I obtained lists of those institutions offering grants for expeditions and wrote to several. All were unsuccessful. They seemed more interested in scientific work than in exploration for its own sake. Laudable though such scientific work might have been, the adventure seemed to me, somehow, to have gone out of England. In retrospect I conceded that had I received communication from an unknown lunatic requesting assistance for such an apparently madcap scheme, the letter would almost certainly have taken the shortest route to the waste paper basket.

Throughout the year I managed to find a little supply teaching, filling in for absent staff, but as winter approached once more things looked bleak financially. A couple of short jobs just before Christmas helped a great deal, and I sold whatever else of value I owned, which wasn't much.

My cheapest way, it seemed, was through Spain and over to Morocco, thence to Algeria and down the same way as last time. I was on the tightest budget yet, having barely enough to buy one good camel and some scraggy sacrificial beast on its last legs: this provided I didn't eat much and steered clear of bars. I thought about hitching through England, France and Spain, but decided that it would cost me as much in food to do this as the bus fare would cost, quite apart from the draining of much needed strength as a consequence of hitching such a distance in the middle of a European winter. I booked an open return to Algeciras, on the southernmost tip of Spain, with Magic Bus.

My Wake was combined with Christmas amongst friends in Oxford and between then and New Year I travelled south. On New Year's Eve, at nine-thirty in the morning, I disembarked at Ceuta, that foothold of Spain on the North African coast. I boarded a bus to the Moroccan border and alighted in torrential rain.

Customs formalities completed, I took shelter in a café on the Moroccan side. Unfortunately the border bank was closed so I had no dirhams, the Moroccan equivalent of money. A young man who spoke some English introduced himself as Mohammed and chatted. Could he perhaps change some money for me, I asked? Not here, he said, but he had a brother in Tetuan who would change it. Mohammed would pay my fare to Tetuan and when I had changed my money I could repay him. Since I had to go to Tetuan anyway this seemed like a reasonable arrangement. As this was Morocco I knew that, somehow, I was about to be ripped-off, but I was quite used to the ins and outs of North African business, so figured that I could handle it; in any case, as the American gambler said, 'I know the game's crooked, but it's the only game in town.'

We boarded the bus, which was packed with all manner of people and parcels. Goods of all kinds were available duty-free in Ceuta so the Moroccans paid frequent visits there. The entire bus was solid with contraband. A seat was lifted and a sack of grain shoved underneath. Various goods were distributed amongst friends to fool the border guards.

I was introduced to Mohammed's friend, a young Moroccan with an Afro hairstyle and evil, piercing eyes. His name was Omo. I didn't like Omo.

The bus splashed on through the rain and stopped at a road-block where the border guards swarmed, bee-like, inside. Various illicit items were detected and confiscated, and several unsuccessful smugglers led, glum faced, away. We continued towards Tetuan.

Mohammed and I chatted about various things. What did I do for a living? I was a teacher. Was a teacher paid much money? Not much, and many teachers had no job. Why was I in Morocco? For a holiday. He told me that he was a student who worked for his brother, a tailor. The bus sped south on its hour-long journey, past village and pine forest. Coca-Cola signs, in Arabic, were everywhere.

We arrived at Tetuan's bus station and I followed Mohammed through street after street into the Medina, accompanied by Omo. I tried to keep track of direction, but soon gave up on this, relying on my guide to get me through. It was the usual Medina scene of shops and stalls in narrow streets and alleys with exotic aromas and sounds. Finally we arrived at the shop of Mohammed's brother. It was quite a large shop selling mostly brightly coloured Moroccan clothing and all kinds of intricately worked leather goods. We sat in a back room and tea was brought. Another young man joined us. We were introduced, but his name escapes me.

I needed a *bou-bou*, a loose Arab robe, for the desert. Mohammed's brother showed me several, one of which I liked. We bargained for it, and I finally got it for less than ten pounds which was not too exorbitant. In my back pocket I had around eighty pounds in sterling, the rest of my cash being hidden in my pouch. I paid the man and received change.

Mohammed asked me if I liked *cous-cous*. I certainly did, so he invited me over to his house across the street to eat. He led the way through a door into a small courtyard, then through another door into a small, windowless room. A single bare light bulb lit the room dimly, showing benches around a low table. Omo joined us and tea was brought by a lady of the household. It was all very pleasant.

An older, well dressed man entered, was introduced, and joined us in tea. After a while there was a lull in the conversation. Mohammed said, in a friendly manner, 'How much money have you got?'

A strange request, I thought.

'Not much,' I replied, hoping that this would suffice.

'There is much money in your pocket,' he said, indicating his own back pocket. He was still smiling, but only with his mouth. His eyes had become hard. The other two were staring intensely at me. I began to understand.

'Give me your money,' said Mohammed quietly. I watched with loathing as Omo pulled a flick-knife from his pocket, clicked it loudly open, and busied himself with his nails, glancing up at me with as evil a look as I have ever seen.

'Why?' I asked, lamely.

'Give me your money or we will spill much of your blood, and we will damage your eyes.' By this time I was standing. Mohammed grinned, his face close to mine. It was obvious that this was a well-used script.

'Don't be frightened,' he said, solicitously. His hand pulled at my beard. 'Just give us your money, or we will take it, and everything, and we will kill you.'

I knew from their confidence that they were capable of this. No one knew where I was. I would not be missed for several months. I would simply vanish without trace. My eyes flicked to the heavy door. 'The door is locked from the outside,' beamed Mohammed, 'It will be difficult for you to leave.' My mouth was dry and my hands tingled with fear, as they had when I'd climbed into the pit as a child. Old Baldie had arrived and was grinning somewhere in that room; I knew he was grinning.

Then anger began to well up inside, swamping the fear. I thought of the years that had gone into this trip, the hopes and fears, the dangers faced, all to be brought down by three scum, by three little scrapings from the gutters of Morocco. I knew that there was every chance I would die in that room, whatever happened, but I wasn't about to go without a fight. I became calm, as on the rockface just before my backbreaking fall.

The bulge of my father's sword was visible through the side of my rucksack. There hadn't been time to put it on. However, the army had taught me several nasty blows which, no matter how severely provoked, I had never used. Now seemed a good time to start.

Omo had to be put down first for he had the knife. With him out of the way the odds would be considerably improved. I moved away from Mohammed to get within striking distance of

Omo, saying something like 'OK! You can have it.' When I was positioned correctly I let Omo have one in the throat with every ounce of my weight, strength and controlled anger behind it.

He dropped like a sack of rice. I aimed a kick at Mohammed's kidneys, but missed. Things became confused after that. The older man joined in from behind. There was little room to manoeuvre. Some of my blows connected imperfectly, some of theirs likewise. Limbs flailed about in all directions. Then my spectacles clattered to the floor and I knew I was lost. Without them I am, for all practical purposes, a blind man. Vague shapes were all I could see. I lunged at one, making a grab for his clothing. If I could feel him, I could fight him.

It was hopeless. The other one hit me in the kidneys and I went down. They kicked me to the verge of unconsciousness. I indicated that I'd had enough. They had a few more kicks and stopped, more for a rest than for reasons of humanity.

'Your money!' screamed a demented Mohammed. I took the money from my back pocket and threw it in the direction of his voice. I hoped that this would satisfy him. There was about seventy pounds, enough to convince him that this was all I had.

'My glasses?' I asked. I could taste blood.

There was a pause, and a discussion in Arabic. Then my glasses were handed to me in two halves. They were not broken, simply unclipped. I clipped them back together and put them on. My nose hurt, and my left ear.

Omo was on the floor, gasping for air. I was annoyed that he could still move. It was gratifying to see blood streaming from Mohammed's nose. He handed my money to the older man, evidently the boss, who limped a little. If they were going to kill me they would have done so by now, I reasoned.

Omo was helped from the floor onto a bench. When he was slightly recovered he made a lunge for me, but was stopped by the boss. I stayed on the floor. There is a time for humility, and it appeared that this was it.

There was a gold ring on the third finger of my right hand. The boss pointed to it and spoke to Mohammed.

'He would like your ring as a present,' he said in a not impolite manner.

The third finger of the right hand is the marriage finger in

Islam. 'It is from my wife, before Allah,' I lied, hoping this would stir something inside the boss. Mohammed translated. The boss shrugged, and the subject was dropped.

A short time later, when Mohammed had ceased to bleed and Omo could breathe, I was ordered to get up and given my rucksack. Aches and pains abounded. My bad knee had suffered a blow and felt severely damaged.

'No police!' said Mohammed. 'We have many witnesses.' I knew that the police would be of no help in this part of the world. As likely as not they were in the pay of the boss who was obviously running an efficient organisation. If I did complain, more than likely I would be incarcerated for several months on suspicion of some diabolical crime. That is the way of Morocco, the most corrupt country in the whole of North Africa. I knew Morocco of old.

I staggered out of the room, escorted by Mohammed and Omo, inadvertently leaving my *bou-bou* behind. In the courtyard a schoolgirl of about eleven in gym slip and white ankle socks was reading a book. She smiled prettily as we passed. The whole thing seemed, somehow, to increase in wrongness.

Outside, in the street, were people. I have never in my life been so pleased to see people.

'We will take you to the bus,' said Mohammed. It was a statement of fact, not an offer. They escorted me down several alleyways, obviously getting me confused as to direction. They succeeded in this. I doubt if I could ever find the place again.

Suddenly I noticed that we were entering an alleyway devoid of people. It wasn't over! They wanted more, either of my goods or my guts. I made a fuss. They tried to drag me down the alleyway, but I wouldn't go. People began to look. I shouted and kicked out at the two gangsters. They fled down the alley.

Eventually I found the bus station. I had five dirhams, the change from my *bou-bou* transaction. The next bus out of Tetuan was for Tangier in an hour's time. The ticket cost three dirhams and the remaining two I spent on a pot of tea to wash out my bloody mouth. I could feel my pouch against my chest containing my documents and the rest of my money, and from this derived some comfort. It was two p.m. I had been in Morocco for two hours.

The bus arrived. As I was about to board, an arm shot out, barring my way. I looked along it and there was the face of the other young man from the shop. He was chewing gum with his mouth open, chomping it like a cow chewing cud. He was grinning.

'You have money,' he said in broken English.

Still it wasn't over. A great sadness came over me.

'I have no more money,' I said, wearily.

The rest of the queue had walked away, pretending to busy themselves with other things. They were obviously very frightened.

'Give me money!' demanded the rat.

I saw red. I snapped. I boiled over. I was mad with rage. I grabbed that little rodent by the hair and the neck and banged his face repeatedly on the side of the bus with the strength of ten men. There was a join of the metal on the vehicle's side, overlapping and riveted. When I released him it was dripping blood and parts of his nose were adhering to it. I kicked him on his way. A substantial trail of blood showed the direction of his retreat. For the rest of his life, every time he looked in a mirror to shave, he would remember me.

No one saw it. No one was looking. A police officer was standing about twenty yards away, not seeing anything.

I boarded the bus. Everyone quickly did the same. The driver jumped behind the wheel and we were off, quickly, down the road. The bus was quiet. Nothing was said. No one looked at me.

I took out a cigarette to calm myself down. As I searched for my matches the elderly Moroccan sitting next to me flicked on his lighter. I lit the cigarette and thanked him. He smiled, and nodded, and that was that. A small gesture, but it said much. The rest of the trip was conducted in silence.

I knew Tangier quite well, but I had never known it so quiet as it was that evening when I stepped off the bus. Since all the banks were closed I changed some money, illegally, on the street. There was no way out of Tangier until morning, either by land or sea. I would have to stay the night. By now I knew that the rodent would have spoken to Mohammed and friends, and they would have spoken to their friends in Tangier. I needed to hide out somewhere until morning. Several touts wanted me to go with them to a hotel, 'a good hotel.' A cheap hotel? I knew where I was going.

The Hotel Tan Tan on the edge of the Medina had a few rooms on the roof. From this roof there was a good view of the bus station, the harbour gate and the promenade. I booked into one of the rooms.

In the room I stripped off and inspected my injuries. There were two large splits inside my mouth, a cut on the bridge of my nose, another on my left ear where my spectacles rested, several bruises on my body and arms, a large bruise on my left thigh near the groin, my right shin was grazed and covered in dried blood, and my left knee hurt like hell. There was a sickening pain around my left kidney, making lifting and walking difficult. My knuckles and the heel of my right hand were sore and swollen, but I didn't mind that.

I feasted on bread and lemon curd, and brewed a cup of tea on my solid fuel stove. Belatedly I donned my father's sword.

It was time to think over the events of the day. Many people would say that I was stupid to go into a back room in the first place. During the thirty years or so that I have been travelling I have been into countless back rooms and had no problems whatsoever. Indeed, I have spent many happy hours in obscure little back rooms from Tangier to Istanbul and beyond. Does one refrain from crossing roads because of the possibility of being knocked down?

As to the first fight, should I have hit out, or just given them the money? From a practical point of view, and in hindsight, the latter would have been preferable, but at the time I didn't know if I was about to live or die. Such people as those are, by their very nature, unpredictable. Were I presented with the same problem again I was sure, and am still sure, that I would do the same. Indeed, had I been wearing my father's sword I would have used it to its fullest effect and felt fully justified in so doing. Vengeance may well, in the final analysis, be the Lord's, but in that room there were three gangsters, Old Baldie and me. I am normally a peaceful person who lets others alone and likes to be left alone. However, I am not a pacifist. It passed through my mind that if the judges and magistrates of Britain were just once to be the victims of a mugging, they would not be so lenient in their sentencing.

As to the fracas in the bus station, technically I was guilty of assault, but there are many kinds of assault other than physical. Had the Moroccan not mentally assaulted me I would not have physically assaulted him. He got what he asked for, and I was rather pleased about it.

It had just turned midnight. Here was 1982. At home all would be jollity and merrymaking. I wished myself a Happy New Year, chewed a humbug and dragged my battered, sober body to bed. Outside it was pouring with rain. I was sure I heard Old Baldie snoring in the corner.

In the morning I knew I had to get out of Tangier fast. I was up at five. From the roof of the hotel I could see several shady characters hanging around the harbour gate. This was not entirely surprising since on any street in Tangier are shady characters hanging about. I didn't particularly want to leave Africa yet as I wasn't absolutely sure whether the expedition was on or off. I sneaked out of the hotel and bought a bus ticket for Rabat, the administrative capital. There I should be able to get lost, and find a Malian Embassy to obtain a visa.

There was brilliant sunshine when I arrived at the ancient walls of Rabat. I passed through the gateway into the Medina and booked in at the Hotel Saada. The Tourist Information Office was my first port of call, to find out if there was a Malian Embassy in town. One would think that such an office would be located where the tourists went. One would be wrong. I finally found it in a residential suburb a couple of miles the other side of town. It was Friday, and it was closed until Monday.

The pain in my knee was excruciating and I ate painkillers like sweets. Coming back through the Medina to the hotel, a kebab in my hand, I started to get pains around my heart. This had never happened before and was very worrying. Was it just lack of acclimatisation, or something more serious brought on by the trauma of the previous day? I had no way of knowing. I went back to my room and lay down until morning.

During the evening, and the next morning, I tried to juggle my finances into a viable amount with which to continue the expedition. I even thought of selling all my European clothes and dispensable equipment in Mali, but it was no use. There wasn't enough left. So that, unfortunately, was that for another year.

The making of this decision had converted me in one move from a penny-pinching expedition treasurer to a reasonably well-to-do tourist. I went in search of a beer to celebrate my new status and dull the pain in my body and soul. Later I invested in a meal, the first proper meal I'd had since leaving Oxford. Three courses all for about £1.20.

On Sunday I was running very short of dirhams and the banks didn't open until Monday. The trouble with Rabat was that it was an honest, law-abiding city. It was nice to have someone chase after me with a pen I had dropped in the street, but there wasn't a black-market money-changer in town. I passed the afternoon playing the 'little game'. This is a game played strictly between two men and Old Baldie has no part in it. The plot is always the same, but the script varies considerably.

It began as I was having a glass of black coffee outside a café. A weasel-faced gent of about forty-five in a crumpled brown suit sat down on the next table and ordered a drink. After a while he introduced himself and we talked in French. The 'little game' had begun.

First I had to establish my ignorance of the French language to allow for intentional misunderstandings. He told me that he was a high-ranking customs official from Tangier, where he had his home, to which I was invited. I told him that I was a Professor of History at Manchester University, and he must visit me sometime. We pretended to believe each other. I knew that he wanted to con some money out of me. In my pocket were thirty dirhams, worth about three pounds, and two hundred French francs the value of which was about twenty pounds. Before he could con dirhams out of me he would have to organise the changing of the francs, which was what I wanted.

He invited me to a bar. I explained my monetary position.

'No problem!' he said magnanimously. 'I shall pay, and you can pay me back when we change your money.'

I was sure that I'd heard that one somewhere before.

The con-man was called Rashid, or so he asserted. Rashid knew the proprietor of the bar, who didn't seem entirely pleased to see him and wouldn't change my francs. I got the distinct impression that had I been alone he might well have done so. We tried a large hotel, where the desk clerk knew him, without success.

On to another bar we went, where Rashid ordered two more beers, without paying. He had a brainwave. Why didn't I, he said, give him the two hundred francs and wait here in this nice bar drinking this nice beer for just two minutes whilst he went to change it? I didn't understand a word of this. Bogus professors of history are remarkably bad at languages. He tried very hard to make me understand.

Rashid paid for the beer and we went to several more hotels without success. Repeatedly he said to me that when he managed to change it for me I must give him a hundred dirhams. Fifty per cent commission seemed a bit high to me. I pretended a partial understanding and smiled a great deal. On our travels we met at least ten of his friends, including a very seedy-looking, unshaven, fat man who was, apparently, a 'Full Colonel' in the customs service. It was remarkable how many people this customs official from Tangier knew in Rabat. Finally one of his friends changed the money and as we walked off he demanded a hundred dirhams. After much bargaining I paid him for the beers and twenty dirhams for his trouble, a very reasonable commission. He stormed off in pretended disgust.

He made his profit. I changed my money. The 'little game' had been a draw.

By Tuesday I was much recovered from my ordeal and decided to move south to Marrakech, partly to kill time until the heat died down in Tangier, and partly to see Marrakech.

Half way there we stopped at a bus station to stretch our legs. Everyone made a dash for the door. I turned my head around to see if it was worth standing up yet and got a big bare brown breast full in the face. There was the young lady, all veiled for modesty with a great boob sticking out, the nipple trying to work its way up my nose. Strange, I reflected, are the cultural varieties of the meaning of prudery.

Having stretched our legs we piled back onto the bus for 'the show', an entertainment common on buses throughout the Islamic world. A succession of people will get on the bus at the front. Some will sing, some extol Mohammed, some will sell sandwiches, some play instruments, some will simply beg. They pass towards the back of the bus in turn, hands held out for alms or payment, and alight at the rear. A small, very pretty girl led her blind grandfather down the bus, his palm outstretched, praising Allah, his other hand on her shoulder. Here there is no welfare state.

Soon the bus was off again towards Marrakech. Somewhere a transistor radio belted out insistent Arabic music. A woman sang over the air, her voice high and powerful, perfectly controlled through the intricate weaving and lilting of her song. Her vocalising had a sensual quality which was erotic to the point of pornography.

Marrakech was a disappointing town, being extremely touristy and beggar-ridden. I found a room in the Medina for fifteen dirhams and went to bed. Then I discovered why the room was only fifteen dirhams. I had to share the bed, with ants. At least I wouldn't be lonely. The mattress was quite remarkable having its springs on the outside. Considering the amount of wriggling and squirming I accomplished that night I must have lost several pounds before morning.

Very early the next day I was on a bus for Ouarzazate, beyond the High Atlas mountains. The bus sped along the narrow pass. Occasionally we would pass an upturned vehicle which had gone over the edge, one truck with its wheels still lazily turning. I had heard tales of the local bandits ramming tourists over the edge in order to obtain booty from the corpses. This was apparently quite a common thing, occurring several times per week.

There was little to see in Ouarzazate except the old town which was quite picturesque. The next day saw me abus easterly to Ksar-Es-Souk, a filthy little town in the foothills, and the day after I spent eight hours on a bus back across the High Atlas, north to Fez. I had become thoroughly fed up with my touristy existence. It seemed to me that if one required a holiday then the place to have it was in one's home town where one could obtain the food, drink and conversation of one's choice and sleep in the comfort of one's own ant-free bed. The heat should, I considered, be off by now so I was going home.

My ants were still with me, but in reduced numbers. I had devised a method of ridding myself of their company. In a pocket of my jacket I kept a couple of lumps of sugar which attracted my tenants. Periodically I would evict them. Within three days I was ant-free.

In Fez I boarded a train for Tangier at three o'clock. Later, as the train sped north in the dark, I noticed a lunar eclipse in progress, brilliantly visible in the clean African air. The movement of the spheres never ceases to fascinate me. For the rest of the journey I stared avidly at this celestial show whilst my fellow passengers gave it but one glance and buried their heads in newspapers. Some people have not, nor do they deserve, souls.

In the morning I bought a ticket for the afternoon ferry to Algeciras, a *cous-cousier* to make my own Lancastrian *cous-cous*, and some presents. Poised on the tip of Africa, ready to leave Morocco probably for ever, I drank final mint teas and waved away last con-men. There was no sign of local underworld vengeance aimed in my direction.

The afternoon sun shone dimly through the clouds as a boat left an African harbour with a twice-failed explorer on board. It was back to the usual mixture of relief and smiles, of sniggers and jokes. But mostly it was back to a free country where, for the most part, one could walk the streets alone in safety. To leave Africa once more a failure was sad, but I was glad to be going home.

There would be another winter for Africa.

Part Two

EXODUS

6 Tombouctou Revisited

Nineteen-eighty-two was a year of full employment, teaching the children of Moss Side the intricacies of mathematics, English and the finding of non-existent jobs.

It was also a year of terrible illness. Asthma, inherited from my father, and until now dormant and unsuspected, made itself brutally apparent. Weeks were spent fighting for breath, and nights sitting in fear of sleep lest breathing should cease. I was unused to illness and was profoundly shocked that this should be happening to me. Injury I could readily accept, but that my body itself, of its own volition, should malfunction in this way was difficult to come to terms with. However, as Christmas approached once more my health improved, and my finances reached and passed the minimum requirement for the expedition.

The usual publicity was sent to the press and media with little real hope of any response. This time I was to do a little scientific work for Manchester University, consisting of the collecting of sand samples from aklé dunes for the School of Geography. The head of that department supplied me with a letter, in French, explaining to whom it might concern why I was wandering over this obscure part of the globe. Since I had heard that the region around Araouane was a restricted military zone this work, sincere in its intention though it was, would be my 'cover'. No mention would be made in Mali about crossing into Mauritania. Unfortunately, circumstances were to be such that this work did not get done.

Just before Christmas I received a phone call from Alistair Macdonald of BBC North West Television. Could he interview me that afternoon, he wished to know, for that evening's programme? He most certainly could! We got on famously. A narrow, out-door man of six foot odd, Alistair was himself well travelled and exuded an air of capability. Though he knew little of deserts he asked the right kind of questions and treated the entire project in a serious manner, not as some kind of amusing side-show as I had half-expected.

The interview had far-reaching results. People I didn't know would stop me in the street to wish me well. Counter assistants and the school crossing patrolman said, 'Good luck.' There were countless others. I began to realise that it wasn't just a one-man show any more, but that not only were the people of my town with me, I was, in many ways, doing it for them. I was their representative in the field of exploration. It is a strange and a very moving thing to feel both pride and humility simultaneously. The people of Eccles put some much-needed fire into me at this time, and I shall always be grateful for this.

Two days after the interview Alistair rang me again to tell me that a higher power at the Beeb had expressed a wish that a film crew should film me setting off.

'You mean,' said I, 'getting on a number sixty-six?'

This was not what he meant. They wished to meet me in Tombouctou, film my preparations and the approach to, and departure from, Araouane; then go around to Oualata the easy way and film my arrival. All this was to become a documentary for transmission later in the year. Was I in agreement, Alistair wished to know. I stopped dancing long enough to tell him that I was, then resumed. This was the finest publicity for the expedition that I could possibly wish for.

Things moved very quickly after this. Since Alistair was to head the camera crew I gave him a crash course on deserts. There was some filming in a folk club for preliminary footage. Alistair flew to Paris to get our visas for Mali and Mauritania.

Christmas time and the ensuing few days were tense days for me. I was constantly on edge, and occasionally over it. It was a time for setting one's house in order, and the making of a Will; of deep introspection, and of fear.

For Alistair it was a time of enormous organisation. To accomplish what he did in those few short weeks was phenomenal. At his instigation Karrimor, the out-door equipment firm, became interested in the expedition. We made a trip to their Accrington factory and were royally received. My requirements were discussed with the boss, Mike Parsons, and I came away with a sleeping-bag, a 'Gortex' jacket with 'Thinsulate' inner, a pair of 'K-SB-2' light-weight boots which were, in effect, super-plimsolls, a 'Karrimat' sleeping-mat and several elastics with hooks which were extremely useful and versatile. The crowning glory of their sponsorship was a specially built 'Jaguar IV' rucksack with extra straps and, embroidered on the back, the legend, 'EDWARDS Empty Quarter Expedition'. (The term 'Empty Quarter' had been coined for the area by the explorer Tom Sheppard who had crossed much further north by motor vehicle. It was reminiscent of Thesiger's famous 'Empty Quarter' in Arabia.)

The expedition was now thoroughly respectable, being backed by my national TV company, sponsored by a leading out-door equipment manufacturer and endorsed by a major university. I thought that, perhaps, the Royal Geographical Society might give it recognition, so I filled in the necessary forms and despatched them.

I saw the journey as having three distinct phases, each with its own unique problems.

Phase One was the trip to Tombouctou which, this time, should be easier since I would fly to Algiers, but was still a formidable task which I wasn't looking forward to.

The second phase was the buying of camels in Tombouctou and the long trek to Araouane.

The third and final phase was the crossing of the Empty Quarter and arrival in Oualata.

What happened then was a matter for pure speculation. If the crossing was successful I should be able to fly home on pure exhilaration; if not, then the problem would not arise.

Final preparations were made. I had obtained a Gurkha *kukri*, the curved fighting knife of the Nepalese warrior, which, together with my father's sword, required sharpening. A strap had to be made for the former and a new sheath for the latter. Pills for this and pills for that were obtained, injections boosted, bandages bought, documents checked and, where necessary, renewed, equipment tested and repaired or replaced, log book bought, traveller's cheques purchased, tomato purée procured, toilet paper, batteries, insect repellent, solid fuel, boiled sweets, films, ball point pens, needles, matches, and pencils, etc. etc. etc. collected.

At last, at long last, all was ready and packed. On the morning of Tuesday the eleventh of January 1983 I said goodbye to Alistair at Ringway airport, expecting to see him in Tombouctou in a fortnight or so. Phase One had begun.

Algiers has three separate areas, the Seedy, the Very Seedy and the Extremely Seedy or Medina. It was dark when the airport bus dropped me off on the promenade of the Very Seedy zone and I headed for the Extremely Seedy region in search of a bed. In the dark the Medina can be a very dangerous place for a man alone with a large heavy rucksack and a shoulder-bag. I tried numerous hotels but all were full. Weakness of legs was the order of the day as the previous night's farewell revels caught up with me. All the hotels in the Medina are up several flights of stairs. As I came out of one hotel into the dimly lit street a young man made a grab for my shoulder-bag, but I had a good grip on it. He tugged hard at it, taking no notice of me at all. For his trouble he received the toe of my right K-SB-2 where it would interfere with his involvement in the perpetuation of his race for some time.

Deciding that the Extremely Seedy beat was not, at this time, for me, I made for the Very Seedy, and subsequently the Seedy precincts, both to no avail. There was not a bed to be had in Algiers. By ten o'clock I was completely exhausted. The streets were dark and empty save for shadowy characters in shadowy corners. It was time to get off the streets and mingle with people.

On the Very Seedy promenade there stands an all-night café known to me from my previous trip, a haven of light and safety in a very dangerous blackened city. It was packed and smoky. Three young Frenchmen with similar problems made room for me at a table and we drank coffee, talked, dozed, drank some more coffee, talked some more, dozed again and drank more coffee until about seven o' clock. Then through a wakening city cold with dawn I located a bus to Ghardaia and left on it at eight. I had decided against the train as a method of crossing the High Plateau, the bus being both cheaper and more comfortable.

In the hill-town of Ghardaia, reached ten hours later, again there was no bed to be had. I walked to the edge of the dark, sprawling town, and attempted to sleep amongst the rocks.

There was little sleep to be had, thanks to the noise of traffic, dogs, donkeys, and what sounded like wolves and probably was. At four I was up and shaking the crust of frost from my sleeping-bag. I caught the bus for Adrar at five and, half-awake, was conveyed south-west.

My health had, for a few days, taken a nose-dive. There was some manner of infection in my right lung giving me great pain, complicated by constant asthmatic wheezing and coughing. If I had been at home there would have been no question of attending work. Severe doubts, fuelled by my physical state, assailed me. I must be crazy, I thought, to contemplate this journey in my state of health. Over the past three days I had had about five hours of sleep and eaten nothing solid, there being no appetite in me. Depression settled on me like a sodden blanket.

Adrar was reached at nine o'clock. I was told, or at least I thought I was told, that there was a bus for Reggane, the gateway to the Sahara, at five a.m. I drank a cup of ashtray coffee at the bus stop café and once more went in search of that elusive African bed.

There were two hotels in Adrar, both charging exorbitant prices. Algeria was still a very expensive country. I decided that the bed-price would make too great a hole in my finances and set out for the edge of town where on a large, flat, dark clay area, the clay crunching underfoot to give warning of marauders, I lapsed into unconsciousness.

Next morning the bus came promptly at five – with 'Ghardaia' written on the front in Arabic script. There was no bus for Reggane until next day. Everyone crowded onto the bus and it departed, leaving me alone to watch the cold dawn.

There was no point in staying around for another day. As the sun's disc cast long shadows over the earthen square, and the cold wind chilled the bones, I left the town to try a hitch down to Reggane. After an hour or so a truck stopped and in the early afternoon deposited me on the edge of that town.

Since my last trip there had been changes. A casbah-cum-supermarket had sprung up near the police post and a tap which, occasionally, gave a trickle of water. When I arrived there was a French convoy of Citroens outside the police post with the crews checking in prior to tackling the dreaded Tanezrouft.

Three of the girls were dressed in obviously new male Arab dress, which made them look even more ludicrous than girls dressed in European male attire. The police were highly amused and several members of the populace gathered to stare and laugh.

They couldn't, they said, find room for another traveller. I impressed on them my knowledge of the route and conditions, but to no avail. They departed with ample space on board.

I spent the day trying to obtain transport from any of several European enclaves, but always they were rich enough to refuse the proffered passage money, or were, so they said, knowledgeable enough not to need my services as a guide. The day wore on, and on, and on.

Reggane was where the flies came in winter. They were everywhere, flying into my ears and nose, crawling all over my clothes and punctuating my diary as I caught up with the day's events. Though there was no post-office in Reggane I wrote letters home for posting in Gao, eight hundred miles of desert away.

The police told me of a bus across the Tanezrouft to Borjd Mocktar on the Malian border. This left the next morning and was an innovation. As the sun sank over the praying town I went over to the bus stop café for a meal of barley, potatoes, sand, chilli peppers and a minute particle of some unspecified dead animal, in roughly that order of proportion. It was my first meal for five days. An eating companion asked me the usual questions and I talked an incredible load of waffle about Manchester United. Before we got onto the subject of Blondie I fled to the desert and slept.

The bus was a magnificent affair, being a large insulated van with small windows and thirty-two seats, mounted on a four-wheel-drive Mercedes truck chassis, the whole thing painted in bright orange. There was, however, a problem. I had spent my last dinars on the previous night's meal and there wasn't another bank until Gao. The driver, a reasonable gent, figured that he may as well fill the seats as not, so we agreed that, somehow, I would pay him in Borjd Mocktar. We piled masses of baggage onto the roof and held it tight with a rope net; then south we went, dropping off the end of the road onto the sands of the Tanezrouft.

It was cool in the van and the journey would have been almost pleasant were it not for the weakness of Arab stomachs. The constant bumping over undulations caused several fellow travellers to part company with recent sustenance. Fortunately there was no shortage of sand to stop it sloshing about.

One old man was obviously close to death and had to be laid down in the aisle as the bus bounced south at speed. A considerable proportion of the journey was accomplished by air with the passengers flailing about in free-fall. The dying man's relatives remonstrated with the bus crew about the roughness of the ride, but they made it plain that The Company had contracted to deliver thirty-two bodies to Borjd Mocktar. The number of souls present upon arrival was entirely the responsibility of Allah.

The sound and stench of retching and farting was incredible. Periodically we would stop to eat, pee and pray. On leaving the cool of the bus the broiling Saharan sun hit like a sledgehammer. The mostly flat sand and gravel stretched featureless in every direction to a perfectly level horizon. On and on for hour after hour we banged, and swayed, and sloshed, and at every stop it seemed that we might as well not have moved at all.

There was a Frenchman on board, also heading for Gao. We talked, and shared water. At some time in the afternoon we crossed the Tropic of Cancer. At one point we encountered nomads with camels. The 'town' Arabs on the bus were intrigued by them, and, I think, envied them their freedom. The 'free' men begged cigarettes and matches from those in bondage, so were they really free? Perhaps only the desert is free, and daily its freedoms are being eroded. I supposed that even the sand sampling that was part of my schedule would curtail, to some minor degree, this freedom. That is the way of Man. We are ants moving over the carcase of the Earth, stripping it bare.

Once we stopped to give assistance to the Citroen expedition which had become hopelessly bogged down in the sand. The strangely dressed girls, and one or two of the men, stood around looking helpless as we dug them out and pushed them clear.

It was eleven p.m., after fourteen hours on the bus and four hundred Saharan miles, when we arrived at Borjd Mocktar. There were, Allah be praised, still thirty-two passengers on board in possession of souls, though for at least one the hold was somewhat tenuous.

The Frenchman produced from his copious luggage a European tent which, tourist-like, he commenced to erect. He invited me to share his stale air and body odours but I declined in as graceful a manner as possible. I did, however, share in his bread and jam. My appetite had returned and my health was much improved.

In the morning a large Malian truck piled impossibly high with merchandise, a tramp of the sand seas, offered the Frenchman and myself passage. He would, he said, be in Gao in ten days. Since I wished to be in Tombouctou in about a week I declined, deciding to take a chance on swifter transport. I knew that Alistair and the film crew would be in Africa that evening. The truck swayed and leaned its way south and vanished, eventually, over the horizon.

Borjd Mocktar consisted of a police station, a customs office, an artesian well, an army post, several mud brick dwellings, a school and about thirteen goats. I went through the customs formalities, which took all morning, and paid the bus driver in French francs, which he managed to change somewhere, giving me a few dinars change. I had money. The day wore on.

The French Citroens with the strangely clad women came through in the afternoon, looking somewhat bedraggled. A children's expedition of European origin, mostly French and Swiss, lurched in. As normal they playfully fought each other in the sand. The Arab young just stared at all this barbaric display. Earlier I had watched the local children in the school playground. They did not fight, or make pretence of fighting. Contrary to popular belief the Arabs are not habitual warriors like us uncivilised northern barbarians, but poets and scholars. They are a gentle people, though they can fight when sufficiently roused.

Not until the fourth day did I leave Borjd Mocktar. Life evolved a pattern. Each morning the customs post kitchen boy would give us coffee for sweets. I would direct all traffic to the appropriate officials and try to obtain a ride. The wind would blow the sand everywhere, and I do mean everywhere. The customs officials fed me each night in payment for my traffic control.

I established links with the local army post and was thereby allowed to buy from the army shop, the only shop in town. Choice was a little limited. They sold sardines, sweet biscuits, cigarettes and flash-lights; nothing else.

The customs men offered me the use of their floor on which to sleep, but I preferred the desert where I could burrow into the cool sand in comfort and breathe the clean air. There was a new moon, the horns pointing upwards like my birth sign, Taurus. I speculated as to whether I would see the next new moon. Using poetic licence I had come to see the Empty Quarter as a dragon to be fought, and it seemed to me that the next time there was a new moon either the dragon or I would be dead. This I entered in my diary.

On the Tuesday afternoon, as I was contemplating putting my name down on the housing list, three Peugeots pulled in at the customs post driven by Frenchmen. They were taking the cars south to sell them. A feeling of déjà-vu came upon me. At first there was no room on board, but when the right amount of cash was waved at their leader a place was, miraculously, found in his car. He produced a beer from the depths of his luggage and presented it to me. I cannot remember a finer present. The majority of the populace assembled to shake my hand and wave me off. We pointed the cars south, hoping to cover the hundred miles or so to Tessalit by nightfall.

The leader I shall call Pierre. He made about six trips per year of this nature, and conducted other 'business' in transit. The other two were his hired drivers.

In the early stages we bogged down a couple of times, but soon we were beyond the Tanezrouft sand sea and into the rockier area. The soft tyres were changed for harder ones and off came the exhausts. The trip to Gao took three days, including the conducting of much 'business' and the giving of vast quantities of *cadeaux* along the way. Pierre, wallet bulging, constantly complained about the demands of officials and head-men.

'Cadeau! Cadeau! Always *cadeau*. They will have me out of business with *cadeaux*!'

In the village of Anefis we tried to perform a sumpectomy on one of the cars, the sump having been badly dented by a rock. It was hopeless. The thing just wouldn't come off, so back went all the bolts in the dark.

I tried to sleep outside the head-man's house, but he would not hear of it. I must, he insisted, sleep within his house.

'Here you will be cold.'

'No I won't.'
'It is not good for you.'
'Yes it is.'
'You will be uncomfortable.'
'No I won't.'
'Animals will pee upon you.'
'No they won't.'
'What will the neighbours think?'
'OK. I'll sleep inside.'

I slept on a hard tiled floor in a hot room next to the toilet with a wheezing, snorting old man in the opposite corner, and suffered from asthma all night, but the head-man was happy.

Wearily, on the afternoon of Thursday the twentieth of January, we arrived in Gao where I paid Pierre and departed for the Hôtel d'Atlantide. Madame the Statuesque remembered me, as did some of the staff. The removing of filthy clothes, the taking of a cold shower, the donning of a clean *bou-bou* and the drinking of an ice-cold beer after crossing the Sahara; these are a few of my favourite things.

My old friend Musa was now a handsome young fellow who had become some manner of con-man. His future was assured.

I contacted the fixer, told him I wished to go to Tombouctou and also wished to buy a Mauritanian camel saddle. We arranged to meet the following day, after I had been to the bank. The usual police formalities were set in motion and I ate and slept the sleep of the content, in a real bed.

At the bank the following morning I changed over seven hundred pounds-worth of traveller's cheques, there being, so I thought, no bank in Tombouctou. It is a nervous thing to wander the streets of Africa with the equivalent of twenty-five years' gross income for the average local upon one's person.

After five days languishing in Gao, being constantly conned and let down by the fixer, I decided to by-pass him and left Gao on the Tombouctou road for the police post, about two miles out of town. All Tombouctou traffic had to stop there, so there I would remain until picked up. I was amply supplied with bread, sardines and water, prepared for a stay of several days.

As I walked the two miles to the post I found myself whistling a tune. This was a good sign. My marching tune is a fine indicator of my mood and condition. If my spirits are high I whistle, hum or sing, vocally or mentally, jazz and music hall numbers. As my demeanour and physical state diminish my repertoire goes through the marching songs of England, then Scotland, Ireland and Wales, followed by France, Holland and, finally, when every step must be forced from my body on pain of death, Germany. When I come to the 'Panzerlied' and 'Erika' then things are dire indeed, but the ultimate is 'Horst Wessel', a song about a Nazi yob of that name who got himself killed whilst exercising his naziness upon others (how sad). The thought of fascism and any other extremist creed, be it politically or religiously dogmatic, is anathema to me, but in extreme *personal* circumstances then the *power* of such extremism can be useful. It becomes, briefly, the lesser evil, the means to an end. Even such a mindlessly brutal activity as riding to hounds has produced some fine chorus songs.

My tune that day was 'The Stripper'. My health had improved dramatically and I was on the last leg of Phase One. I estimated that the film crew would have been in Tombouctou for several days awaiting my arrival. The sky had been hazy for a couple of days, a sure sign of a sandstorm brewing. There was a cold, strong wind blowing as I slept that night beneath a boabab tree.

A hazy dawn crept in, chilly with wind. The police and staff thanked Allah for its arrival and went about their business. They gave me tea.

Presently an ancient truck which was entirely held together by wire, string and wooden wedges, lurched out from Gao. The driver said he would take three days to deliver his cargo of Taiwan charity rice to Tombouctou and offered me a place in the cab, with food, for about fifteen pounds. I took it. It could be several days before another truck arrived.

The old girl may have been tatty in appearance, but she had a heart like a lioness. Every fifteen minutes or so the driver would leap out of the cab and hammer home several wooden wedges which, together with a quantity of string, formed an integral part of the suspension system. The tyres were remarkable, being for the most part completely treadless. In some cases even the canvas was much worn through. There were no brakes but a couple of wooden chocks which the driver's boy, Kassim, rammed dexterously beneath the wheels whenever we stopped. But her diesel heart never missed a beat as we lumbered slowly but surely down the Tombouctou track.

There was a road of sorts for the sixty miles to the small town of Bourem where we spent the night. We ate meat, bread and rice, then slept on our cargo of rice sacks, the truck parked in the main square. In the morning the sky was even hazier. From Bourem there was no road. Mostly there was not even a track from there to the environs of Gourma-Rarous a hundred and twenty-five miles along the Niger's bank. We drove through the scrub making new tracks in the sand. Occasionally we would bog down and have to dig. Sometimes we would follow other tracks for a while, but generally we simply went west.

The Niger was beautiful, wandering the plain below us, wide and lazy, an occasional pinnace ploughing its lonely groove up or down river. The sun was hot by ten o'clock, having risen above the sand-haze into a clear sky. We stopped beside an east-bound truck for lunch and recommenced at around three.

It was about five-thirty when we pulled onto a large sandbank on the shore of the river where three other rice trucks were parked. As the sun dipped behind the sand-haze the whole world became red. The wind had dropped as I took an evening stroll along the bank, watching great storks fly low over the water, their brilliant blue and white wings lazily wafting the air. The driver had told me that in Mali too, storks were responsible for babies. Various other water birds swam away at my approach, protesting ritually. All was peace and beauty.

The sandstorm hit the following morning, and hit with a vengeance. Visibility was down to a few yards as the sand was forced from the ground by the great gusting winds. Two tyres had deflated in the night and had to be changed despite the conditions. Then we sheltered in the cab for the morning, watching the sand swirl past.

The drivers held a meeting. They decided that the storm could last for several days. It was impossible to continue on by truck to Tombouctou until the storm abated, so they decided to send their rice upriver by pinnace. My driver explained the position to me and refunded about five pounds, which was fair. I would have no trouble, he said, obtaining passage by pinnace to Tombouctou.

By mid-afternoon the storm withered somewhat. The trucks were moved to a different part of the bank where an eighty-foot motor pinnace, black and narrow with brilliant paintings on its long, pointed prow and stern, was moored thirty feet off-shore. There was a large crowd gathered, mostly young men and children. The atmosphere was festive.

Four of the young men girded their loins and waded out to the pinnace, sinking in mud to their knees, the water up to their chests. A great iron set of industrial scales was unloaded from the pinnace onto their shoulders and they carried this impossible weight onto the shore where it was placed with reverence. Village dignitaries were in attendance. The doctor took charge of the tally, assisted by the head-man and watched by the captain. A truck was backed up to the scales and the transfer of rice began.

First there had to be an argument. The more I see of the Third World, the more I am convinced that it isn't the poor soil or the lack of natural resources that keeps them poor, it is a basic lack of any ability to organise. Black Africans and Arabs will far rather argue about doing something than actually get around to doing it. Eventually the argument was temporarily settled and rice sacks began to fly from the truck onto the scales. They were weighed, recorded, and carried on heads at the trot through the mud and water to the waiting pinnace. When they finally got going they knew how to work.

Occasionally a sack would tear, spilling rice onto previously laid mats. The children would swarm like ants onto this, gleaning it into bags and tins to take home. A man was kept busy sewing up damaged sacks. Meanwhile a kitchen had been built and rice was put on to cook. Children sold biscuits, sweets, cigarettes and matches. Somehow tenuous order emerged from total chaos.

The first truck was emptied, driven away and replaced. Then the argument was resurrected, run out of steam, and laid to rest once more. I amused the children, and not a few adults, with some mild coin magic as the pinnace and the sun sank lower.

The pinnace would not be sailing for two days so I would have to go to the village which was across the Niger. Eventually all the rice was loaded and several small boats arrived to ferry us over that arm of the river. Shoes had to come off and trousers be rolled to board and disembark. The sun vanished as we began a five-mile hike towards Gourma-Rarous. We boarded another mini-pinnace and set out into darkness on the great river. First we were propelled by poles, then, as the water became deeper, by paddles. It was strange to sit in that ancient craft which could well have been one of those in which my companions' ancestors had chased, and killed, Mungo Park's expedition.

Eventually dim lights became visible ahead and we arrived at the village. There were many pinnaces moored along the shore, but enquiry revealed only one leaving for Tombouctou the following morning. The Captain swore to have me in Tombouctou the following night. For five pounds I booked passage and embarked.

The boat was about forty feet long with branches laid on the bottom to raise the cargo above the bilge water which was sloshing about. Mats were placed over the branches to form a kind of undulating deck. Other branches were bent athwart the hull in hoops like a Wild West covered waggon, over which were spread rush mats to form a sheltering canopy. The general appearance was like unto an aquatic Nissen hut.

I lay down to sleep, the stench of bilge in my nostrils. During the night I felt a quite large animal with a feline-like tread walk over my feet. 'The ship's cat,' I thought. In the morning I discovered no ship's cat, nor did I remember having seen a cat in this part of the world. I concluded that it must have been an enormous ship's rat.

The ship's company, discounting the rat, consisted of the Captain and the First Mate, both black Africans in their early twenties. Their language was unknown to me, possibly Bambara or Tamachek with a few French and Arabic words thrown in. Indeed they rarely spoke at all, either to me or to each other. The First Mate produced hot rice, grey-brown of colour, sticky of texture and vile of taste. I ate a couple of handfuls to please him and went to buy bread.

At around nine o'clock we weighed anchor, a car axle, and hoisting a small patchwork square sail of rice sacks at the bows, sped upriver in a stiff breeze. Periodically the First Mate would bail out the green bilge slime with an enamel bowl. The old vessel had a rather sieve-like construction.

For a while it was pleasant to recline in the boat, listening to the rush of the water past the hull and the wind creaking the rigging. Occasionally we would ground on a sandbank and, when poling failed, the First Mate would leap over the side to push or pull us clear. Sometimes we would pass a village or encampment. Water birds, inquisitive as children, would fly around us, then, curiosity satisfied, flap lazily away.

As the morning aged the wind strengthened. At first this was to our advantage and increased our speed through the brown water, throwing spray into our faces. Then the strain became too much for the flimsy sail. It rent asunder and flapped uselessly from the boom. Luckily we were close inshore and were blown onto the bank, with help from poles. The Captain repaired the sail, and we set out once more beneath a grey sky, the wind cold and damp. Again the speed and the spray. We left the shore and sped up the middle of the river, the wind almost directly astern. Quite a heavy swell had developed in the normally placid water. The gallant craft splashed through waves, breasting them like some ancient man o' war. The whole experience was exhilarating.

Then the rigging gave way and the mast fell. No longer did we breast the waves, we wallowed in the troughs as the waves breasted us. Water sloshed over the sides as Captain and First Mate inspected the damage. We tried to resurrect the mast but the rigging parted again in the rising wind. Now we were totally out of control, half a mile from shore in gale force winds which now contained sand. Waves higher than the boat occasionally blotted out the shore, which itself was becoming indistinct as the aquatic sandstorm increased its fury. There was a left-hand bend in the river a mile or so ahead. We grabbed hold of bowls and pans and bailed as we had never bailed before as the little stick that was our ship floundered slowly, very slowly, towards the bank. Somewhere in the howling of the wind I was certain that I heard laughter as Old Baldie saw the joke of the Great Saharan Empty Quarter Expedition ending in a fatal shipwreck. I am not a strong swimmer and would have lasted only seconds in that kind of water, so I bailed, and the Captain bailed, and the First Mate bailed. After what seemed like hours, but probably wasn't, the hull was dumped onto the bank with three cold, wet and weary sailors slumped beneath the canopy for shelter.

The storm abated, the mast was rerigged and all the water bailed. The First Mate lit a fire and began to prepare a meal. He took the enamel bailing bowl with which we had been throwing out the green slime, scooped up some river water, which had the appearance of primordial soup, and added rice. Next he went to the centre of the vessel where a mat had stayed miraculously dry. He lifted up each end of the mat and shook all the debris thereon together into the centre. Then, deftly, he flicked the mat. The debris, consisting of dust, sand, dried grass, and things I would rather not think of, rose into the air. With a skill born of much practice he snatched the cloud of muck from the air, went back to the fire and threw the lot in with the rice. So that was how this master of the culinary arts gave his speciality its distinctive flavour.

I ate some bread.

The wind dropped entirely for a while so the First Mate became a barge-horse, walking along the shore towing the heavy boat behind. Then a respectable breeze sprang up and we continued along as before, spray and all. The sun dipped and was gone. We carried on by the full moon shining from a clear, star-speckled sky. I drank some river water from my bottle. Niger water is the only water I have ever tasted that seems sweeter with the addition of purifying tablets. Some hours later we pulled into shore at a small settlement of mud-brick dwellings. I was shown to a room with sleeping slab where I slept very well indeed.

Breakfast was a wooden bowl of gruel, which was not concocted by the First Mate, and which I enjoyed. The Captain said that Tombouctou was about six miles north so I set off into the bush slightly to the east of north. This 'intentional error' is a much used strategy in circumstances where a certain location could possibly be missed. There was a well travelled track running towards Tombouctou from the east which I could not possibly miss. When I hit it I would simply turn left and follow it to the town, which should be about a couple of miles along it at the most.

It was a very pleasant morning. There was a cool stiff breeze blowing from the east and the sky was deep blue and clear. Periodically I would encounter a rush mat hut set inside a

1 My 'father' and 'brother',
Judaean Desert, 1969

2 The Adrar-Reggane-Borjd-
Mocktar bus. A prayer halt on
the Tanezrouft, Algeria, 1983

3 The good ship *Pinnace* on the River Niger

4 The Captain battles with the *Pinnace*'s battered sail just before the shipwreck

5 My historic meeting with Peggy near
   Tombouctou. Hardly love at first sight

6 Pegasus, known to posterity as Peggy

7 Desirable residence with boabab trees
   near Gao, Mali

8 The great trek north to Araouane. The motorway can be seen on the left

9 Early morning, saddling Peggy

10 The Taoudenni salt caravan heading south to Tombouctou: a hundred camels, three men and one small boy

11 A well on the Araouane road. The water was 120 feet down

12 Approaching Araouane, starting-point for the crossing of the Empty
   Quarter

13 Peggy feeling rather tired. Ali doubted her ability to reach Oualata

14 With BBC TV producer Alistair Macdonald
and the girls in Araouane, two days before
the start of the walk across the Empty
Quarter

15 Ali Ould Boy, Le Professeur du Sable

16 A pensive moment in the age-old settlement
of Araouane

17 Lunch-time break on the sixth day into the Empty Quarter. The girls begin to die

18 Peggy's feet in the Empty Quarter. Note the shallowness of her footprint

19 Dune Evelyn. Evening of Day 11

20 The aklé is beaten. Beyond is fixed dune and the Plain of Iron

21 One of the nomads I tracked down on Day 17. Only our humanity did
we have in common, and it was enough

22 The Forest of Arden; Day 18

23 The escarpment; Day 18. Before me, the wrong valley

24 The well at Oualata where the girls had their first drink for twenty days, a world record

25 Journey's end: Oualata

26 The author enjoys his just reward

thorned acacia fence, but no people did I see. The area was well wooded with all kinds of trees, mostly acacia. It was about an hour and a half later that I found the track and turned left along it. The sun had become warm and the breeze dropped. I walked on quite happily, whistling 'The Entry of the Gladiators'. It was quite hard going as the sand was very soft and my pack weighed around seventy pounds; however, the weight was well distributed and comfortable. Since arriving in Borjd Mocktar I had worn no socks and my feet were becoming hard.

After an hour of walking down the track there was still no sign of habitation. I rested for a few minutes in the shade and continued to the tune of 'The British Grenadiers'. Another hour of walking and still there was no sign of Tombouctou. I began to have doubts about my position. Had I made a big enough intentional error? Had I hit the track to the west of Tombouctou and was I walking away from the town? The map was no help since I had been unable to obtain the name of the settlement from the inhabitants, nor did they understand what a map was, so they couldn't point out their position on it.

I sat under an acacia and thought out a plan of action. An inspection of the track told me that the last vehicle to use it had done so that morning, and several had used it the previous day in both directions so it was safe to assume that one would be along shortly. If I continued walking west I could reach Tombouctou soon, or if I found myself going in the wrong direction I could obtain a lift. There were still a couple of hours before the sun reached its zenith and walking would become impossible. I was about to saddle-up again when I heard a truck coming from the West. Minutes later it lurched down the track and stopped at my request.

'*Salaam al laikum.*'

'*Al laikum el salaam,*' said the crowd on the back.

'Tombouctou?' I enquired, pointing west.

'Oui, oui, Tombouctou.'

So far so good.

'How many kilometres?'

'One hundred kilometres.'

'One HUNDRED kilometres?'

'Oui!'

Sixty-two miles to Tombouctou. I imagined my hands around the Captain's throat. I thought of my boot connecting with his buttocks. Since I was so far from my destination there was no point in attempting to walk. I would simply make myself comfortable in the shade and await west-bound transport. They gave me water and departed, waving.

A short time later my transport arrived, a Mercedes truck from Niger loaded with the inevitable rice and assorted humanity. We bargained a price, the better of which the driver got owing to his superior bargaining position.

Sitting on top of the rice, much of the time was spent dodging the lashing acacia thorns which were over an inch long, and pulling them out of clothing and flesh when dodging didn't work. All part of the joys of African travel. Several times we bogged down but the strong Mercedes engine got us out, with a little help from the crew and passengers.

We stopped for noon-day prayers, ate, and drank tea. A small truck came down from Tombouctou disgorging two Englishmen and their wives. They knew of me and my mission. Alistair and the film crew had arrived the previous evening; they too had had to wait for Africa and were a week later than expected. This was good news as I had half-expected them to have given me up for lost and gone home. The Englishmen told me of the magnificent new hotel where the crew were staying, a recent innovation, though I took with a pinch of salt their well-sung praises of the establishment. This being West Africa a hotel with a lock on the door, water in the tap and no used Tampax in the communal shower was worthy of the utmost accolades.

The truck finally pulled into Tombouctou at about eight-thirty. At this late hour of course the streets were deserted. A newly acquired youthful guide took me past the Hotel Campement and there before us, floodlit on a hill, was a large and magnificent single-storey building the like of which I did not think existed in that part of Africa, the Hotel Azalaï. Flags of all nations before its portals. There was a gate-man in attendance. I paid off my guide and, half-expecting the gate-man to boot me down the hill owing to my tramp-like appearance, strolled in through the gate and glass doors to the reception desk as if I owned the place.

Alistair was sent for and, relieved, we shook hands to the

words, 'Doctor Livingstone, I presume.' His own expedition had met with problems both bureaucratic and physical. The five hundred virtually trackless miles from the capital, Bamako, had been fraught with guide and navigation mishaps. Alistair had taken in his stride the jobs of expedition leader and treasurer, with all the worries and people problems that these positions entailed; thankless tasks either one of which would have broken lesser men. This he would continue to do for more than another month, as well as producing a film in one of the worst areas on Earth for film-making. The strain was written on his face, but still he managed to remain cheerful. A remarkable man, Alistair Macdonald.

Within the hour I was clean, had drunk beer and was eating steak. I had come to believe in Shangri-la.

Phase One was completed. After three years I was back in Tombouctou with the money and ability to mount the expedition. My next minor miracle was the buying of two camels and the journey north to Araouane, one of the world's remotest settlements, described by Caillié as 'a detestable place'.

My thoughts were on that 'detestable place' as I fell asleep that night.

7 The Approach

Tombouctou had changed little since 1980. The streets were still dusty and beggar-ridden. The market hall now came a poor second to the Hotel Azalaï as the most magnificent building in town, but the town was mostly untouched. Tombouctou is one of the very few places I have ever seen which could only be improved by tourism.

The expedition had seemingly taken over the town. Alistair's crew was of formidable proportions, consisting of Fin the cameraman, Bill the assistant cameraman, Alan the soundman, two local drivers and Chek, a government fixer who smoothed paths and eased passages. Alistair organised and directed, delegated, and caused things to happen.

That first day in Tombouctou much was accomplished. First to the police station to inform the Chief of Police of my safe arrival. The previous day he had radioed Tessalit to check if I had got through safely. He was delighted and there were handshakes all round. Forms were filled in and the deception of omission consolidated. The film crew were here to film 'Monsieur Le Professeur' as I conducted my scientific experiments.

There was a little filming around town which was closely inspected by every child for miles around.

Mali owned a tourist agency, called SMERT, the job of which was to make straight the way of the visitor. The local representative was one Ali who spoke reasonable English and most of the local dialects. I had dealt with him before and he was very useful indeed. Ali knew everyone. He had a friend who would sell me camels and equipment.

We met his friend, an Arab camel dealer and general businessman, and drove down beyond the airfield to search out some camels, hobbled somewhere in the bush. They had recently returned from Algeria and were busy fattening up and recovering. Camels in Mali, indeed throughout the Sahel, the area south of the Sahara, were at best scrawny beasts since between 1968 and 1973 there had been the great drought which killed quarter of a million people. There had been precious little rain since.

All Ali's friend's camels were veterans of the dreadful Taoudenni salt run. Taoudenni is to Mali what Siberia is to the USSR. Five hundred miles north of Tombouctou it is inhabited by political prisoners who can be hired at forty pence per day to dig rock salt. This is loaded onto camel trains of upwards of a hundred camels, each camel carrying four large slabs, two either side, with a total weight of a third of a ton. Only the toughest survive.

From the land-rover we spotted a couple of beasts just south of the airfield. The first was a wiry white cow, a sorry sight with bones sticking out and practically no hump. She was tick-ridden and covered in healed scars from the brands of various owners and from the rubbing of salt on flesh. A badly deformed upper lip gave her a comical appearance. On the good side she was young, about ten years or so judging by her teeth. Though she was docile, for a camel, I wasn't keen on her at all.

The second made the first look like a thoroughbred. Ingrowing toe-nails, an even bonier body and an extremely nervous disposition. Ali informed me that this was not a camel for the desert, but for hauling river boats. I doubted its ability to negotiate Southport beach.

After much searching we managed to run three others to earth, all cows. One was very nervous and another downright belligerent. This she displayed by catching me a swift kick to the groin, which automatically ensured her return to Taoudenni.

Another, however, was a large and muscular animal, brown of colour and gentle of manner. She was of about fifteen years, approaching middle-age for a camel, and seemed disinclined to murder. I decided on her and, reluctantly, the white one with the deformed lip, being mostly influenced by her docility. I had enough problems to contend with without frequent kicks to the groin.

Some hard bargaining followed, with much shaking of heads. Their owner was a tough customer, but we of the north are not inclined to submit easily. I offered a price and he threatened to eat them. He postulated a prince's ransom at which I laughed loudly. I upped my derisory offer. He expressed a wish to

donate them to the Polisario rebels. Had he a Mauritanian saddle
and a baggage saddle, I wished to know. Yes, he had, and
produced the merchandise which appeared to be serviceable.
Eventually I got the two animals, the saddles and a tatty old
guerba for 650,000 Malian francs, about £650, not a bargain, but not
exorbitant either. We shook on the deal. He would bring them to
the hotel on Monday afternoon. Ali spoke with him, then said to
me, 'He says he can tell you now. You know camels like an Arab.'
He did not know how seriously I hoped that there was truth in
this.

A guide was required to lead us to Araouane, the starting-
point for my Empty Quarter crossing. The man from SMERT
told us of one Ali Ould Boy who was the best in the area and
whom he would try to obtain for us.

That evening, as I was walking towards the hotel, I was
accosted by a man with a saddled camel.

'Ride the Touaregh camel, Monsieur?' he proposed, thoughts
of wealth on his mind.

Said I, 'That is a Malian saddle, not Touaregh. You are not
Touaregh, you are Arab. Besides, I have two camels of my own.'

With a superior smirk I left him standing with open mouth.
Pride of ownership is a fine thing.

The next day Alistair dropped his bombshell. On his journey
to Tombouctou he had come through Bamako where he had
spoken to a Frenchman about the true purpose of my journey.
This Frenchman had told him that two winters previously a
friend of his, together with a fellow French ornithologist, had
crossed from Araouane to Oualata by camel with two guides.
Their route was uncertain, and Alistair had no further information, but it appeared that mine was not to be the first crossing of
the Empty Quarter.

It was a serious blow to my mounting ego. Alistair was at pains
to point out the importance of my trip as the first solo crossing,
indeed the first single-handed desert exploration by camel, but
the information threw me down, taking the gilt from the gingerbread of potential victory. Still, there was naught to be done. A
reduced victory is better than no victory, so the plans would be
unchanged.

The guide, Ali Ould Boy, was employed as a well-digger by a

Belgian charity, the local head of which came to the hotel to meet us. We pored over maps and discussed routes. There was on my proposed route across the Empty Quarter a well named Zourg Oukendera, the position of which was uncertain and which had been known as a 'lost well'. I was desirous of finding this well as a part of the expedition, and marking its exact position. It had, I was informed, been recently located and visited several times by Ali. Again some of the gilt went from my gingerbread.

The route to Araouane was, apparently, straightforward with a barely discernible track to follow. This would, of course, finish in Araouane and I would have to make my own way from there, relying entirely on my navigational abilities. I still thought it a good idea to go via the Zourg Oukendera well as this would give me a good point of reference in the largely featureless desert.

Four new *guerbas* were bought in the market on Monday. They stank abominably and spread muck and sand all over the hotel bar's floor. Prodigious quantities of sardines and luncheon meat, peanuts and spaghetti, sweets and onions were acquired, and an excellent twisted hide camel stick which served as a riding crop. To step outside the hotel was to run the gauntlet of souvenir-sellers. One small boy had spent three days trying to sell me a cheap copper ring. I bought it out of sheer admiration for his doggedness.

My animals duly arrived and were parked beneath a tree outside the hotel. I bought hay for them and fed them a couple of bales to build them up for their long walk. The young white one had acquired the name of Pegasus since she had been found near the airfield. Very quickly this was shortened to Peggy. As yet the other one was nameless. Desert peoples do not name their camels as a rule, except for their best racing beasts. A camel is looked upon as a tool and an asset, not a being or a pet. Like a tool it will be well looked after, but worked until worn out and broken. Nonetheless, as with a tool in the hands of a craftsman, the best work is done by using the tool to its best advantage, and no two tools are alike. It was not to be long before I found the differences between my two tools and treated them accordingly, but on that Monday evening they were just two camels.

The camel is a tanker of a beast which can store up prodigious amounts of water within its body, even in its bloodstream. One

was once seen to drink 176 pints in ten minutes. Estimates of
how long they can go without water vary considerably from as
little as three days to as much as fifteen and, perhaps, a day or so
beyond. Camels are as individual as people in ability as well as
personality.

I grew up with a camel story which goes thus.

A man wished to go to a town ten days' journey away and went
to the local second-hand camel-dealer in search of a ten-day
camel.

'I have no ten-day camels in stock,' said the dealer, 'but I have
this excellent seven-day bull camel which will get you there if you
brick it.'

The traveller bought the camel and, not wishing to appear
ignorant, did not inquire as to the meaning of the verb 'to brick'.
He watered his camel at the water-hole, ignoring the two house
bricks near the well, and set off.

Seven days later his camel died. He was picked up by nomads
and returned to his starting-point where he sought out the
camel-dealer and told him of his camel's demise.

'Didn't you brick it?' he asked, not unreasonably.

'What do you mean?'

'At the well there are two bricks. You take one in each hand and
when the camel has almost drunk its fill you clap them smartly
together on its testicles. The camel will go 'ssschlrrrp!!!' and
suck in enough water to take it the three extra days.'

'Doesn't it hurt?' asked the man, in concern.

'Not if you keep your thumbs out of the way,' replied the
dealer casually.

Tuesday was the day of departure for Araouane. We made a
late start owing to problems at the filling station with petrol
supplies, and a little filming of my departure. Ali the guide had
arrived and was piled into the Land Rover whilst most of the
crew's gear and personnel were put into a small blue truck. Ali
pointed out the way through town and I led the cavalcade to the
northern suburbs followed by every small boy in that part of Mali.
I walked, leading Peggy with the baggage saddle and baggage,
whilst the brown camel with the riding saddle brought up the

rear. Tombouctou had turned out to see the Nazrani pass and many were the derisory comments about why I was walking rather than riding. There were two reasons why I had chosen to do this at that stage. Firstly I did not wish to tire out the girls on the approach, and secondly if, as had been my habit in the past, I was to practise my famous 'Flying Mount' technique I wished there to be as few people as possible in the vicinity. Stoically I ignored their jibes and continued onward regardless.

Outside the town the trucks overtook me and headed north through the bush leaving instructions for me to follow their tracks. It became their habit to drive on for five miles or so, then film my approach to their position. This was fine as long as they didn't want any retakes, which were a bind.

After an hour or so of walking it was obvious that Peggy was not ideal as a lead camel. My pace was a steady three miles per hour which was slightly faster than camels normally walked, but I insisted that they walked at this pace and training had started immediately. The local harness consisted of a slip knot on a rope pulled tight around the bottom jaw, a stick passed through the rope just below the knot to prevent slipping. It was simple but effective.

Peggy was very reluctant to come. Obviously she had some idea of the trials ahead. Maybe she remembered that whenever she had passed this way before she had been en route to Taoudenni. Be that as it may, she pulled back as much as the non-dislocation of her bottom jaw would allow, saliva and white froth blowing from the left, downwind side of her mouth. I tried it with my brown one in the lead and, though there was still some reluctance, it made walking much easier.

By half past one we had covered nine of the 150 miles to Araouane and I stopped, very tired indeed, waiting for the heat to pass. The sun was big and hot with temperatures in the eighties. I unloaded the girls and flopped in the shade of the truck whilst Alan, the sound man, ministered to me with tea (no milk, three sugars) and luncheon meat. One of the main joys of that northern trek was Alan's *Lip-ton's*. This was what the locals called it, and we followed suit.

I talked with Ali, mostly via an interpreter as neither could understand the other's version of French. He said that my camels were good camels and recommended alternately an hour's walking and an hour's riding. We talked of the distance it was possible to cover in a day in those conditions. He said that he, Ali, son of Boy, could cover thirty-two miles per day without problems, but he would not expect me to do more than twenty-five. My pride was bruised a bit at this.

Somehow he had got wind that I was going to Mauritania. Perhaps he had heard some careless talk. Alistair reported to me an earlier conversation when Ali had picked up one of the myriad scarabs, said that if I went to Mauritania I would die, and at the word 'die' had emphasised the point by crushing the unhappy beetle between thumb and forefinger.

Too soon it was time to load up and go. A little cloud covered the sun which blunted its sharpness. It was not long before three when I tugged at my lead camel and we sallied forth once more.

The country was quite wooded with acacia, and scrub grass abounded. A solitary vehicle had passed this way a couple of days previously so I followed its tracks. Sometimes I would pass travellers going south, somewhat amazed at meeting a *bou-bou*-clad Nazrani alone with two camels. Small boys drove massive haystacks which had the legs of donkeys. There were herds of goats and of camels. I informed a mini-herdsman, melodically, that if he could see what I could see, a window cleaner he would be, if he could see what I could see, when I was cleaning windows.

As the sun's glow dipped to my left I was happy with my physical condition and my spirits were excellent. I was managing the camels all right. Phase Two was looking good. All systems were GO. It was about six-thirty and dark when I pulled in at the camp fire near the well of Jefal. I had covered twenty-two miles during the day, which wasn't bad at all considering my late start.

Not until I had unloaded and hobbled the girls did I realise how much the day had taken out of me. Quickly I began to stiffen. Despite the cloud of the afternoon my arms were badly sunburned. I felt slightly feverish and, though excellent lamb and rice had been cooked, I had no appetite. Copious quantities of Lip-ton's slipped down my gullet, and a nut bar, and I slept like the dead.

At dawn I awoke to a sleeping camp and put the kettle on,

wishing that my legs were someone else's. Generally I felt fine and knew that the stiffness in my limbs would go as soon as I began to use them. Breakfast was cold rice and lamb. Alistair helped me to look for the girls, but search as we would we drew a blank. We found a strange camel, but not one of mine did we see. Tracks were everywhere, this being a well.

I was becoming concerned when Ali appeared over a dune riding Peggy bareback and leading the brown. He had found them three miles away. This worried me somewhat as to have to chase them three miles each morning would considerably lengthen my journey.

That morning, I had decided, was to be when I would try to ride. I couched and saddled my brown. With an expertise born of not having been near a camel for two years, I boarded, telling Alistair, under pain of death, to keep his cameras packed.

She roared, and rose. Miraculously I stayed on. Then she simply stood. I dug my heels into her shoulders to urge her forward. Nothing happened. I whacked her smartly on the rear with my camel stick. She roared, but didn't move. Everything I knew I tried, but to no avail. Finally she decided that she had had enough and couched herself like a bag of beans. I gave up, tied her to my waist and stalked off muttering about the recalcitrance of women.

On this day my brown acquired a name. She was very nervous about motor vehicles, in fact any kind of engine noise worried her greatly. I had first discovered this at the hotel when she was very reluctant to pass the generator building. Her fear stretched to the extent of fearing vehicle tracks in the sand. I experimented with this. When I walked away from the tracks the rope went slack, but when I turned towards them it tightened as she pulled back. Because of this fear of progress I named her 'The Traditionalist', which quickly became 'Trad'.

Owing to Trad's reluctance I took to walking some couple of hundred yards west of the track. Alistair wanted to do much filming that morning and wasn't too happy about this. Neither was Fin, the cameraman. For about half an hour Alistair walked with me, so I handed him the rope to let him understand my problem. He admitted that camel-hauling was damned hard work.

The day was one of starts and stops. Trees and scrub were still there, but slightly reduced in frequency. The route for most of the journey was a series of gentle up slopes of half a mile or so with a sharp drop of about fifty to a hundred feet at the top, thus it seemed that almost the entire trip to Araouane was an up-hill slog in soft sand dragging a heavy weight under a very hot sun.

An hour and a half of rest around noon was enormously welcome, especially with Alan's Lip-ton's. At six-thirty we gave up for the night and ate a rabbit which Ali had shot. Always, within minutes of stopping, Ali would be preparing Whisky Saharienne, the sweet tea of the desert which, like Scotch, was designed not to quench the thirst, but to stimulate the senses. I had thus named the drink, to much local mirth. My admiration for the competence of this man grew. Everything he did was done calmly and with precision. He was a craftsman at the top of his trade, and was recognised as such. His trade was desert travel and all things connected thereto. I took to calling him 'Le Professeur du Sable – the Professor of the Sand'. It was not an exaggeration since he knew more about this subject than most academic professors knew about theirs.

The next day I saddled Peggy for riding and loaded the baggage onto Trad. Ali came with me as I wished to pick his brains. We walked for an hour through the scrub. Trees were very sparse now. There was a mountain, lone and grey to the east. I verified its name, Tadrart, via the map and Ali.

At about nine Ali suggested that we ride. I mounted Peggy and Ali threw a blanket over the baggage saddle of Trad, which he sat on. We rode side by side without any problem. Occasionally it was necessary to administer a quick whack to the girls' rear ends, camels being basically lazy creatures who would grind rapidly to a halt without encouragement.

I learned to guide by foot pressure and by waving the stick near the eye. Peggy seemed as happy as a camel ever gets with a man aboard, and ever after this she wore the riding saddle.

For five hours we rode. After two, my backside, despite the comfortable and well padded saddle, began to complain. My back too began to ache because of the peculiar swaying motion of camel travel. After three hours I wished to walk, but decided to stick it out. My body must be hardened for riding and there was no gentle way to achieve this. For many years, since my Nijmegen days, I had believed in the 'Baptism by Fire' principle rather than the gentle build-up of training. Using this method one simply hammers the body into conformity. For a short initial period there is much pain, but as the body adapts to the continued activity the pain recedes and dies. Usually it works.

Just after two o'clock we pulled in at the well of Dâyet en Nahârât and I collapsed under the nearest shelter from the blistering heat.

It was two hours later before I found the courage to reload the camels. I mounted again and rode off alone with Trad tied behind. This was the first time I had ever ridden a camel alone and I felt the occasion. It was a great step forward. All was fine until we topped a rise and there were the vehicles parked below with Fin and his camera in close proximity. Peggy refused point-blank to approach the vehicles. I couldn't drag her there as was possible when walking. All I could do was try to persuade. She would not veer in their direction try as I would with everything that I knew. Eventually I dismounted and led her by the rope.

Ali, who had been watching the performance, strolled over and asked for my stick. He then commenced to belabour Peggy savagely with it. She grumbled a little, but took it stoically. Then he handed the stick to me and told me to do the same. Reluctantly I gave her a couple of half-hearted whacks. My guru waved his arms and shook his head sadly. He made violent whipping motions in the air. 'What the hell,' I thought, 'If Ali says it must be done, then undoubtably it must be done.' I set to with a will. We both mounted and rode towards the vehicles with no problems whatsoever; indeed it was to be quite some time before there were any problems again.

Ali stayed with me for the rest of the day. For a while we went at the trot, a new experience for me, and one which was much easier on the more battered parts of my anatomy. I was very pleased with the day.

As the sun was about to set we topped another rise to see our camp below. We dug our heels into our mounts' shoulders and charged, yelling, down the hill like Lawrence at Akabar. Most of the time I was kept in the air above Peggy by massive blows from the saddle. It was wonderfully exhilarating.

Immediately I dismounted I began to stiffen and ache. Walking was difficult. I began to understand the peculiar gait of the cowboy. Supper was sheep, rice and painkillers. We had covered about twenty-five miles that day.

I had brought with me two Edwards Patent Camel Finders. These were strips of fluorescent red material about six feet by one with strategically placed eyelets. The idea was to tie them around the camels' necks so that they could be spotted at great distance. It was remarkable how a tree or a bush at some distance could look like a camel, and vice versa. The theory was sound, but they were of little practical use. Tracking was still the only method. I simply found their tracks and followed them. Sometimes this meant walking a great meandering course across the desert, but eventually there the girls would be. They would greet me with a great gurgling roar which sounded for all the world like a deep-throated 'Hughie-ughie-ughie', which, roughly translated, meant 'Oh Hell! It's the boss again!'

The first job then was to put the rope noose around the bottom jaw, a simple procedure involving jumping up to grab an ear some eight feet in the air and hauling the enormous head down. The lady in question would open her mouth loudly to protest against this indignity, thus allowing the other hand to throw on the noose and tighten it.

That was the basic theory. Practice was complicated by each camel according to its peculiar talents. Trad, being the taller of the two, would, upon sighting the rope, raise her head an extra foot. It was then necessary to throw one end of the rope over her head and pull down until her ear was within grabbing distance. Peggy used the deterrent method. You will often have heard it said that camels spit. This is incorrect. They vomit. From somewhere deep in their innards they can bring forth a great jet of brilliant green, evil-smelling slime, which they can direct with amazing accuracy. Peggy would loudly protest about the rope and as I was tightening it, would squirt this jet over my hands and up my arm.

Upon the morning of Friday I found the girls a couple of miles away, both together as was usual, camels being very gregarious creatures. I had put the rope on Peggy and taken off her hobble.

To stop her wandering off whilst I attended to Trad I tied her to my ankle. Several times I leaped for Trad's ear, but each time she flicked it away. Over her head went the rope, down came her ear and I grabbed it. I will swear that there had been collaboration between those two beasts for at this point Peggy decided to walk away in one direction taking my leg with her, and Trad set off in the opposite direction with me hanging on to her ear. It must have been quite a sight to see, this Nazrani hopping on one leg in a horizontal position, loath to let go of a hard won ear whilst Peggy, for good measure, vomited profusely on my raised leg. Thankfully the cameras were miles away.

We were loaded and away before eight, I walking owing to pain. An hour later we came to a water-hole where we converged with an Arab and a lone small boy of about seven, each on a camel. They drew water from the forty-metre deep well using a pulley and camel power. The pulley and leather bucket with rope are always carried to the well by the water-seeker so that he can guarantee they will be there. The wooden pulley on a wooden axle is fitted to two arms of wood or metal on the well rim. The rope is then thrown over the pulley and the end attached to a camel. Bucket and rope are dropped down the well and, some time later, a muffled thud is heard from the depths. Then the camel is driven away from the well bringing the full bucket to the surface.

We watered our camels and replenished our supplies. I gave cigarettes and matches to the nomads and an extra present of chewing gum to the boy, who had to be shown its purpose. He tried it and found it wanting. A fair comment on certain aspects of our society, I thought.

As I left the water-hole I somehow missed the track. When I realised it I was probably half a mile or so west of it. I turned north-east hoping to pick it up, but without success. There was not a sign of the vehicles and the terrain had become very barren with just an occasional clump of grass. Nothing but rolling dunes could be seen in any direction.

I wasn't unduly worried as I knew exactly where I was and my next water-hole at Tâgânet was about two days away. There were about four gallons of water on Peggy and I had food, map and my two compasses. Because of the wandering nature of the track I was almost certain to cross it before Tâgânet, but if not I would still be able to meet Alistair and his team there the next evening, I took a bearing and pressed on.

A couple of hours later a Land Rover full of very worried BBC men appeared on the horizon and sped towards me. Ali had spotted me, a dot amongst the nothingness, from about five miles away. I rejoined the main track which was by now about a mile or so away, and we stopped for lunch. It was the hottest day so far.

The truck had gone back to Tombouctou that morning for supplies. In the evening, after a sweltering afternoon, we ate the last of the sheep and drank gallons of Lip-ton's and Whisky Saharienne.

Ali and I talked. Someone asked him the direction of Araouane. He flung out his right arm in his economical and precise way, sighted down it, and announced, 'Araouane.' I glanced at my wrist compass and at the map. 'Not quite,' I said, with confidence, for had I not at my bidding all of man's modern technology whilst he had but his guesswork? I made my bid for the direction of Araouane, flinging out my arm four or five degrees away from Ali's direction.

Ali smiled, shook his head, put out his arm again and repeated, quietly, 'Araouane.' This called for proof. I laid out my map on the sand, took my optical compass, and accurately plotted the position of Araouane. Ali was absolutely spot-on.

At about nine-thirty, as I was falling asleep in my bag, the truck returned, headlights blazing, and almost ran me over IN MY OWN BEDROOM.

Next morning I rode for a couple of hours. It was very painful but I did not realise the extent of the damage until I dismounted to rest. The saddle was covered in blood. That, I decided, was my last bit of riding for a while. The days were becoming hotter and by lunch-time I was exhausted.

Ali had shot a bish – a local species of gazelle – so we ate excellent bish stew. Prodigious amounts of tea and water vanished as I lay panting in the shade. It was a reluctant cameleer that dragged himself out of the lunchtime camp.

I drank more and more water, but still my mouth was dry. Soon I found myself staggering with weakness. Then it dawned upon my tiny brain that, owing to the heat, I had been eating little, and there had been a sparsity of salt in that little which I had eaten. I was badly desalinated.

The next time I encountered the camera crew I asked Alistair to make me a salt drink. He did better. He produced some special salts for athletes which he added to water and fed to me. This replaced all the lost salts and half an hour later I was ready to run to Araouane with a camel under each arm.

Alistair was becoming anxious about the time factor. My progress was not as swift as either of us had anticipated and since there was little filming to do before Araouane he wondered how I would feel about Ali taking the camels overnight to Tâgânet, thus saving us a day. I was happy with this as the approach to Araouane was never considered by me as anything more than a training period and other than that it was a necessary evil. Ali trotted out of the firelight and was gone.

We were up at five, followed the camel tracks in the dark, headlights blazing, and were filming (another necessary evil) near Tâgânet at dawn. Peggy changed her tactics slightly that morning. She vomited on my head. One can, however, get used to anything in time. What a week previously I would have considered revolting was now merely irksome.

It was a pleasant morning's walk before the heat became oppressive. The land had become extremely barren with occasional areas of coarse grass half a mile or so wide. These grass areas I dreaded since they were the homes of enormous numbers of flies. I had ceased to wave away these airborne annoyances, simply allowing them to crawl around my mouth and eyes. In the Moslem paradise it is said that all flies shall have perished save one, and this one to exist in order that one may derive pleasure from wafting it away. One fly may indeed be pleasurable, but ten million are most definitely not.

At the mid-day halt we decided to come clean about my plans to cross into Mauritania. Ali revealed that he had been the chief guide on the previous expedition. I might have known that the

Frenchmen would have wanted the best guide there was, and that was undoubtedly Le Professeur du Sable. This was good news. There was much more of his brains to be picked.

There were areas of bare skin from half-way down my calves where my *bou-bou* finished, to the tops of my boots. These places, despite massive and constant applications of the strongest barrier cream, had become very badly and deeply sunburnt, causing great pain. The crew convinced me that they were worse than I had thought, and dressed them with great pads of lint and antiseptic cream.

Peggy lay on the sand with her long neck and head stretched along the ground in fatigue. Ali expressed some doubt that she would make it to Mauritania. This worried me greatly as I had come to regard the word of Ali as gospel.

The days were becoming hotter as we entered the desert proper, being at least into the nineties. The gentle breeze from the east hit my right shoulder hotly like a blast from a furnace. I switched to automatic and hovered musically between France and Holland.

At five o'clock I turned the camels over to Ali and went on by Land Rover to Sidi El Mokhtar. This was pure desert with not a blade of grass in sight. We had brought wood with us and soon had a fire going, sending dancing shadows over the desert. We had hardly settled down before Ali arrived in the firelight, unannounced, and commenced to unload the girls.

Despite my various pains I slept well that night, happy in the thought that the following day, Allah willing, I would be in Araouane.

An early start was essential owing to the expected heat. Soon after dawn I was on my way, plodding over the low dunes, happy in anticipation of Araouane, 'that detestable place'. The morning was largely uneventful. At one point an Arab woman materialised like a djinn out of nowhere and set her path to converge with mine. I greeted her, but she kept her distance. She asked for something, her hands outstretched, but I was unable to understand. It was probably some kind of medication, usually that was the case, but the barriers of language and culture were just too great. I tried every trick in the book to establish communication, but it was hopeless. Finally she gave up and went back over the dune from which she came. That was the only time I can remember a total breakdown of communication.

The air was as clear as crystal. There was no greyness caused by distance. The wind had ceased and all the world was in perfect silence. If I stopped moving the silence was oppressive. To cough was like making the first mark on a large sheet of pristine paper. A mere movement of the feet in the sand was a statement. We who are of the so-called civilised world are unused to silence. It worries us. I sang, and I talked to the camels, anything to end the encroaching nothingness. And always there was the sun. It seemed to shoot rapidly to the zenith in the morning, there to remain for the day until an hour or so before sunset when it would drop like a stone. Shadows were either very long or almost non-existent. I cannot recall any other kind. But always there was the sun, and with it the heat. I sucked on boiled sweets to give interest to the barren hours. It is amazing how important the flavour of a barley-sugar can be.

In the late morning I topped a rise and saw the two trucks, sharp, dark and distinct on the horizon. It seemed that I would reach them in twenty minutes or so. In fact it took me over an hour and a half. They were parked on a high brown dune with ridges of brilliant white sand running in streets east to west. Those sand colours reminded me of palamino ponies. The light was incredible in its intensity and the beauty of it all was breathtaking, like a Hollywood movie set for Heaven. It seemed sacrilegious that people should be there. My first words, when I arrived at the vehicles, were, 'Didn't I tell you she was beautiful?'

But the finest thing of all was to the north, on the horizon. There sat Araouane, little black dots in the distance, a mere five miles away. There she was, waiting for me to take her. For almost four years I had dreamed of this moment, and the beauty of it excelled all my expectations.

We ate and drank for a couple of hours to let the sun blaze, lying under the truck for shade. Then I saddled up and set off on the final stage of Phase Two, the trucks going ahead to prepare the way. Half-way there, despite my painful rear, I mounted Peggy. It was fitting, I considered, that I should ride into

Araouane for such an arrival demanded dignity.

Araouane was dominated by a block-house on a hill with what appeared to be a flag on top. It looked like a fort, Beau Geste style. This, I considered, housed the massive military presence spoken of by the IGN official in Paris. In fact the only military presence in Araouane throughout my stay there was a brief visit some days later by members of the Polisario rebels, the rag-tag army fighting for the independence of the North-Western Sahara. The 'fort' turned out to be the guest-house and the 'flag' a windsock.

As I arrived at the well the village children descended *en masse*. I couched Peggy and dismounted, surrounded by about thirty small boys of Arabic and negroid extraction showing brilliant rows of teeth. It was a joyous greeting.

We were led to the guest-house and watched closely in every-thing we did. I unloaded the girls and hobbled them outside our new home. After a decent interval to allow us to sort ourselves out we were visited by the Headman, introduced by Ali as Mohammed Ould Sultan, a magnificent name by any standards. He was a quiet, smiling, elderly gentleman, white of hair and beard; a man with the air of dignity befitting his position. He welcomed us to his village and bestowed the blessings of Allah.

There were other dignities to meet, one of whom was Moulaie Mokhtar, the other guide on the previous Empty Quarter expedition. Whenever one thinks of a desert Arab it is of Moulaie that one thinks. He was an archetype with dark skin, magnificently curved nose, neat chin-strap beard pointed at the front, and crow's-footed, far-seeing eyes. He would be around forty-five. I came to know him, and his son, quite well. Also, I came to like him.

It was Sunday when I arrived in Araouane and Thursday when I set out into the unknown. In all this time I found no indication as to why Caillié had called it 'a detestable place'. The people were the friendliest community I have ever met. We were invited to their homes, fed royally, helped in any way they could devise, and all with complete open-faced honesty.

Araouane's situation was magnificent, the dunes rolling into the distance in all directions. There did not seem to be any reason why Araouane should exist at all, there being no crops, or possi-

bility of crops, and no natural resources whatsoever apart from
the 120 feet deep water. Everything had to be imported. The
nearest animal fodder was two days away. Yet here lived a
community of some three hundred souls, and it had lived here for
millennia. The evidence for this was the hundred-foot mound on
which sat the guest-house. It was man-made and composed
entirely of bones and potsherds, and sand of course. For thousands of years this had been the rubbish tip. Some day an
archaeologist will dig a trench in that mound and learn of the
history of Araouane, but for a few days that ancient refuse heap
was to be my home.

There were no streets in Araouane. There were simply twenty
or so single-storey, flat-roofed, mud-bricked buildings dotted
about on the desert floor without any plan. Between them the
sand blew unhindered. Within each building were several rooms
and a small enclosed courtyard. Doors usually consisted of the
steel of oil drums, split and flattened, the wind blowing the sand
beneath and around them. The floors were sand, and when
guests arrived rush mats and mattresses would be placed upon
the ground for their comfort. There was a mosque, which looked
just like the other buildings, and an adjacent graveyard which
Alistair and I found ourselves inadvertently walking through the
middle of since there were only one or two small stones as
markers and the desert had tried to reclaim it. We wondered what
diabolic taboos we had broken by so doing.

Near that ancient cemetery, and the bone-hill, was evidence of
even earlier occupation. The sand was littered with countless
sea-shells, the remains of a once thriving aquatic community
which died millions of years ago when the Sahara ceased to be sea
bed and dried to become a drifting sea of sand.

Twice daily food, steaming hot, was sent to us. We were the
honoured guests of the village. Always we were pursued by
small boys demanding cadeaux. As is the way of small boys they
stole lumps of sugar. Whenever Lip-ton's was made they would
beg the tea bag and go away happily sucking it. Alan referred to
this mini-regiment as 'the early morning cadeau squad'. For
them it was like having a carnival in town. These men in strange

dress who did strange things with strange equipment had to be observed in detail throughout the day. It was impossible to do anything without a dozen wide-eyed faces hovering close. Defecation posed a problem of privacy if not accomplished before the first rays of dawn, since it was done on the open desert. I talked long with Ali and Moulaie about the Empty Quarter. They had taken the two Frenchmen over in eighteen days, and themselves returned in fifteen. I had already realised that a ten-day crossing was extremely unlikely and was now aiming at about sixteen days. Bravado made me promise a fourteen-day crossing, but I recognised this for what it was, though did not rule out the possibility. Ali, contrary to his original statement, now accepted that the journey was possible for me, but it would, he said, be very difficult. I wasn't expecting a picnic. He gave me a pulley to draw water. It was a symbolic gesture. We both knew that I had neither bucket nor rope. It was all that he had, and that was the importance of it.

This was a time, supposedly, of rest, but there was much to be done. The baggage saddle had to be rebuilt, final letters needed writing, camels required feeding, more filming was necessary. I was supplied with a 16mm movie camera and tripod and given final instructions in its use. A short-range walkie-talkie was handed over for warning of my approach at the other end, though I must confess that even then I realised its purpose to be more psychological than practical. A listening schedule was set up. Alistair would begin to listen on my fifteenth day. Until day eighteen he would listen for ten minutes at six a.m., noon and six p.m. After this he would listen every hour from six to six. I told him that if I hadn't arrived by day nineteen then I would probably be in trouble and would appreciate whatever rescue mission he could possibly mount.

There were other letters to write, in case I didn't make it. This was a time of great introspection. They were very difficult to pen. I gave them to Alistair to deliver personally, if necessary, then went for a long walk over the dunes in the dark.

We filmed a little on Monday, including a monologue of my thoughts and feelings about the trip and its success. I felt like a frog in a school laboratory, cut and displayed, as I spoke to posterity from the refuse mound of Araouane.

On Tuesday the truck left with the crew, leaving Alistair, Ali and the driver. On Wednesday they shook hands and departed, leaving me in Araouane. As they were boarding the Land Rover I felt a few spots of rain. This we considered to be a good omen. Rain in the desert is always a good thing. I watched them get smaller as they bounced to the horizon and went over the edge, wondering if I would ever see them again. Suddenly, then, I felt the whiteness of my skin beneath the unnatural tan, and it became a badge of inadequacy amongst the casual competence of the ebony-badged ones around me. I realised how much I had come to rely upon Alistair's strength and competence over the previous couple of weeks.

Moulaie's son brought food and we talked of the world. Was there much desert in my country? He was amazed to hear that there was none, and that no camels roamed the wild places of my land. He could not conceive of a green field, or moorland. Snow was an entirely alien concept, though he had seen ice once in a box in Tombouctou. How was the hunting, he wished to know, in Salford? The thought of shooting bish from the top deck of a number fifteen in Regent Road filled my mind for an interesting few minutes.

Moulaie's son was an intelligent young man who, in another environment, would doubtless have entered a profession. His mind was lively and quick to assimilate. He understood that I was not French, doubtless from my diabolical French accent, and had even a vague idea of global geography, though his understanding of the relative sizes of countries displayed room for improvement. He had heard of the Falklands conflict, even in Araouane where I never saw a radio.

'Is not Argentina small, and your country big?'

'No. My country is small and Argentina is big.' I etched out the relative sizes in the sand.

'Then you are great warriors,' he said with admiration. I tried to explain the relative technical and economical differences, but since I didn't really understand them myself, let it go.

Moulaie joined us and advised me not to bother with the well at Zourg Oukendera as the route there was barred by aklé. He suggested that I follow the line of the streets of dunes south-west for a few days until I hit aklé dune, then turn west. This had been my original planned route in my solar still days. He did not appear to know the extent of the aklé and as far as I could gather their route had been to the north via Zourg Oukendera. According to my maps there was a definite dune line running west to what I called Aklé Corner when it went north-west and rounded a great knob of aklé. Finally I could head south towards the escarpment. This route would unfortunately be about fifty miles longer.

The main problem with taking this route was that if I got into difficulties on the new route then Alistair would assume me to be on the more direct Zourg Oukendera route and would direct any subsequent rescue mission there. However, it seemed to me that if I encountered major problems in the middle of the Empty Quarter then the chances of being found were so remote as to be negligible. I thought that I may as well make the journey as easy as possible and increase my chances by so doing.

In the late afternoon I took my ladies to have their last drink and to fill up my four plastic jerricans with water. They drank surprisingly little considering that they had not been watered for over a week. I had thoughts of using a traditional method to increase their intake, but they were the wrong gender and not a brick was to be seen near the water-hole.

The village boys were there, leading, slapping, and riding my camels. There was a sense of great occasion. All the village knew of my mission and wished to help with advice, some useful, some not.

'Keep out of the aklé,' impressed Moulaie, 'or in three hours you will be dead.'

I did not really know what aklé looked like or felt like. There had been the experience of the low aklé in Tunisia, but apart from seeing the thousand-foot dune in the distance on my first Algerian trip I had no knowledge of big aklé. Soon, Moulaie assured me, this lack would be rectified.

Physically I was feeling fit and rested. My sunburnt calves were still extremely painful, but on the mend. A great thick scab covered my coccyx, but this was no problem as I had no wish to ride for at least a week until the weight of water on the girls' backs had diminished somewhat.

Moulaie expressed concern at Peggy's condition. She was

obviously very tired and spent hours with her neck stretched out on the sand. Like Ali he did not think that she would arrive in Oualata. It was too late to do anything about it now, even if it were possible. I could not afford another camel, even on a part-exchange basis. To all intents and purposes I was broke, almost my entire worldly wealth being tied up in livestock. The only thing I could do was to put the bulk of the weight onto Trad and save Peggy as much as possible for subsequent riding. As it turned out that decision probably saved all our necks.

As I pottered about in final preparation a thousand djinns whispered to me of destruction. Was the water enough? Did I know sufficient about camels? What if I broke a leg? Would there at last be snakes and scorpions? Had the maps gone out of date because of drifting sand? Just how bad was aklé? Did I have enough rope? Could my knee hold out? Supposing I broke my spectacles and lost my spare pair? Supposing . . . What if . . . Maybe . . .

Suddenly I found that I had nothing to do. It had all been done. I brewed some Lip-ton's and smoked an American cigarette from a packet left by Alistair as a parting gift. My confidence returned. I knew that I could never be as ready as I was at that moment. I told myself that the journey was a series of one-day excursions, and I had done many of those. Failure and death I would not allow myself to think on. There would be time enough for that if they presented themselves convincingly on the journey, but for now the subject was taboo. I was concerned only with success, and how I would achieve it. The question was not '*if*?' but '*when*?'

The sky had clouded over and one or two lonely raindrops were falling gently, spotting the sand. I tried to read some Azimov, but couldn't concentrate; so I sat and looked out over Araouane, and smoked, and drank tea, and thought of home.

8 The Holiday

I was up at five and began the loading in the dark. Moulaie and son, cameleers to the demented, assisted and advised. All the water went on Trad with two jerricans either side. Most of a load must be carried by the front legs, but care must be taken to reduce chafing as much as possible. Peggy carried the food and most of the other equipment. Sixteen gallons of water seemed enough for the journey. Since a camel's survival is measured in days rather than in miles I could not afford to hang about. The aromatic *guerbas* that I had purchased in Tombouctou, and which I had not been looking forward to using, I gleefully gave to Moulaie.

Mohammed Ould Sultan and the village elders assembled to give me a civic send-off. There was much shaking of hands. I tied Peggy to Trad, and Trad to me, and as the sun scraped above the horizon I walked off the bone and potsherd hill into the Empty Quarter. I did not look back for about twenty minutes, and when I did so Araouane, the guest house and the people were gone. I was alone.

It was pleasant in the early morning. The sun was hidden behind a cloudy blanket and the ground was flat. I walked between two rows of white dune, their tops twenty feet or so above the land and about a hundred yards apart. Camel tracks were everywhere, and the tracks of goats and donkeys. There was some initial trouble with the baggage, which was soon rectified. The girls and I were working as a team, each knowing and supplying what was required for our smooth passage through the desert. On sand one walks in short, quick steps, perpetually in low gear. My rhythmic tread and the creaking of the camels' loads echoed through the quiet valleys.

In mid-morning the cloud thinned and was gone, leaving the sun a clear passage to scorch the earth and all that was on it. By noon the temperature was well into the nineties with only a slight breeze from behind. Sparse clumps of grass had appeared which the girls eyed hungrily. They had eaten only dried grass for about a week so they needed fresh green food. I stopped, unloaded them leaving their saddles on, and hobbled them. They went away to eat.

I built a shelter from my space blanket, tripod and jerricans, and lay beneath it waiting for early evening. Lunch was corned beef and garden peas, both of French origin. Of all that is bad which is produced by France, their corned beef has to be the worst. It is virtually inedible, but it can be forced with an effort of will and washed down with water. The peas were, however, excellent, eaten cold from the tin after drinking the beautiful juice.

As the sun moved west, so the shade moved east and I had to move with it. There was no time to sit and contemplate. The log had to be kept up to the minute and notes spoken into the tape-recorder. Photography was practised, both still and ciné. At three-thirty everything was repacked and I went off to find the girls, now out of sight beyond some dunes. I tracked them for a mile or so and brought them complaining to my camp. Soon after four we were on our way again, walking into the sun, the baggage creaking and the ten feet shushing through the sand.

Camel tracks were becoming less frequent as we went on. There were occasional tracks of bish, cloven and meandering. The terrain was as bare as before with occasional patches of vegetation. It was a happy time. The journey, so long in the planning, was finally in progress and so far I could see no major problems. I was supremely confident and the atmosphere was almost festive. The work was hard and the girls had to be hauled along, but the songs were happy songs which owed much to the ancient sport of the egg-shaped ball.

As the sun began to dip the sky clouded over again. I was very tired at six-thirty when I decided to call it a day. There was a vast plain all around me with the dune streets in the distance in every direction. A wind had begun to blow quite strongly from the north-east. I unloaded the girls and hobbled them, taking care to close-hobble Trad. Close-hobbling is done by hobbling in the usual way, then couching the beast and tying a rope around a bent foreleg to prevent it being straightened. There was no vegetation of note around so I didn't want Trad, who had wanderlust, to be several miles away by morning. There was no need to close-hobble both at this stage as they always stayed together.

I had found a little brushwood and made a fire on which I brewed Lip-ton's and boiled water for something freeze-dried. The wind I kept off me by building a wall of jerricans. That day I had covered about fifteen miles which, considering various teething problems with the baggage, wasn't bad. Henceforward I decided that my bare minimum per day must be sixteen miles giving me, at worst, a twenty-two day crossing for the 350-mile journey. I fell asleep contentedly staring at the bejewelled Orion.

In the early morning, just before dawn, I was awakened by the great rumbling of thunder. Rain was falling quite heavily but dried as it hit the ground. It was a magnificent production with streaks of lightning striking all around from a very angry sky. It was as if the desert gods were warning the pretentious Nazrani who dared to enter their domain. It occurred to me that as I was on a very flat plain covering several square miles then the girls and I were undoubtedly the highest point for miles. If I were to stand then perhaps the local gods would do more than merely warn. I lay for a while listening to the rain pattering on my space blanket. Eventually, as dawn slid in and the storm moved east, I leaped out and brewed up. The girls were together about a hundred yards away chewing their cud. At six-forty they were loaded and we were on our way.

The morning was cloudy and quite cool with an occasional shower. Between the streets of dunes the valleys became deeper and there would be a definite end to them after a few miles, which had to be climbed out of. Soon after eight I encountered the biggest and deepest valley yet, some two hundred yards wide and the valley floor a hundred feet below the dune tops. At its entrance a great outcrop of iron ore stood sentinel. A curly-horned bish leaped from a hollow about fifty feet away and bounded off down the valley. Since I was almost certainly the first European to see this valley I solemnly named it 'Bish Gully'. I followed it for its four miles on the dune's rim which was quite solid and more level than the gully bottom.

The land was barren. This worried me slightly as according to my map I should have been going through an area of scrub. Several miles later I hit an area of grassland. This had me more concerned since if this was the grass on my map then I was walking much more slowly than I had estimated. I pushed the thought from me, remembering my first rule of desert travel, 'Be meticulous in navigation and trust your results.' I had been meticulous.

There were camels scattered over the area, grazing happily. They raised their heads to watch us go by, they carried on with their refuelling. These beasts would spend a week eating, then be rounded up and taken to water at Araouane, after which undoubtedly Taoudenni would be their destination. I informed my girls of their luck in encountering me who, Allah permitting, would take them to a new and fatter life in Mauritania. No more would they tread the Taoudenni trail. Perhaps my speech lost something in the translation for they seemed little impressed.

I had begun to talk to the ladies shortly after leaving Tombouctou. Every move I intended would be aired in public and they were included in any decision-making. They would reply, presumably by telepathy, often with sound advice. Each had her own personality. Peggy, the scatterbrained teenager, resented every move she had to make and was prone to sulking, moaning and the occasional tantrum. Trad was the capable, if not perpetually willing, house-keeper who would go about her tasks stoically but would not stand for too much nonsense.

At noon I unloaded them and sent them to graze, myself tucking into beef luncheon-meat and cold peas. We had covered twelve miles that morning which was excellent. For two hours I stayed where we were, doing the usual small tasks that had to be done, then I rounded up my reluctant entourage again.

'Why - can't - you - leave - us - alone - I - don't - want - to - carry - any - more - of - your - SILLY - food - and - where - are - you - taking - us - anyway - look - at - the - time - I'm - tired,' said Peggy, vomiting up my arm.

'A woman's work is never done,' sighed Trad, ritually trying to keep her ear away from my hand.

Shortly after setting out I saw a cairn of iron ore about four feet high. Always men build cairns; cairns to show their passing, cairns to departed souls, cairns to local spirits. There was

perhaps a little of all of these things in my act of placing my
stone on top. Then I walked away from it. Apart from some
evidence of camels this was the last sign of humanity I was to see
until I had crossed the Empty Quarter.

The afternoon was cool and cloudy also, ideal for my task.
Every time I breasted a rise the new vista would give me a thrill in
the knowledge that mine were probably the first European eyes,
and possibly the first human eyes, to see it. It is a feeling difficult
to describe, like a collector adding something of great value to his
collection, but much more; like a lover seeing new aspects of his
adored one, but much deeper. There was, in my case, an element
of selfishness in the feeling for I did not have to share it as other
discoverers had had to share their finds. Later I would share it on
film, but the first eyes were my eyes. Since there was no one
present to pat me on the back it couldn't have been an ego-trip.

Why people should wish to go to the desert with others was,
and still is, beyond me. One must go to the wilderness alone. To
be alone in the desert is to feel safe. Certainly the desert must be
treated with respect, a great deal of respect, but unlike people
she is predictable. To be with people, even those one thinks one
knows intimately, is to be, to some extent, wary.

Worry has never been my strong point. I have a bank manager
to worry about my finances and a landlord to worry about my
roof. These two I allow to share what should be my ulcers, and
pay them well for their trouble. But still, the leaving behind of
civilisation completely was a great burden removed. I was now
living a completely separate life which had begun in Araouane,
and the only problem I had in the world was to reach Oualata.
Nothing else mattered. I cannot remember ever being so deeply
and quietly happy.

The light began to dim as I came to the end of a valley. There
was a little grazing about so I decided that this would do for
tonight's camp. I had run out of wood and had seen none all day.
For over a week I hadn't seen a tree, but sometimes there were
low shrubs which yielded morsels of fuel. Not, however, on this
day.

I had with me two packets of solid fuel for emergencies. One of
these had perished into a powder, either from old age or the
heat, or even from physical pummelling on camel-back. At

lunch-time I had used half of this powder to brew my Lip-ton's. Clearly a more substantial source of fuel had to be found.

In various books I had read of dried camel dung being used as fuel. At the end of this valley there were a few patches of dried dung which came in handy marble-sized little lumps. I collected a quantity of these, and some dried grass, and lit a fire. The dung caught instantly, blazed quietly, and settled down to a charcoal-like glow. Tea brewed on a camel dung fire is very pleasant. I became an ardent camel dung collector. From the top of that valley alone I collected half a stuff-bag of fuel.

Cigarette rationing was in progress. One smoke per day was the rule, and this I had with my second cup of tea. It was the calmest time of the day, when there was nothing else to do but enjoy the desert. As I slipped into sleep on the evening of the second day of my new life, the last embers of my fire glowing steadily, it began gently to rain.

The morning was, thankfully, dull and my ladies close by. I tried to film myself leading my caravan out of the valley, but it was pretty hopeless. First I set up the camera on the tripod and wound up the clockwork motor. I had then precisely eighteen seconds to run to Trad who was out of shot, drag her into shot and out of the other end.

'What's - going - on - now - I - was - all - right - where - I - was - having - my - breakfast - and - I - didn't - want - to - be - a - film - star - anyway - you've - not - got - my - best - side,' moaned Peggy.

'Let's stop going around in circles and get on,' said Trad. I agreed with Trad, packed the gear and away we went in the cool morning.

My calves had almost healed, most of the scabs having fallen off. My other scab was flaking at the edges. I was in danger of coming down with a severe case of health.

Though the day was pleasant the walking was difficult. There were two kinds of ripple in the hard morning sand, the first being small ripple such as can be seen at Blackpool when the tide goes out and presents no problem to the walker. The other, large ripple, had its crests at just below, or just above the length of my stride. The difference in height between the crest and the lowest point was an inch at most, but anyone who has tried to walk along a railway track on the sleepers will understand the problem. Almost all of it was large ripple.

Trad, always the brainy one, tried an experiment. She would overtake me to the length of her rope, dip her head down to a clump of grass, tearing it up bodily, then resume her walk before the rope tightened. That was the theory, and it seemed to be working so it was fine by me. However, she failed on a couple of occasions to resume motion in time, resulting in my almost cutting myself in half on my waist rope. I had to put a stop to it. A few judicial tugs as her head went down and she soon got the message.

Despite the large ripple, when I found a good campsite that evening I had done twenty-two miles, a very acceptable distance.

The site was a well grassed little hollow sheltered from the wind, which was nothing more than a breeze. I decided not to close-hobble Trad, but allow her a little freedom that night. If she was miles away by morning I would think seriously about doing it again. Supper was sweet and sour something with rice, finished off with biscuits and Chinese haw jam. The jam was in a glass jar and it seemed a good plan to empty it before it was broken. A jar of free flowing jam in one's rucksack is second only, in its ability to cause misery, to a soft boiled egg mixed in with a camera.

According to my calculations it was possible that late on the next day I would sight the aklé.

It was a warm night and around midnight I was half asleep in my sleeping bag, contemplating what to do in order to cool off. It seemed like a good idea to stick a leg out of the bag so I dopily shoved out my right one. I felt a slight sting but thought nothing of it, assuming it to be a bit of grass or some such. Within a very short time, however, a great acid-like pain began to spread throughout the lower leg and up beyond the knee. It was as if someone had spilled boiling fat on my leg. It had to be a scorpion sting. I knew of nothing else nocturnal that would do this. The pain required painkillers, which I took. They had little effect. A couple of hours later there were pains around my heart, the sort of thing one must expect from a scorpion sting. I was glad that I had done my homework and knew that the situation was not serious. It certainly felt serious, but I told myself not to worry. Scorpion stings were very rarely fatal, and then only if the victim was very small or very weak. I was neither.

Sleep was somewhat spasmodic after that. The pains around my heart receded and by morning were gone, but my leg was still painful. There was, strangely, no visual evidence of the problem. At dawn I discovered my next setback. Sometime during the night one of my jerricans had fallen over on the soft sand. The cap was well worn and ill fitting so a considerable amount of water had leaked through it. I was now down to ten gallons. It was not an accident, but carelessness on my part. I knew about the leaky cap and should have piled equipment or sand around the can to stop it falling over. It was an expensive lesson.

It was not, however, a major disaster as I had been using only six pints per day and at that rate I should have enough to finish the journey comfortably, providing nothing else happened to reduce my water for there were now no reserves. From now on there was to be no washing except for my crotch, or use of water for anything other than consumption. I knew my water intake exactly as each evening I would fill a one-gallon container and drop purifying tablets into the grey murk which looked and tasted like thin mud. This would be my supply for the next day, from which I would fill my water bottle, cook and brew. Always, without design, there had been a couple of pints left after the evening meal and Lip-ton's.

Trad and Peggy were about ten feet away. There had been no reason for them to go anywhere as there was much lush vegetation nearby. They were saddled and loaded and we were on our way on the fourth day by seven o'clock. From the very start of this day Trad became bolshie. She hung back and had to be dragged energetically along, her head and neck stretched horizontally. I tried sharp tugs, I tried coaxing, and I tried swift whacks to her rear, all to no avail. She would not even bring the matter to arbitration in order to air her grievances. Finally I had to suspend her from her position as lead camel and tie her on behind.

Peggy was not much better and travel was really hard work. The sun spent some time blazing past the clouds, which did not help one bit. Later in the day we began to encounter low, soft dunes in which my feet sank to the ankles. I normally had to stop every half hour or so to empty sand from my left boot. My right boot didn't seem to fill. I had put this down, on the approach, to the wind which blew from my right, but this theory no longer held water as the wind was now from behind. I concluded that I must have some peculiar way of walking. On the soft sand I had to empty both boots frequently, as to walk in sand-filled boots is to invite blisters.

There was, towards evening, a definite change in topography. The streets of dunes were giving way much more to soft, rolling dunes, heralding the aklé. I mounted a large dune hoping to sight the aklé in the distance, but could see nothing of note; just an undulating sand sea which looked much the same in every direction. When I lay down that night I was absolutely exhausted, but yet happy with my progress. On reaching the aklé I would be able to confirm my speed and distance. My stung leg was back, more or less, to normal.

I thought again about my love for this desert that had provided me with so much enjoyment, and even with my fire. Where some other European desert travellers seemed to have gone wrong was in not loving the desert, but treating it as an enemy to be battered into submission. I preferred to move with it, for it was far too great to submit to me. As for my insistence on being alone, to take a knowledgeable companion to the desert and hope to understand it through him is as difficult as trying to understand God via a priest. Each has his rituals, and his explanations for those rituals, but does he really understand? In any case, should not lovers be alone?

I slept happily and deeply that night.

I did not, however, sleep for long. Soon after midnight the monsoon began. The rain poured. It rattled on my space blanket. It clattered into my pan. It thudded against my jerricans. It patted onto the sand. The thunder clapped the endless staccato symphony for percussion. For the rest of the night I cowered beneath the plastic blanket, trying to stay dry. Sleep was somewhat erratic amidst that great cacophony of sound. When dawn showed tentative signs of arriving it slackened a little. I leaped out of my damp bag and packed it.

There was not a sign of my ladies anywhere – literally that! All traces of their tracks had been battered out of existence by the heavy raindrops. The whole ground was a mass of deep little craters; and it was wet, the dryness of the sand being insufficient to soak up that quantity of water immediately.

This was, I concluded, likely to be a long job. Meanwhile I thought that collecting a little water would be a good idea. I spread out my space blanket and using two jerricans together with other articles, channelled the falling water towards a hole in which I placed my pan.

Now for the girls. I was in a roughly circular hollow about five hundred yards wide. They must have got out somewhere so it seemed to me that I should walk along the rim looking for evidence of their passing and possibly I might spot the girls somewhere. The sand was very barren with just a few stalks of grass poking through here and there, like reeds in a polluted pond. It took me half an hour to circumnavigate the hollow without seeing a single sign of their passage. I returned to camp, emptied my now full pan into a jerrican, and reset it.

The situation was now serious. I was beyond the point-of-no-return since the chances of walking back to Araouane and finding that speck on the desert were remote indeed. Ali could have done it since he knew every dune within a day's journey of Araouane by heart. I did not. To miss Araouane was to wander over the sands until death intervened. Old Baldie was around somewhere. He never gives up, Old Baldie. He knows that he can't lose.

To be able to carry enough water to get me to Oualata was improbable to say the least. I was less than a quarter of the way across with almost three hundred miles yet to go. I had to find those camels.

A camel's foot is designed not to sink into the sand so that, at best, it leaves very shallow footprints. There are, however, two great toe-nails which leave twin holes about an inch and a half apart. Very often, even in ideal conditions, those holes are all that can be seen. There were millions of similar holes made by raindrops all over the desert floor. What I had to find was the vestiges of a series of these holes in the correct regular pattern.

I had a brainwave. When a camel goes uphill it has to dig in its toe-nails for traction. The place to look, therefore, was not on the tops, but on the steepest part of the slope itself. It was still raining steadily. I tied my wet skirt up around my waist and resumed my search.

It was when I had almost completed another circuit that I saw the regular pattern that I was seeking. Just by intense looking I would not have seen it. One must, when in a tough tracking situation like this, 'half-look'. It is a technique I had learned as a child tracking rabbits through early morning grass. Close scrutiny would show the same green grass everywhere, but 'half-looking' would reveal a distinct line where there was not quite so much dew clinging to the blades of grass. Here I saw the pattern of marks revealing the girls' passage.

I followed them into the next hollow, lost them, picked them up again, and eventually found the damp ladies chewing cud unconcernedly in a little hidden hollow about two miles from camp. To say that I was relieved would be massively to understate my feelings.

'I - thought - *you'd* - turn - up - just - as - we - were - having - our - bath - and - now - I - suppose - you - expect - us - to - carry - something - for - you - in - this - weather - and - me - with - wet - hair - and - I - can't - do - a - *thing* - with - it,' said Peggy through the slime.

'We didn't *really* want a day off anyway,' said Trad in a sarcastic tone.

Eight-thirty saw the girls loaded and the great trek continuing. A cool breeze blew and the rain came in patches of gentleness. An hour later, after mounting several hump-backed dunes, I looked back and saw that several of these dunes fell away on their western side in steep crescent slopes. I was in amongst the aklé and hadn't realised it. The sand was very soft underfoot, despite the hardening effect of the rain. 'Keep out of the aklé,' I heard Moulaie say, 'or in three hours you will be dead!'

I turned on a compass bearing north-west. Those dunes, though deadly, were incredibly beautiful, even unto paradisic. I soon learned to read them. As I came up a gentle slope I knew that there would be some parts which would drop steeply from a sharp edge, and other parts which would slope gently onto the next rise. There would appear an almost undiscernible haze above the gentle slope and for this I would make with confidence.

It took me an hour to drag the girls out of the aklé, an hour of very exhausting travel as my feet sank and hot sand covered my calves. Trad was lead camel again and she did not like aklé at all.

When I checked on the accuracy of my navigation I was amazed to find my estimate of distance to be correct to within very fine limits indeed. As near as it was possible to check on my small-scale map I was within a hundred yards of where I had calculated. This was fantastic news and it filled me with confidence.

Before me was a long valley going my way, so down it I went. Except for periods around mid-day when the sun was out I mostly didn't wear my *chèche* on my head, but let my hair blow around at will. My skirt I had hoisted up into a sort of mini so I had the appearance more of an ancient Greek than an Arab. My navigational confidence had put a spring into my previously weary step and I actually skipped for a while down that valley.

At noon the girls went to graze and I sat on a rise looking out over a grand grass-dotted hollow some two miles across. For lunch I made spaghetti to celebrate my arrival at the aklé, the sauce consisting of tomato purée, onions and sardines. It was excellent! The sun came out and I spread out my wet gear to dry. The world was a wonderful place. I told Trad all about Manchester United, and Peggy all about Blondie, this taking several seconds.

Just after three we set off down the slope into the great hollow. Beyond it was a smaller one, then the whole terrain settled down into a regular series of valleys about a quarter-mile wide and a hundred feet deep, dotted with scrub grass and lying across my line of march. This was *dune fixée*, or fixed dune according to the map.

Happiness abounded. I strode along singing old jazz numbers I had almost forgotten, dragging them from the depths of memory. Jazz had been my first love in the musical world and in my youth, with a pianist friend, I had entertained in pubs for free beer. I pleaded with Bill Bailey to come home, also with my melancholy baby for was not love just around the corner come rain or come shine. That old black magic had me in its spell, but it was just one of those things. I was feeling misty when I happened to look round.

I was a camel short! Peggy had slipped her moorings and her

rope was dangling empty from the back of Trad. I had been going for about an hour and a half and had no idea when she had departed. She wasn't in sight. There was nothing for it but to close-hobble Trad and track her down.

For three quarters of an hour I followed the tracks of a man and a single camel, crossing valley after valley, until I finally found her happily munching not far from the tracks. She raised her head, had a grumble, and resumed eating, unconcerned.

'Say baby, what's da big idea huh?' quoth I.

'Didn't think much a da sounds man, so I split!'

Everyone wants to be a critic! She made her protest in the usual emerald fashion and we returned to Trad.

It was now just after six. Thanks to the troubles of the day we had come only sixteen miles, but I was finished. There was grass below in a valley, and even a little brushwood, so this was as far as we went on day five.

As I was so exhausted I didn't get around to close-hobbling Trad, thinking to do it after supper. However, when I looked for them by torch in the pitch-black they were not to be seen. Another lesson learned. They would probably be miles away by morning, giving me another late start. I prayed for a fine night with no rain.

When returning with the prodigal my bad knee had begun to give trouble for the first time. The pain was very severe so I took painkillers. As I was dropping off I registered the thought that I might have to ride the next day so I must keep Peggy's saddle clear.

It rained. Maybe I was out of practice with the praying business. I searched the area for tracks, but it was as before. Finally I found the pattern I sought on a slope and followed it, 'half-looking' ahead. The two sets of tracks constantly split up and converged. I tried to follow Trad's tracks, these being the biggest. If I was going to lose a camel I did not wish to lose the hard-working Trad. A few times I lost the tracks and had to backtrack to pick them up again. Much of the tracking that morning was subliminal. I could not explain in detail why I was going in a particular direction as there was mostly nothing to be seen on the ground, I simply knew that they had passed this way.

It took an hour and a half to find them. They had travelled almost four miles in the night. Peggy had broken her hobble and set off, the gallant Trad, loyal in friendship, struggling in her wake. We grumbled at each other in the usual manner and I made a mental note that close-hobbling was to be the practice from now on. Moulaie had said to me, back in Araouane, 'After nine days you must close-hobble as they will go looking for water.' They had begun early.

By nine o'clock I was back on my route with my camels laden. I had already done seven miles at least, and accomplished nothing. There was intermittent cloud throughout the morning with, at other times, the sun beating heavily down. The pain in my knee had become bearable so I continued to walk taking care not to limp. If I had allowed myself to limp it would have thrown my body out of rhythm causing problems somewhere else, and slowing me up, thus giving me difficulties with my estimation of distance covered.

The terrain itself had slowed me down a little. *Dune fixée* was still here but with much soft sand as well. Occasionally I would pass an isolated patch of aklé to the right or the left. The quarter-mile-wide valleys had become much deeper and the sides correspondingly steeper. I was having to meander quite a lot to make my route as little uphill as possible. Soon I gave up the practice of actually going *to* my sighted object, that which I had selected as being *directly* on my intended line of march, in favour of greater progress in a general westerly direction. In fact any inaccuracies inherent in this new method were largely evened out by keeping a mental note of the direction in which I had erred and correcting it by a reciprocal error the next or subsequent time. This is what practical navigation, as opposed to going by the book, is all about.

By lunch-time I was ready for a good rest. I had walked non-stop, except for boot-emptying operations, for four hours and estimated that I had covered ten miles. Unloading the girls I sat down to eat. At this point they would usually make for the greenest clump of adjacent grass and commence to consume it. This time they didn't. They just stood where they were, not moving at all, not even chewing their cud. They had begun to die.

That morning, whilst I was tracking them, I had noticed that they had not stopped by any grass, but had just continued walking. When I found them they were not eating, which was unusual. This was not an unexpected problem, but I didn't want it just yet. They had seemingly reached the point where they had insufficient moisture in their bodies to digest food. How many days would they last now? It seemed inevitable that two or three more days was all I could expect from them. That would bring me to half-way and then I would have to test my ability to walk out carrying my own water. This had always been a possibility, but in spite of my trials in Tunisia, now that it was becoming a probability the task seemed enormous.

I knew that I would have to get as many miles per day out of them as possible. Unlike cars camels work on miles per day rather than miles per gallon. Night travelling was, unfortunately, not practical. There was a new moon but it was rarely visible because of cloud and to walk in the dark was to risk injury to legs or ankles which could prove fatal.

The lunch-time halt was short and I moved out on a bearing due west. As on the approach to Araouane there was a series of shallow slopes upwards leading to sharp drops so that I was almost continually walking uphill. My knee was giving me much pain but owing to the condition of the girls I elected to walk in order to preserve what strength remained to them. They were really fatigued, particularly Trad. When I stopped to empty my boot she would immediately flop down and lean over on her side, but when I stood then so would she and, without complaint, continued. She didn't seem to have the strength to moan.

Just before six I found a sheltered spot in the crescent of a large isolated aklé dune and set up camp at the base of the steep sand wall. The wind was quite strong and it was pleasant to be out of it. There was a little wood around which was useful as I was almost out of dung and hadn't seen any for days.

I hobbled the girls near the top of the hollow, allowing them a short period of freedom. Thankfully they began to eat. This was wonderful. As it became dark Trad decided that she didn't like that particular area and set out for pastures new, followed by her shadow Peggy. I caught them and close-hobbled them both near some greenery. There could be no further freedom to waste their strength.

The moon, new and Taurean, shone through a gap in the clouds. I remembered my diary comment of a month previously: 'Next time there is a new moon, either the dragon or I will be dead.'

We were still both very much alive, but the battle was yet to come.

In the morning I overslept. It was all of six o'clock when I awoke, and daylight. Still, I must have needed the rest and I certainly felt better for it. My ladies were where I had left them the previous evening. It was nice not having to conduct hiking and tracking exercises first thing in the morning.

Just after seven, under a hazy sun, we were on our way. The cloud had thinned out and the sun was visible through it, warming the still air of morning. Scrub grass abounded and the girls seemed much fresher and more willing; not exactly enthusiastic, but more willing. The land was much more level than on the previous day and the morning saw good progress, despite a very painful knee.

This pain I despatched by mentally banishing it. Periodically it would return, but I would send it away again with strict instructions not to disturb me whilst I was working. I was using a technique which I call a *mind trick*. Pain is simply the body telling the mind that something is wrong; but the mind does not have to hear. In normal circumstances the warning would be heeded and steps taken to solve the problem. These, however, were not normal circumstances. The only thing that I could do to solve the problem which was causing the pain would be to stop walking; but I had to cover sixteen miles per day minimum and my girls were very tired. So I allowed the knee to hurt and refused to heed its complaining. I imagined that it did not hurt, and because imagination is far stronger than will-power, it did not.

Soon after eleven, the temperature having risen to above 90°F, I saw a tree, the first tree I had seen for many days, since before Araouane in fact. Trad's eyes bulged and Peggy drooled. Beneath that tree was shade, a valuable commodity in the heat of the day.

Since I had already covered thirteen miles that morning and was unlikely to find another tree for some time, I called a halt and unloaded the womenfolk who immediately set about the delicate task of pruning.

This type of tree must have been the favourite food of camels. It stood about ten feet high with narrow branches sprouting out of the sand culminating in spiky, very green, pine-like needles. These needles, and the entire device, were loaded with sap which replenished the moisture in the camels' reservoirs and spoke of an enormously deep tap root. The thing was, of course, merely a shrub, but to me, in the context of the undulating plain speckled with scrub, it was a giant redwood towering to the skies. It was curious that for the rest of my journey one of these would very often appear at a convenient time for the lunch-time or evening halt, so I came to know them as 'Manna trees'.

Curiously enough, some weeks later back in England, I was perusing a book of desert growths and came across a picture of such a tree, under which was the legend 'Tamarisk.' Later still, in another volume I chanced upon a reference to the Tamarisk. It had indeed a deep tap root, over a hundred feet in depth if needed, and its branches and leaves oozed sap. The Arabs, the book said, would collect this sap, dry it out, and make the residue into cakes to eat. This they would call *Manna*. Sometimes the world takes on a strangeness one does not expect.

I had been going so well in the morning that I had neglected to empty my boots as often as I should, the result being that I was now the proud possessor of a blister on the ball of each foot. My method of dealing with a blister is simple, direct, and painful. I sterilise my father's sword by fire, burst the blister, cut off the dead skin, put antiseptic cream on the raw flesh and a couple of strips of plaster over the lot, then ignore it. Once mobile this hurts much less than the original blister and heals faster. I thus treated the left foot and decided to leave the right one, it having only a small problem which, with diligent boot-emptying, should go away by itself.

There was dead wood to collect and burn. I put on water to boil and dug out two packets of freeze-dried food with which to regale myself. The labels had worn off, this being their fourth trip to Africa. One was obviously rice, but the other was a lumpy white powder giving little clue as to its ingredients. I assumed it to be prawn or pork something. It turned out to be mashed potato. For desert dessert I ensured my protein intake by opening a can of sardines and thought fond thoughts of steak pudding, chips and mushy peas with gravy, sprinkled liberally with salt and non-brewed condiment.

Half past two saw us on our painful, hot, but quite happy way. The view was uninspiring, the novelty of new vistas for mankind having wallowed under a blanket of utter boredom. When you've seen one scrubby, sandy valley, you've seen 'em all. This was, I am convinced, why the mystics of old came to the wilderness. True, at night the heavenly vista would inspire them to great revelations, but during the day the sheer visual boredom of great stretches of desert would force their minds to seek within for stimulus. I myself thought long and deep about the Holy Trinity – scrumpy, Guinness and Boddington's bitter.

The pain in my knee went away unbidden in the afternoon. I concluded that the nerves had finally worn through. Dusk put on a beautiful red-streaked display as I burned Manna wood and boiled water for Lip-ton's. I had accomplished nearly twenty-two miles that day, a very respectable distance, and I was pleased with the way things had gone. With luck it was possible that I would camp on the Mauritanian border the following night, and I might even reach half-way on the evening after. I close-hobbled Les Demoiselles de Tombouctou downwind, their perfume being not of the finest, and thought trinitarian thoughts.

On the morning of day eight I awoke with a cold. I sneezed on the baggage as I packed it, sneezed at the orange sunrise and sneezed at the adjacent Manna tree as I collected its dead wood. There had been a heavy dew and everything was damp.

'Atishoo!' I said to Peggy as I bent to untie her ropes.

'Don't - you - give - me - that - cold - I - don't - know - where - you - got - it - you're - all - the - same - you - foreigners - we'll - all - be - ill - I - wish - I - was - back - in - that - nice - Tombouctou - it's - terrible - the - way - you - treat - us.'

'Your complaint has been registered and will go through the normal channels.'

Her green slime missed me completely. I was getting good!
'Atishoo!' I reiterated to Trad.
'Bless you!' said Trad, not unsympathetically.
'Thank you, Trad.'
'Think nothing of it,' she mumbled, contemplating another hard day's slog.

At seven-fifteen we moved off to the west, the sun struggling with sparse clouds, an enormous scrubby plain the first item on the agenda. Tracks were everywhere. I saw darting green lizards leaving lizard tracks and scarabs doing likewise with beetle tracks. A desert fox, light of fur, its body no more than nine inches long followed by an enormous brush, darted from behind a clump of scrub and sat beyond a rise, its enormous rabbit ears betraying its presence. Large raven tracks were common, and occasionally the ravens which made them. An ungainly, tatty, badly designed, utility sort of bird is a raven on the ground, but in the air she becomes a three-dimensioned ballerina conducting her dance with grace and precision. She is the desert's dustman, the skyborne scavenger whose job it is to keep the desert clean and sterile. At enormous heights she will glide the currents looking for something in the process of dying. She is not averse to assisting in this process as she has a great preference for warm, fresh, newly dead meat.

Always there were the flies. They were difficult to ignore. They would buzz inside ears, crawl over lips and around nostrils and eyes. The girls' eyes and rectums were moving carpets of black flies jostling for position like last-minute boozers.

I topped a rise and the plain just went on, and on, and on. Tramp, tramp, tramp went my feet as they blazed new frontiers, sounding much like feet on Southport beach. This area reminded me of where I used to play as a child. Here the dunes were of sand and there they were of iron slag and pit dirt, rounded by wind and rain, but still small clumps of poor grass poked through and managed to survive. Yes, we did have deserts in England. I felt strangely very much at home.

A line of ants marched to and fro along my direction of march, busily doing the things that ants do. I crossed a bed of lava, dark grey and hard, about a hundred yards by twenty-five, and another; there were many.

By nine o' clock the temperature had already touched the eighties, the sun blazing from an almost cloudless sky. Isolated aklé dunes had begun to spring up in my path and my feet continually sank into the sand as the girls showed reluctance to continue. It dawned on me that exploration was much like genius in that it was ten per cent inspiration and ninety per cent perspiration.

There was a flash of movement just where I was about to place my foot and I caught a glimpse of the biggest spider I have ever seen, fully three inches across, thick legs with black and white fair-isle markings on its body. In a fraction of a second it had dug itself into the sand and was gone.

At half-past ten I had covered nine miles and decided on a short rest. The temperature was now well over 90°F and the sky a deep, flawless blue from horizon to horizon. Not a breath of air ruffled the sand and no sound disturbed the peace. I needed that rest. This had never occurred before. It was literally impossible to continue without it. My basic reserves of strength were in short supply and this was the first real evidence of the fact. Since leaving Tombouctou seventeen days previously I had hardly rested other than at times spent actually sleeping. Almost every day had been a seventeen-hour one, and a hard seventeen-hour one at that. Now the price was becoming evident, and payment due. I wondered how much longer I could operate at anything like full efficiency. From now on I decided that frequent short rests would help to preserve what strength remained.

Twenty minutes later I was on my way again. According to my calculations I was only fifteen miles from the Mauritanian border. That was my goal for the night. After a while the refreshing effect of my short rest began to wear off and I became 'dune happy'. This is my term for a condition whereby if I saw an uphill slope then, if I did not concentrate, and in that heat concentration was difficult, I automatically headed up it to the summit. This played merry hell with my navigation, though I tried my best to correct it on each occasion.

Other mistakes were beginning to manifest. According to my tape-recorded diary, which I was on this occasion recording as I walked, I was still walking at ten past twelve with the intention of stopping at one o' clock. In my written log it states that I stopped at eleven-fifty. The log is more likely to be correct.

Most of the lunch-time 'rest' was spent filming and repairing a sand-filled tape-recorder. At three, in a temperature which must have been over 100°F, we set out again over the hot sand. Down into a great hollow we went. No breeze blew and the air, hot in my nostrils as I breathed in, was noticeably cooler on its way out. There were other desert foxes around, bouncing over the dunes. I wished them luck as I marched on through the vast oven, Dutch marching songs in my head.

At five I had to rest. The sun was directly in front of me, burning into my eyeballs. A slight breeze had built up, but it was so hot that it was like walking past an open furnace door. Seconds after stopping Trad folded herself onto the ground. Peggy didn't seem to have the strength to collapse. She just stood and stared. On the next day, if the weather was like this, I knew that I would have to ride. Though the girls were tired, I was more so. After a very few minutes I stood up and we continued.

As the sun dipped before me the air rapidly cooled and the going became much easier. I calculated that though I was just over a day from half-way across the Empty Quarter I had already come over three hundred miles with the girls from Tombouctou and had a mere one hundred and eighty miles yet to go. It was a sum that made me a little happier.

At twenty to six I found a Manna tree with a great deal of dead wood on it. This was as far as I was going. I was still five miles away from Mauritania but we were all tired and hungry. The tree, and its sap, were essential to the well-being of my bonny lassies, and they must have first consideration if we were to arrive in Oualata.

That night as I drank my tea and smoked my cigarette, as the fire's embers glowed beneath the stars, I knew that the holiday was finished. Up to that time the days had all been filled with hard and consistent work, but there had been a cheerfulness and a light-heartedness about it. Now that my, and my ladies', strengths were ebbing the exhilaration of the past few days was ebbing with them. I was still extremely optimistic about the success of the venture, but I realised that whatever happened from this point on the task was going to increase in difficulty day by day and would require greater determination as Oualata came closer.

The honeymoon was over. The battle was about to begin. But the battle would not be with the desert; that was to be the focus, the battleground. My opponent, the dragon, would be myself.

9 The Dragon

We entered Mauritania at quarter past eight on day nine. There was a Manna tree, complete with shade, instead of a border post. I took advantage of its shade for twenty minutes whilst the girls reduced its area. The day was, if anything, even hotter than the previous one, the perfect canopy of blue framing the flaming golden powerhouse of the sun. There were problems with slipping baggage at nine o' clock which took half an hour to rectify.

I slogged on, forcing each footstep forward. Again the baggage slipped, and was rectified. By eleven I was at the limit of my strength. My legs would carry me no further and that was that! I led Peggy to the head of the caravan, shushed her down and took off my boots.

Peggy knew what was coming and voiced her reluctance.

'I - don't - know - you - bring - me - out - here - and - work - me - every - day - and - wait - until - I'm - tired - and - then - you - want - me - to - carry - you - well - we'll - see - about - that - the - cheek - of - it - all - I - ask - you.'

'Sorry m'dear,' I said in reply to her somewhat justifiable tirade, 'but owing to the scheme of things you, the camel, are the servant whilst I, the human, am the master. Therefore I am entitled, at the express wish of Allah, to ride whenever the whim takes me.' This last I emphasised with a flourish of my camel stick.

Using my sleeping-bag as upholstery I swung myself aboard. Peggy turned her head and roared with all her might into my face, 'I won't – I won't – I won't!'

A judicial whack to her rear made her rise somewhat reluctantly, grumbling the while. She stood, solid as a monolith, and despite my efforts refused to move. Another whack and she let out a pitiful moan, but didn't budge. This was no time for delicacy. I gave her rear a hefty swipe and she lumbered forward.

So far so good. Unfortunately we were heading north and we

needed to go west. I pulled her head around with the rope. She turned around and walked south. I touched her left flank and she headed north again. This was repeated several times. On two occasions she turned east, but in no way could I get her to walk west. It was ridiculous. Finally, with a wail of anguish, she dropped down onto the sand and lay on her side, pitching me unceremoniously from my perch.

There was only one thing for it. I would have to resort to the Ali Ould Boy method of obedience training. Reluctantly I administered this to the sad animal, then looked her in the eye and said, 'Right! Let's try that again!'

Into the saddle I leaped. Before I was properly settled, up she rose, giving a final shrug at the end of her rising. I wasn't prepared for that last shrug and flew backwards through the air to land on my back in the sand.

I may have been momentarily unconscious, but my brains were certainly scrambled. For a few moments I lay there, mentally checking for breakages. I was badly shaken and winded. When I tried to get up a great pain shot through my back on the left side. I had had broken ribs before; my first thought was that I'd done it again. That was what it felt like. Almost simultaneously came the thought, 'Thank God the pain is on one side and not in the middle. My back is all right.'

There was a Manna tree close by and I crawled over to its shade where I lay for a while to think about this new problem. After about half an hour I knew that I could go no further that morning so I dragged myself over to Peggy, who was looking sorry for herself, hobbled her and Trad, and unshipped my rucksack from Trad. The movement and lifting caused excruciating pain from which I almost passed out. The rest of the gear, except for my one-gallon container, I had to leave on board. Then I crawled back to the shade of the tree, dragging my rucksack behind me. The whole operation took over half an hour.

Tea was required as a matter of urgency. I built a fire and brewed up. Shock was setting in as I lit my last American cigarette and sucked in the numbing smoke. My hands were trembling as I held the cup of hot, sweet tea and sipped it carefully. A dose of painkillers was washed down with hope and I brewed another cup.

Time passed slowly. I filled in my log-book, reported my accident to my tape-recorder, and smoked a tatty Malian fag as a sort of penance, thinking that perhaps the pain it induced in my throat would somehow delete from the pain in my back. The afternoon dragged on.

I carefully weighed up my situation. There were six gallons of water left and I had about a hundred and seventy miles to go. Roughly that meant that at six pints per day, the bare minimum for this heat, I had eight days' water left. To do the remaining distance I would have to average about twenty-one miles per day, a daunting task even without injury and fatigue. I dared not risk riding again for a while because the camel's motion would induce too much pain, so whatever happened, pain or no pain, at three o' clock I had to start walking, and walking at my regulation pace. About this I had absolutely no choice. It would be several days before there was enough light at night to walk safely.

Dutifully, just before three, I packed my rucksack and loaded it onto Trad. The pain had become a general numbness and I concluded that the ribs were not in fact broken but badly bruised since I could not feel broken ends grating together. In fact they *were* broken, I discovered later, and took many months to heal, but at the time my main pain seemed to come from my kidney which shouted when I lifted anything or walked.

Tying Trad to me I walked on, ignoring the pain and not favouring my left side in any way. Immediately I was marching to German songs. 'Erika' was vocalised loudly at my enemy, the pain. The hard painful miles of Nijmegen were on my mind as I stamped my way westward. Soon, as is the way of pain, it subsided with use and I continued at three miles per hour in the windless heat.

Over half an hour later I looked behind me and saw only Trad. Peggy had gone away again. Half of her rope dangled free from Trad's rear, broken and tattered. There was hardly any emotion. I simply noted these things and automatically set about doing something about them. Close-hobbling Trad I retraced our tracks over the fixed dunes until I found Peggy quite close to the place of our lunch-time halt. She was still reluctant to go west. It passed through my mind that I might have to dump Peggy before her recalcitrance killed both Trad and myself.

I led her back to where I had left Trad and she too had gone, her broken rope lying like a dead snake on the sand. Their ropes were of Malian manufacture, weak of structure and rough of texture. I would, I decided, have to make new halters from British cord of which I had a quantity. Trad had fortunately taken off in a westerly direction, which was the first good thing that had happened all day. It took half an hour to find her and I immediately set about making two new halters. Minutes later we were on our way again.

Aklé was becoming more frequent as we neared Aklé Corner. There were thoughts of the possibility of crossing the aklé rather than going around it, but to do so I would have to dump both camels and this I was reluctant to do. Without the girls I could probably cross the forty or so miles of aklé as I would be able to take a straight course going up the dune's backs and sliding down the steep western sides. This would, I thought, be impossible with camels. It was not idle thinking for one must think well ahead and consider every contingency.

I found the ancient skull of a bish, bleached obscenely white, its great curled horns pointing to the sky. The other bones were widely scattered where the scavenging ravens had left them.

Soon after six I calculated that I had done my original bare minimum of sixteen miles and thankfully, with this as justification, gave up for the day. Immediately I stopped walking the pain took over again, making it very difficult to unload the baggage, but unloaded it had to be. The pain definitely raged around my left kidney and it was difficult to find a comfortable way to recline on the ground.

I was now off my large-scale maps and onto the smaller scale 1:1,000,000. According to my log I was about six miles from half-way and a little more from Aklé Corner, both of which I should reach the following morning. I took painkillers to help me sleep and bruised, battered and bent, but alive, slipped into slumber.

Half past six in the morning, the morning of day ten, saw us once more striding west. At first there were the usual fixed dune valleys, but by nine o' clock, at my estimated half-way point, I found myself in aklé. According to my calculations I should not have hit aklé for another two or three hours, but here was Aklé Corner. This meant that either the aklé had moved east some five to ten miles since the map had been made, or, the more likely explanation, I had underestimated my distance walked. In any case I had to change direction and head north out of the aklé.

For twenty minutes I rested, couching the camels and sitting in the shade of Peggy's saddle, the only shade around. Then onward over the massive piles of sand, now heated to an enormous temperature and pouring into my boots. After half an hour of this I was exhausted, but I knew that I must keep going. I picked out gentle slopes for the girls to walk down and zig-zagged to and fro over the burning white sand.

There was a heart-rending howl of lamentation from behind and there was Peggy, the saddle having slipped forward onto her neck. The rope from the saddle to her tail had broken allowing the saddle, baggage and all, to slide forward. The girth was tight around her shoulders and as I tried to untie it, it parted, dumping saddle and equipment onto the sand.

Repairs took over half an hour and we continued on through the mountains of sand, a strong wind blowing into our faces and whipping the stinging sand into them. The pains were there, but were gradually becoming absorbed into the normal condition of existence. And always the impossibly hot and brilliant sun hammered down.

At eleven-thirty, after over two hours in the aklé, we staggered into fixed dune. There was a Manna tree just ahead, a lonely blob of brilliant green on the rolling sea of sand. I collapsed in its shade after unloading, and brewed a greatly needed cuppa.

We set out early after the lunch-time break as I wanted to finish the day's work well before dark. There was to be a party that night, and a flag-raising ceremony to celebrate the half-way point. For this purpose I had brought with me a Union Jack, and four cans of lager purchased in Tombouctou for the grand sum of six pounds.

The fixed dune petered out and became a vast tabletop of a plain, level and dotted by scrub. This was a welcome change, almost a rest compared to the morning's aklé. Such was my relief that I even reverted to British marching songs, a sure sign of comparative physical and mental well-being. My left knee had begun to trouble me again earlier, but now this pain had blended with the rest of my pains giving me a sort of general dull ache on the entire left side of my body. This was strangely more manageable than any one of the various pains that it comprised. To complement it the wind from the east, hot though it was, had resurrected an ancient rheumatic pain in my right shoulder and upper arm. This was a legacy of years of teenage winter camping with inadequate ground insulation, and had lain dormant for most of my adult life. I left these pains to battle it out as best they could and continued north.

At about four o' clock, the sun dipping redly to my left, I saw two small Manna trees about a mile away. I judged that by the time I arrived there I would have completed my quota for the day, and there was supper for my girls and wood for my fire. Twenty minutes later I was unloading. I took the two camels and the million or so flies over to the smallest tree and close-hobbled them; the camels, not the flies.

I erected my tripod, contrived a pole using it, my camel stick and some camera tape, and soon the Union Jack fluttered grandly over the centre of the Saharan Empty Quarter. It was a proud moment.

It was a moment that needed something more. Should I perhaps sing 'Rule Britannia', I thought, but watching the sand being blown over the small rippled waves made the idea seem ridiculous. There were footprints, lonely and remote, around the tripod's base which were somewhat reminiscent of another expedition in another place. I cleared my throat and made a short speech to posterity via my tape-recorder:

'This has been one small step for Mankind, but a dirty great stride for one man.'

Next on the agenda was something I had been promising myself for days . . . a bath. I had not washed anything other than my crotch since leaving Araouane ten days previously. True, the rain had freshened me somewhat, but of late the girls had taken to turning away their noses and I had noticed that they were beginning to smell quite pleasant in comparison.

I had agonised greatly and long over the quantity of water needed for this operation. My water situation, though not quite desperate, was none-the-less somewhat serious. However, as much for psychological reasons as anything, I decided to sacrifice about three-quarters of a litre, just over a pint, for this purpose, justifying it to myself by reference to the four cans of lager I was about to consume instead of vast quantities of tea.

With my hands I dug a small hole in the sand, lined it with my space blanket, and poured in the precious liquid. Then, systematically, I cleaned every part of my body, including my teeth. My hair I let go fallow, it being so filthy and matted that only vast quantities of hot water and professional attention would make the slightest impact upon its condition.

The feel of a clean(ish) body after such toil and sweat is indescribable. Its psychological effects were dramatic. I laughed, seemingly for no reason. I even did a little dance, naked on the wind-blown plain.

I noticed, this being the first time since Araouane that my body had been perused in detail, that there was very little flesh, and absolutely no fat, on my bones. The skin clung close to the frame and my watch flopped loosely on a strap that in Tombouctou had been tight around my wrist. This state of affairs had been anticipated. I had left England a stout fourteen and a half stone on the principle that if camels could exist on their fat, so could cameleers. The girls, too, were much thinner, their great barrel chests deeply corrugated and humps long converted into energy. We must have looked a sorry sight.

But it was a time for jollity. I ate spicy beef and mashed potatoes, with an extra portion of potatoes. My beer cans I had wrapped in wet tissues and placed in my washing water to let them cool by evaporation. There were ten Malian cigarettes left, and a handful of boiled sweets. I laid out three cigarettes and four sweets on my sleeping-bag. These, together with my beer, would constitute the party.

There seemed no point in dressing for dinner, so I lay there starkers. As the sun vanished, snuffing out the long shadows, I drank the vile, gassy beer, smoked the cigarettes and ate the sweets. Then, coughing, belching and farting, I fell asleep as the last embers of the fire glowed redly. I fell asleep content in the knowledge that I had made it to the centre of the Empty Quarter, and that it was all downhill from now on. The last sound I heard was the flapping of the Union Jack, wafting lazily in the night breeze.

At seven on the morning of day eleven I struck out north-west. I thought that something had crawled into my mouth during the night and died. Still, the going was good and I made excellent progress. For three hours I walked over some very pleasant country with an occasional quite green valley, or a wide shallow hollow to break the monotony. Bounding foxes abounded and, because of the general flatness of the plain, the sky was enormous.

I was, in fact, walking away from Oualata, in order to circumvent the great knob of aklé. I did not wish to increase this distance more than was absolutely necessary, so at ten o' clock I decided to go west in the hope that I was already level with the northern extremity of the aklé. If I was not, then I could always go north again for a few miles.

The day was again incredibly hot. I had, I estimated, more than a hundred and fifty miles to go with only four gallons of water left. At six pints per day that would give me five days' supply at a comfortable rate of consumption. This meant that I must aim at thirty miles per day. There would be a half moon that night, after which it would be gibbous leading to full a week hence. This would give sufficient light by which to travel at night, strength permitting.

I kept going until one-thirty, looking for shade but finding none. Finally I couched the camels sideways on to the sun, a relative term since the sun was practically overhead, and inched into the shade of Peggy's saddle, which managed to get the back of my neck and head into shadow. Almost nineteen miles had been accomplished in the morning's heat, each mile forced from weary limbs, collected and hoarded. There were signs of aklé, a few isolated dunes here and there. It was seeming very probable that my assumption of the previous day at Aklé Corner, that I was much further west than I had estimated, had been correct. I decided to continue west to see if I hit any substantial aklé, then to act accordingly.

After an hour's rest I brought my protesting entourage to its feet and we plodded on. An hour later we were undeniably in dense aklé. I sat down atop a great crescent dune, close to the almost vertical western slope dropping two or three hundred feet to the level sand below, and worked out my next move.

There seemed to be aklé in every direction, great piles of shifting sand towering high and barren. To the north, about four kilometres away, was a massive multi-crescented dune fully five hundred feet high, the highest that I had seen on this trip. I had promised my maternal parent that I would name something on the desert after her, so I solemnly named it 'Dune Evelyn'.

I talked with the girls about our position and they both agreed with the evidence that we were much further west than I had thought. Judging from the time that we hit the aklé we were somewhere between ten and twenty miles west of our estimated position. The immediate evidence suggested that the error was nearer the greater distance, so I entered a new position in the log and on the map. According to the map the only way out of the aklé was north, so, reluctantly, we turned our backs once more on Oualata and trudged into the open desert.

The going was hard. I tried to keep to the tops of dunes, but we all sank into the soft sand, so I went for the lower regions. At half past four we were level with the towering presence of Dune Evelyn which kept the breeze from us, making us gasp for air in the stifling heat. Shadows were beginning to lengthen at five when my legs gave out. I considered riding Peggy, but she and Trad collapsed onto the sand the moment I stopped walking. There was no doubt that here we would spend the night.

Slowly and very wearily I began the great task of unloading. First Trad, who was the more heavily burdened, had to be relieved. The ropes were untied in what had become a ritual. Without the round turn and two half-hitches, learned so diligently as a boy, desert travel would be impossible. My water was now in two jerricans, one on either side of Trad. These I removed, together with my rucksack and camera bag, and placed nearby on the sand. Then the baggage saddle came off, all this done with adverse comments, loudly proclaimed from Trad, about the discomfort thus caused, for there were one or two raw patches on her flesh.

Then to Peggy. The food was removed, and the *kukri*, followed by the saddle itself. I walked around to Trad and pulled gently on her halter. She rose gracelessly, followed by Peggy. As we moved off I heard a *clump* from behind. It seemed that Peggy had staggered into the gear, knocking over a jerrican. I went back, shooed her away from the equipment, resurrected the jerrican and, shaking my head, shuffled away a couple of hundred yards where I close-hobbled the beasts.

Returning, I set about ordering my camp. There was no wood about so I would have to burn great quantities of dried grass. This I collected and piled in a great heap near the site of my fire. Then I noticed a dark patch of sand around one of the jerricans, the one that Peggy had bowled over. I leaped over to it and lifted it in time to see the last drop of water drip from a split in the bottom seam onto the damp sand. Peggy must have trodden on it and burst the seam. I should have checked this, but in my weariness I had simply chosen to assume that it was fine. Such short cuts are expensive.

Carefully I measured out my remaining water. In all, including what was in my water-bottle, I now owned fifteen pints. This was disastrous.

Rapidly I checked my map. That day we had covered twenty-five miles, which meant that it was now a hundred and twenty-five miles to Oualata, providing my adjustment was correct.

I was very thirsty and would have to drink at least a pint that evening to stay healthy, leaving fourteen pints with which to complete the journey. Rationing was not the answer. I needed to operate at the fullest efficiency for as long as was possible and hope that I would make it through the inevitable waterless days at the end. There might be nomads, I thought, towards the escarpment. If I asked myself, each time I reached for my water-bottle, how much I was in need of that drink, this would probably give me three days of top efficiency and a very few more of hope. One thing was clear. I could not afford to walk away from Oualata for one more step. The next morning I had to turn west.

But 'sufficient unto the day is the evil thereof.' Those were problems for the morrow. At that moment I needed a drink.

Then the second major blow of the day hit me. I realised that I was down to four tea-bags. Did you know that one can make four cups of tea from one tea-bag?

Dawn came gently to day twelve as the sun's disc, hidden behind Dune Evelyn, turned the sky blue. I packed my gear, drank a little water, and went to where I had left my transport. There, on the ground, was Peggy's close hobble, torn asunder. The girls had gone!

Their tracks were not difficult to follow. Trad had stuck with Peggy under the 'Loyalty to Species' rule and, close-hobbled as she was, had churned up the sand to an enormous extent as she struggled to keep up. After half a mile I found her close hobble, broken but knottable. A further mile away, on the rear slopes of Dune Evelyn, they stood, docile as labradors, too tired to comment as I roped them up and led them back to camp.

This was another setback. They were both obviously fatigued from the rigours of fighting their hobbles. To enter what promised to be a rough day with worn-out camels was not a pleasant prospect.

It was almost seven-thirty when we left the camp site and turned west. The terrain was a sort of semi-aklé with extensive patches and hills of soft sand overlaying a bed of fixed dune. The walking was hard work and the girls had to be hauled along behind like sledges. I sucked boiled sweets to keep my mouth wet and lurched on like an automaton. The sun battered the sand and the three weary travellers. 'Erika' sang through my brain, and the panzer song, but not yet 'Horst Wessel'. I knew that things would get worse, and 'Horst Wessel' was to be kept in reserve for the direst emergency.

The seemingly perpetual hot wind was now, mercifully, from behind helping us, however little, forward and not blowing the sand into our eyes. For over four hours without a break, except for the emptying of boots, we waded on, and on, and on. It seemed that the whole of life was concerned with placing one foot in front of the other, as indeed it was.

Mid-day was approaching as two Manna trees came into view, right on schedule, and we made for their hospitality. Twelve miles had been accomplished that morning; a mere twelve, largely because of the late start, but I did not intend to go out in the heat of the day as I had the previous afternoon. That had been, I was sure, the main reason for my fatigue of the evening. The hot-time sun saps body and soul and makes dead cinders of living things. I huddled in the sparse shade of the Manna tree and waited for Sol to lessen his fury.

Since I had now but three tea-bags a brew of Lip-ton's was not possible until the evening. With me I had some powdered milk which had had everything removed from it but its whiteness. I mixed some with a little water and drank it down. It was a pleasant taste-change and any intake of foodstuff could only be good. The heat made food unpalatable and I had to force a tin of sardines down my throat to fuel the glowing embers of life within.

About three-thirty I stirred myself and commenced loading the girls. As I was lifting my rucksack onto Trad's saddle it slipped from my fingers onto the sand. I simply hadn't the strength in my hands to hold it. Until that moment I had not realised how weak I had become, and the revelation shook me rigid. It came upon me for the first time, as I looked at my rucksack lying in the sand, and at my hands, thin-fingered and shrivelled of skin, that I might not see Oualata. The black embroidered rucksack legend, 'Edwards Empty Quarter Expedition', borne so proudly but a month previously, now had the aspect of an epitaph. I leaned on Trad for support and actually *looked* for Old Baldie. It would not have surprised me in the least to see him standing there in the sand, eyeless sockets looking, lipless teeth grinning, great curved scythe and hourglass glinting in the sun, but the sands were barren save for the two Manna trees, bending a little in the hot wind.

I brought forth thoughts of trees. A few days before my departure from England I had found myself in a local park which I was using as a short cut on some errand. There had been trees there; sycamore and beech, oak and elm, stark and bare in their winter dress. A realisation came that I had paid little attention to trees of late, so engrossed had I been with the things of deserts. I had stopped, and sat, and looked at those trees, hungry for them, with a thought somewhere in a recess of mind that this could be my last opportunity.

I brought myself back to my present. Somehow I picked my rucksack from the sand and, using knees and hips, tied it in place. Then, the camels being loaded, I set out again west, my mind drifting inevitably to friends, to things I had known, and to sycamores.

A very miserable six miles of semi-aklé later, I simply stag-gered to a halt. There was nothing left in me, either physically or mentally. All I wanted was to rest. Nothing else mattered, not survival, nor the future, nothing mattered but rest.

During that worst of all days to date I had travelled a paltry eighteen miles, and it just didn't seem important as long as I could rest. I brewed tea on a grass fire and forced myself to eat rice and potatoes. Choice of food was becoming very limited, but this did not matter. Food was fuel. Only the French corned beef was not to be tackled yet. I hoped I would arrive in Oualata with that.

Over my evening cigarette, more a ritual than an enjoyment, I perused my supposed position on the map. It appeared that I was now level with the end of the aklé knob and that if I were to turn south-west in the morning I would find myself on fixed dune. Against this action was the thought that if I was not as far west as I thought then I would find myself in solid aklé out of which I was sure that I had not the strength to escape. The point at which I turned south-west was a life or death decision. To turn too soon was risky, and to turn too late was to use up what little strength remained to no avail.

'Turn as soon as we set off!' advised Peggy, impatient as ever. Trad, however, advised caution.

'Wait a little for the turn. Wait five miles.'

I decided to continue west in the morning, peruse the terrain and play it by ear. When I lay down to sleep the thought upper-most in my mind was that one more mishap – the girls wander-ing off in the night, more aklé, anything at all – would finish me.

My girls didn't wander off and on the morning of the thirteenth day they were still where I had put them, chewing consistently, if not contentedly. We were on our way by half-past six when the air was still a little cool.

Soon the topography began to change. There were fewer bare aklé dunes and the land was becoming flatter. After an hour there was hardly a crescent to be seen.

'Is this the time to turn?' I asked the committee.

'We - should - have - turned - at - dawn - yes - hurry - up - and - turn - why - don't - you!' admonished Peggy.

'Yes. This looks like the right time,' sighed Trad.

I agreed, so, resetting my wrist compass and noting the map and field bearing in my log, I set off south-west on a 222° field bearing. It was hot and the wind was warming up, but my spirits were high. According to the map another forty miles or so of flattish fixed dune should bring me to twelve miles of valleys running in my direction, after which was a vast plain leading to the escarpment. The going should be easy from now on.

I had noticed that my emotions had become much more intense, doubtless due to the tension brought about by a basic position which was not, by any stretch of the imagination, good. But now I was running for home, coming closer to Oualata with every step. There was even a spring in each one of those steps. I sang music hall songs, and even dredged up a few jazzed-up hymns, learned as a less than angelic choir-boy, in defiance of the local gods.

I should have known better. Four hours and twelve miles later, in a very selpulchral tone, I spoke into my tape-recorder. This is the unexpurgated transcript of that entry.

'Day thirteen, half past twelve . . . I've just stopped on top of a rise . . . and I've discovered . . . aklé dune as far as the eye can see . . . I think I'm a dead man . . . I'm in aklé dune now . . . If I go back north to get out of it . . . I haven't got enough water to survive . . . until I get to the first water-hole . . . I doubt if I've got the strength to get out that way anyway because there's . . . there's dune as far as the eye can see that way too . . . I've only got one chance . . . one chance at all . . . That's to carry on . . . on the line I've been taking . . . carry on south-west . . . Still I've got to wait till this sun goes down . . . Just keep right on going south-west . . . Just take it as it comes . . . Live or die, that's the way I've got to go . . . That's the direction of the next water-hole . . . I've just got to go that way . . . OK . . . If I die in the dune, I die . . . Moulaie, who ought to know about these things, Moulaie the guide . . . reckons that about three hours in aklé is about all you can take . . . Three hours and you've had it . . . I'm coming up to some pretty solid aklé right now . . . so I'll see . . . I'll have to tackle it tonight . . . whatever happens . . . Just have to keep on going . . . There's no other way . . . Just keep on going . . . Keep gooin' wi' t' yed deyn . . . You never know, I might just be

on the corner . . . I might come out of it after a couple of k's . . .
Three hours . . . in any case . . . three hours . . . that's fifteen
kilometres [nine miles] . . . Not . . . Not in aklé it's not . . . You
walk three kilometres to gain one . . . and all that's in soft sand
. . . Anyway we'll just have to risk it . . . Well [here a chuckle] it's
not a case of risking it. It's the only chance I've bloody well got!
. . . Ah well . . . I've got myself into it. I've got myself out of
it . . . Right now I'm having a rest until the sun goes down . . .
Signing off.'

For an hour I rested in Peggy's shade. I knew that my decision
to turn south-west at the point at which I did had been, owing to
the evidence, the correct one. It was a calculated risk, a gamble
that hadn't paid off. Decisions were now out of my hands.
Circumstances dictated that I had to continue south-west.

At one o' clock I did just that. For two hours I ploughed that
mountainous sand sea, thinking of nothing but going on . . . on
. . . on. I had little hope, but if I did not go on there was no hope,
so I went on, the sun burning, the sand burning, the air burning,
and the wind burning, I could feel my strength ebbing as I
dragged my legs out of the clinging sand.

Soon I stopped wandering around the dunes and meandering
along the arms of the crescents. I took a straight line south-west,
dragging the unwilling girls up dune slopes and down almost
sheer cliffs of soft sand causing enormous avalanches of sand,
camels and equipment. I don't know if this new tactic gained me
any miles, but it gave the illusion of greater speed and that, at
least, was something positive.

I was no longer living with the desert. The desert was now the
enemy and we were at war. The beauty of those dunes passed
unnoticed as I ploughed on, carving a great gash over their
pristine surfaces. I brought 'Horst Wessel' forth, and sang it
loudly at those towering dunes, sang it savagely at the wind and
the sand. I was angry with this desert that it should delay me, that
it should try to keep me from my appointment in Oualata. I
yelled at Old Baldie to come out and fight! I was enraged and I
screamed my hatred into the teeth of the dragon!

And the dragon capitulated. Suddenly, there it was, a great
flat plain before me, dotted forever with scrub grass, on and on,
just beyond the next dune.

I stood on the plain, the aklé ending abruptly in a definite line, breathing heavily and grinning. I reported to my tape-recorder, in a voice of unrestrained joy and triumph, the following.

'It's five to three . . . I've just ploughed my way through the worst load of bloody dune in my life . . . and I've beaten it! I've cracked it! – I set off at one o' clock . . . It's three o' clock . . . In two hours I've moved about four or five kilometres [3 miles] . . . up to my knees in red-hot sand . . . and all that . . . But I've cracked it! It's here! . . . Dune fixée, as it says on the map . . . Fixed dune . . . It looks all fairly level to me . . . There's vegetation all over it . . . it's all level plain . . . I can't . . . can't see any sign of aklé all over it . . . It just goes on, and on . . . Yea, there's a little bit . . . a little bit of aklé right, oh, about five . . . seven or eight kilometres away . . . just one lump . . . one blob . . . Here it is, dune fixée . . . Ah! Beautiful! . . . Well, all I've got to do now is get beyond that lot and I'm on the plain . . . It's great . . . Hey! Maybe this *is* the plain . . . Can't see any dunes even . . . Maybe that's the plain . . . The girls are knackered. They're just squatting down . . . I'm not surprised . . . Right! . . . Going to have five minutes . . . then move on over this lot . . . Signing off.'

Whilst resting I checked my position. I now knew almost exactly where I was on the map, right at the edge of the aklé. It appeared that my original estimate of being twenty miles further west than I had calculated had in fact been somewhat exaggerated to the tune of fifty per cent. I adjusted my map position accordingly. Now I needed to go southerly, straight for the escarpment. I adjusted my wrist compass and away we went.

There were several patches of very low aklé which from time to time presented themselves, but these were more of a nuisance than a problem, being no more than ten feet high. The real problem was a huge plague of flies which always inhabited grassy regions. For a further hour I continued, the joy of my triumph still with me, but at four-fifteen my legs informed me that this was where they wished to spend the night. Riding was out of the question, the girls just flopping down where they stood and stretching their necks along the ground. The aklé had taken its toll of us all.

My tea that evening, despite water, tea-bag, and now sugar

rationing, was sweet indeed. I was only a piddling seventy-five miles from my nearest water at Amersâl, just below the escarpment, and just ninety-five miles from Oualata itself. It seemed that in three or four days at the most I would be with people once more. Whilst this thought brought me joy, there was also a sadness that this great adventure was coming to an end. The enormous feeling of loneliness which I had expected to assail me had not materialised, but what had was a period of time in which I had lived life at an incredible intensity, day by day living on the edge of survival, the adrenaline never ceasing to flow. And now this was coming to an end and I must return to a normal, mundane existence for a while. Yes, I realised once more, I did love this bitch of a desert, would leave her with sadness, and would always return. I loved her for what she was and for what she could do to me.

Little did I realise that she had not yet finished with me, and that the real battle was yet to be fought.

10   The Final Battle

When morning arrived on the fourteenth day most of the euphoria of the previous day had drained away into the sand. I was undeniably weak and still had a long way to go. Much of my weakness stemmed from dehydration since I had drunk only four pints per day for the previous two days. I was going against my decision to drink at my normal rate to keep myself as fit as possible. This was purely psychological since I had it instilled into me that water is life, and to have no water is to die. I was not so much rationing my remaining precious water as hoarding it as a symbol of life itself. Whilst I possessed water I would live.

Early, at half past six, we were on our way south. At eight I even managed to do a little filming of sand blowing over the dunes. There was beauty there and the twenty minutes or so spent capturing it would not greatly influence my chances of survival. There were isolated patches of low aklé which, for the most part, I managed to skirt. I noticed occasional outcrops of iron ore; great, flat, rusty slabs, the bare bones of the planet thrusting through the flesh.

Day fourteen was without incident, a day for preserving water. A day for becoming increasingly fatigued. I was eating little but sardines, being reluctant to use water for cooking. It would still enter my body with the food, but would not give my senses as much pleasure as actually drinking it. At lunch-time after a particularly bad bit of aklé, I saw the first acacia tree since several days before Araouane. Acacias do not give as much shade as Manna trees, nor are they so palatable to camels, but this was the only shade of any kind around. The day was mightily hot, each successive day becoming hotter. I stayed in the shade until four o' clock, then continued.

At six I rested for five minutes, then continued as the sun dropped out of sight, leaving a brilliant moon to walk by. It was pleasant to walk by the moon's light, casting amazingly stark,

black shadows on the white sand, the air rapidly cooling. Only
sheer weariness brought me to a halt near seven o' clock. I
flopped, and the camels flopped.

Grass was still being used as fuel. I used one of my two
remaining tea-bags to brew four cups of life, and didn't bother
with a smoke as it only made me thirstier. I was now, after the tea,
down to about three pints of water. That day I had covered
almost twenty-three miles. It wasn't good enough. I was
seventy-one miles from Oualata, three days' march at my
present pace. My nearest water-hole, at Amersâl, was only
fifty-three miles away according to my calculations. Two days'
hard walking should get me there.

There was, of course, no guarantee that the water-hole was not
dry. If it did contain water then, since it was below the escarpment, it should not be too far down, probably close enough to the
surface for me to tie all my bits of rope, cord, string and bootlaces
together and lower my water-bottle, weighted with a stone or
something, down the hole to it.

The added advantage of heading for Amersâl was that, since it
was thirty-seven miles west of Oualata along the escarpment
then that would give me a sufficiently large intentional error
should the increasing abundance of iron ore influence my compass, as I had been told it might. There was also the strong
probability that there would be people about. All in all to head
for Amersâl seemed my best prospect. My mouth was dry as I
fell asleep that night. It did not seem vital to wet a mouth that
was about to be unconscious of that wetness.

To load the girls on the fifteenth morning was a Herculean task
for one in my condition, and when it was done I was thoroughly
exhausted. I set out for Amersâl at six-twenty with little over two
pints. The terrain was quite flat with the perpetual scrub grass
dotted around. After an hour of walking I noticed that my camel
stick, the symbol of my authority, was not in my hand. I had left it
at the site of last night's camp. Normally I would automatically
check the ground thoroughly before leaving, but by now such
things were beginning to be forgotten. There was, of course, no
question of returning for it, so I went on, symbol-less.

Rest stops were becoming frequent, at first hourly, then half-hourly, just for a few minutes. I would not even untie Trad from me, but just flop down onto the ground and lie there, still as death, resting every bone and sinew. The girls, too, would flop down, grateful for the respite. On one such occasion I lay, eyes half open, staring into the desert, when a shadow blotted out the sun. I looked up and there were a pair of ravens, wings outstretched, gliding down to inspect what was, apparently, lunch. They were just ten feet above me. I yelled at them and they kept their distance. They must have spotted my staggering series of collapses from somewhere high in the sky and thought it to be their birthday. Two camels and a man, bony though they were, would make a fine feast for a couple of hungry ravens. I had heard stories of these birds carving out the eyes of victims not yet dead.

The next time I collapsed I had my still camera at the ready, but though they did investigate they were a little more wary. I managed one reasonable shot from about fifteen feet, good enough to identify the murderer at any subsequent trial.

At eleven-twenty, after covering fourteen miles, I could go no further. Leaving the girls loaded, for there was no strength in me to do otherwise, I crawled beneath an acacia after removing most of the thorns from the ground and spreading out my karrimat. The shade was sparse, but better than nothing, and the flies buzzed choruses in my ears. I augmented the shade with my *chèche*, opened out and impaled on the acacia's thorns. For hour after hour, in the mounting heat, I lay there, barely conscious. I thought I heard voices in conversation, but dismissed it as the onset of delirium, a trick of the mind transmuting the sounds of flies into human speech.

It was about half an hour later when I heard the unmistakable sound of a camel's cough. The sound had come from entirely the wrong direction for one of my ladies to have made it. It seemed to have come from beyond some dunes.

I had to investigate. Summoning all my strength I crawled out from under the tree and in bare feet walked across the blistering sand towards the source of the sound. Again I heard it, louder this time. Rounding a small dune I saw them, two camels with Mauritanian saddles standing near a small Manna tree beyond which I could hear the murmur of the spoken word. People! The first I had seen for over two weeks. I had crossed the Empty Quarter! I had done it!

A man and a boy, Arabs, squatted on the ground.

'Salaam al laikum,' I said, grinning all over my face. They were surprised and suspicious. A Nazrani out here, dressed like an Arab?

'Al laikum el Salaam,' they chanted, and we went into the long rigmarole of the Mauritanian greeting ritual. This was complex and varied from place to place. Mainly it consisted of each wishing the other in turn no evil upon himself, his people and his goods. I had never learned it properly and found that a certain amount of mumbling when required to speak, with the oft repeated *'Le-bass* – No evil,' enunciated, sufficed. It was a ritual, and no one ever listens to rituals.

They had an ancient shotgun with them. Suddenly I felt very vulnerable. My only armament was my father's sword, hanging at my left hip. The *kukri* was hanging from Peggy's saddle.

We had no common language, and they were obviously very nervous. The man, probably the teenager's father, looked like a shrewd and crafty old bird, almost to the point of evil. He smiled with his lips, but not his eyes. I needed water and by signs I conveyed this message. They understood, but they had none with them. They were out hunting bish.

Where had I come from? I told them. They understood, but obviously did not believe. Where was I going? Oualata. This they accepted. Suddenly, without warning they got to their feet, jumped expertly aboard their camels, and without so much as a wave, trotted off north leaving me alone once more. I think they just wished to get away from this mad Nazrani. I reflected as to how I would feel if I were accosted by a lone Arab in the English Lakes who spoke no English, conveyed by signs that he had just walked over from Frankfurt, and asked me to buy him a pint. I would be extremely wary of such a man.

Returning to my acacia I stayed in its shade for a while longer until just after four. I reloaded what little I had taken from the backs of the girls and set out again. After fifteen minutes I collapsed onto the sand, not one iota of strength remaining. I couched the camels and crawled into the shade of Peggy where I stayed for some time. My body would no longer obey me. It was time for some major decisions.

First I must decide if I was to live, or to die. The pain in my body from my multitudinous ills was phenomenal, and death, swift and clean, seemed a very viable alternative. Not to have to endure it again for minute after minute, for hour after hour, for mile after mile, for step after step; not to have to feel the thirst in my body, thirst that it is impossible to describe, thirst that allowed no spittle to dampen my mouth, for this to cease then death was the only immediate solution. If I judged that there was no hope, then to end it there, quickly, as I had decided so long ago, by the insertion of my father's sword into my heart, was far preferable to a lingering death, fading away in agony over perhaps several days.

The decision had to be made there and then, within the hour, for I knew that as my body had ceased, I hoped temporarily, to obey my mind, so my mind was beginning to lose control of itself. In a very short time, probably measured in hours rather than days, I would be incapable of making any rational decisions. Therefore I must decide in that place and at that time, and instil that decision into my brain, programme the computer to do what had to be done so that it would instruct the body in precisely what it must do.

The question, then, was simple. Was there any hope of survival?

There were forty miles to Amersâl, a hard day's walk under British conditions. I had about a pint of water left. There was no strength in my legs, certainly not for day-time walking.

'You can walk at night,' said Trad.

'Oh-what-will-happen-to-us-if-you-die?' moaned Peggy. True, I had responsibilities.

Peggy, against whose great body I leaned, though a shadow of her former self, still possessed powerful muscles. I felt them, running my fingers over her legs and through the curly hair of her shoulders.

'This hair is good,' Ali, the man from SMERT had said. 'It means that she is strong.'

'Will you carry me, Peggy?' I asked. She was silent.

My mind wandered to what I must do if I decided to die. A

message must be left on the tape-recorder explaining that I crossed the Empty Quarter before I died. Also I would cut the girths and ropes of the girls' saddles to give them freedom and the possibility of survival. My mind wandered also to England. I had with me a few photographs and artifacts from people at home. I took them out, looked at them, felt them, remembered.

The sun sank and was gone. The air cooled almost percept-ibly. As it cooled then strength began to return, and with it came hope. Yes, there was hope, and whilst there was hope, there must be life. I put away the photographs and stood, unsteadily. I decided to live.

There was an acacia not far away, visible in the moonlight. I needed the strength of tea and food. Slowly I walked the girls over to it and left them to prune it as I collected dead wood and made a fire. The fire blazed as I boiled half a pint of my priceless water, holding the handle lest it tip up and spill the merest drop. I ate something. Maybe it was sardines; almost certainly it was sardines. There were onions and tomato purée. I ate any-thing that needed no water in its preparation. Then came the tea, hot, strong with my last tea-bag, and sweet with my last sugar. I sipped it at first, then took a great gulp of it, feeling it running hotly down my throat and into my innermost plumbing. It seemed to permeate every crevice of my being. I was a walking sponge of tea, a Lip-ton's Man. The last drops of tea were savoured and I packed away the pan.

At half past seven we moved out over the black and white landscape, my last half pint of water sloshing in my water bottle, carried by Peggy in case by carrying it myself I be tempted to drink. I was marching not in hope, but in conviction. I had decided to live. Therefore I would live! There would be no further discussion on the matter!

After ten minutes I was exhausted. I decided that I had to keep moving so I reached a compromise. For twenty-five minutes I would walk, then for five minutes I would lie on the sand, then up again and repeat the process. I ignored my body's pleas for clemency and marched on towards Amersâl.

Looking frequently at my watch I tramped over the plain, endless all around. At the rest time I sat on the ground, whipped off my boots, even dug a hip-hole with my hands to increase my comfort for I have never been one for roughing it, and burrowed into the very cold sand. To lie there feeling the coldness enter my body was luxurious indeed. Sucking a boiled sweet had become possible as a little spittle dampened the inside of my mouth.

Every second of these five minutes was wreathed in gold, but all too soon it was time to go. I emptied my boots, replaced them and stood again. The girls had remained standing throughout. That five-minute halt had allowed a recovery out of all proportion to its length, albeit a temporary one. For ten minutes life was almost pleasant, then the basic weariness surged back and each step had to be forced.

There was a roar from Peggy at the back. I stopped to look behind and saw that Peggy's saddle had slipped forward, her tail rope having parted again. This had happened several times and repair was routine. However, this time, owing to my fatigue of body and mind, I forgot to make the first move; I forgot to untie myself from Trad.

I went back to minister to Peggy and Trad came with me. Peggy, annoyed at the weight and restriction of the saddle on her neck, was now confused by having her bottom jaw pulled in a new direction. She roared at Trad and reared up. This confused Trad, who took this as a personal attack and went for Peggy. With teeth, heads and legs they joined battle, almost two tons of confused and angry flesh whirling about in the sand, and myself, still tied to Trad, being flung about like a rag doll. This was a drastic situation. I tried pulling Trad away, but the puny strength of a man is nothing compared with the strength of an angry camel. I had to get loose before serious injury resulted. The knot was impossibly tight, and behind me, so I drew my father's sword and cut myself free, a very chancy manoeuvre.

For some seconds more they milled and roared, and tied themselves in knots of necks and ropes and limbs, then they gave up as fast as they had begun and stood, shivering with fright, their eyes rolling with whiteness. I spoke soothingly to them, and cut several tangled ropes to separate them, then led them to separate clumps of grass to calm them.

The site of the battle was a mass of equipment, saddles, broken and cut ropes, and churned sand. I searched for, and found, my water bottle. The thick leather strap had broken in two places, but, miraculously, the cap was still on and my half-pint was still inside. I took the merest sip of it to calm myself, and set about the business of reconstruction. It took forty minutes to collect, knot and repair the various damages, and to reload the animals. It was almost nine o' clock when we again continued south.

Onward we went through that night, the moon making its great sweep across the heavens. Polaris, the static pole star, was low on the horizon to my rear so I would choose a southerly star as a marker, checking it frequently by compass and changing it from time to time as the Earth ponderously rotated. I found myself traversing a series of long, narrow, shallow valleys with acacia trees often in their troughs. Horst Wessel was never far away, but progress was being made and the distance to Amersâl was being whittled down with every painful step.

By two o' clock in the morning of day sixteen that distance had become a measly twenty-two miles, a morning's stroll in my native hills. I was finished for the night, my legs having given their all, but since the previous morning I had covered a full thirty-two miles. Despite my condition I had equalled the daily distance of Ali Ould Boy. As I lay to sleep I smiled to myself at this little triumph.

I was up at six and breakfasted on two boiled sweets. I dared eat nothing else for a food intake increased the water requirement of the body. It took all of an hour to organise the girls and it was seven when I celebrated my readiness for travel by taking a sip of water. I was now on a flat plain again with an increased number of trees, mostly acacia, about. Iron ore split the surface with greater frequency and patches of gravel punctuated the endless sand. There was an air of change about the terrain as we neared the escarpment, like the approach to a coast, sensed rather than seen.

I kept the twenty-five-minute schedule going as the world became once more a furnace, but by nine-thirty it was obvious that further progress that day, until the sun vanished completely, was out of the question. I was on the night shift, and that was that!

There was an acacia nearby, with a branch curving over to

touch the ground. This had potential as a shelter. I unloaded the girls and took them to another acacia a little way away, then set about making myself as comfortable as possible for the next ten hours or so. First I swept away thorns on the ground, then laid my karrimat down. Next I spread my space blanket over the bent branch and tied it down, giving a small black patch of shadow in which to lie. I took out a strip of brilliant red cloth, one of the Edwards Patent Camel-Finders, and tied it as high in the tree as possible for a distress signal. If a nomad were to wander past within a few miles he would, I hoped, see it and come to investigate. Then I settled myself down for the day, my boiled sweets, my remaining spoonful of water, and my insect-repellant within reach.

The insect-repellant, though useless for its intended purpose, was an excellent cooling agent, containing alcohol as it did. It had become very precious to me indeed.

The day wore on and became hotter, and yet hotter. In that heat I wilted and shrivelled. From time to time I adjusted my position in order to stay in the shadow. The wind rose and became a sandstorm, whipping the sand along the surface of the land and partially burying me. And still the heat mounted. I learned later that on this day the temperature reached over 120°F.

By noon I was clinging to life like the climber that I once had been, but I would not let go. I had decided to live, therefore I would live.

To stay sane I decided to talk to my tape-recorder, to make statements to it, to assert my life and my future, to tell Old Baldie to piss off. This transcript will give a better picture of my mental and physical state at that time than any amount of retrospective ramblings. It was spoken in a quavering voice, sometimes loud, sometimes inaudible, and speech was interspersed with sounds of shallow, panted breathing and the roar of the storm.

'It's day . . . sixteen . . . DAY SIXTEEN . . . It's mid-day . . . I have done ten kilometres [six miles] today . . . Ten kilometres, in the heat . . . Ten kilometres . . . I HAVE BUILT . . . a shelter . . . from the sun . . . [here a sigh] . . . There's a sandstorm blowing . . . I'm twenty-five . . . kilometres from water . . . I WILL NOT DIE! . . . [here a sigh] . . . MY NAME . . . IS TED EDWARDS! I WILL NOT DIE! I will not die . . . The temperature . . . is into

the hundreds . . . The wind is scorching hot . . . I will not die . . .
I have some . . . insect-repellant . . . There's alcohol in it . . . It
keeps me cool sometimes . . . It stops me from dying . . . I will
not die!   My body's finished . . . Mind isn't finished . . . I will
not die . . . I have to wait . . . till the sun goes down . . . have to
wait . . . till six o'clock . . . seven o' clock . . . I have to survive
. . . till seven o' clock . . . I managed . . . to unpack . . . the
camels . . . I think I hobbled them right . . . Put them near
another tree . . . I don't know . . . My name . . . my name is Ted
Edwards . . . Ted Edwards cannot be killed . . . I will not die . . . I
suck . . . vitamin C tablets . . . Sometimes . . . sometimes . . . I
can make spittle . . . sometimes . . . [here sounds of attempted
spitting] . . . [something weak and indistinct] like Hell . . . I
WILL NOT DIE!   I WILL not die!   I will not die . . .
[whispered] I will not die . . .'

The day, the longest day I can remember, lumbered on.
Periodically I would spray myself with insect-repellant, on the
face, behind the neck, on the feet, in the small of the back and,
best of all, under the arms. My tongue was like a wooden peg in
my dry cavern of a mouth. I had tried chewing liquorice root,
brought over from England, but all I got was a mouthful of wood
shavings.

All the rules state that one should not go naked in those
temperatures as one will simply get hotter and lose more body
fluids. It didn't seem to me that it was possible to get any hotter.
As an experiment I stripped off my *bou-bou* and lay naked in the
shade. It did seem marginally cooler, even if this was merely a
psychological reaction, and in any case this was no time to refuse
psychological help. I remained naked for the rest of the day.

In the afternoon I felt a need to urinate. I had not urinated for
two or three days. This urine was bodily fluid. It was a resource. It
must be utilised in some way. I had heard stories of people
drinking their own urine in desperation. Since I was certainly in
desperation I was perfectly capable of circumventing a lifetime
of conditioning and consuming the stuff, but I had also read tales
of stomach cramps and death resulting from such action. Since I
had no intention of dying, then drinking it was out.

I tried to retain it in my body where it would do the most good,
but it wanted out and the more I thought about it the more

insistent it became. There was a great deal of sand on my mat. I wondered if wet sand would act as a cooling agent as the moisture evaporated, as when I had cooled my half-way beer with tissues and washing-water. There was but one way to find out. I gathered together a pile of powdery sand, peed on it, made a mortar out of it with my fingers, and spread it on my body. It worked wonderfully well, indeed it felt almost freezing.

Eventually, after a thousand years, the sun began to descend. As it got lower the black shadow of the space blanket moved away from its place of usefulness. I crawled out and lay in the sparse shade of the tree itself, bare skin on the hot sand and acacia thorns sticking into my flesh. I didn't mind the thorns for the pain gave my mind a focal point, stopping its aimless wandering.

As the sun shone its last for the day, I made another entry in my tape diary.

'It's half-past . . . half-past six . . . Day sixteen . . .'

That was the last speech recorded for the tape-recorder, thoroughly clogged with sand, worked no more. I tried to repair it by selective thumping, but to no avail. It had become a useless lump of metal, plastic and silica.

Since the sun was down it was time to go. I gathered my things together, wondering if there was any point in this since I certainly could not survive another such day; but all things are resources and may, in some way, be useful.

My mind was no longer entirely my own. Despite my situation there was an air of holiday about retrieving the camels and loading them. We were going to the sea-side, to see the sea, to build sandcastles, beyond the escarpment. I even thought of Punch and Judy, and the drum going thump-ty-thump-ty-thump.

I finished loading my donkeys and set out again for the beach, leaving my distress signal in the tree. Before I left I drank the last drop of hot, vile-tasting, beautiful water and put the broken-strapped bottle in a bag.

It says in my log that it was seven-thirty-five when we left the acacia. For a period of time, I know not how long, we continued as before. Even Horst Wessel was forgotten as the walking machine, with its attachments, moved south. Twenty-five minutes and flop. Twenty-five minutes and flop. There came a point when my legs would not move after one of these flops. I rested a little more, then couched Peggy and took Trad behind her, tying her on.

Since I had no camel-stick I tied my waist rope around my left wrist, a knot on the other end. Then I mounted Peggy. She was too exhausted to protest. I tried to make her rise, but had to administer the rope to bring this about. She creaked to an upright position. Forward motion had to be similarly induced and we lurched onward towards a star.

She would veer towards trees and I had to steer her away from them. I could smell, and hear, and sense the sea. There was even a garage, painted sea-side white, with white stones around the fore-court, but shuttered for the night. No-one was home. We went on.

Increasingly it was becoming rocky. The coast and cliffs were coming closer. I was sure I could hear sea-gulls screaming. I could taste fish, and tomatoes, and gallon after gallon of orange juice. There were milk-shakes and jelly and shrimps and ice-cream with raspberry and chocolate and crabs to catch, and a smiling aunt, and sand, and sand.

Peggy stopped. I administered the goad but she was finished. She got down and would carry me no more. I understood and stroked her weary head. My legs were rested so should be good for a few more miles. I moved Trad to the front and we set off again.

At the point where my legs gave up again my watch said it was twelve-thirty. There were many rocks about and my calculations told me that the escarpment was around somewhere. But that was for morning. I unloaded the girls and took them away to another patch of scrub, then returned to where I had just left the gear.

It wasn't there. It had moved. I wandered through the scrub, looking for it, but it was not to be found. Then I realised that I had lost my camels. I stood still, thinking and working out my next move. The night was windless and quiet. First I must find the girls. I listened, but no sound came. I shouted, but there was no response, the sound just reaching into nothingness. Eventually I tracked myself back until I saw them, couched and miserable, chewing grass at each other.

I tried tracking the camels and myself back to my equipment, but the already profuse footprints were increased by so doing, augmenting the confusion. The only way seemed to be to start from the ladies and walk around in a widening spiral until I found my goods. This I did and I was, eventually, successful. It was after two a.m. when I finally caught sight of Peggy's saddle.

I searched through my equipment and food for anything that contained moisture, but there was nothing. Everything I would have given to discover a forgotten can of peas with liquor. My thirst was such that I opened a tin of sardines and drank the oil, but it was no use. The sardines I threw away for they contained salt.

I slept and arose before dawn. At six-thirty-five we were moving again. I knew that this was the last day. There would be no stopping until I reached water, or the prospect of water. I had not had a substantial drink for two and a half days, since the last of the Lip-ton's. I had preserved my last half-pint as long as I could, for occasional sips, purely for the psychological support they gave me. But now even this support was gone. Whatever happened, sun, wind or anything, I had to keep going until I found water.

The land was still flat with patches of iron ore and dark, red-brown rock. I could see for miles in all directions. I do not know how long I walked. My log simply says that I started at six-thirty-five with the added scrawled comment, 'Keep going until water'. There seemed little point in writing anything else.

The previous evening, according to my calculations, I had already passed the point where the escarpment should be. That morning I also passed the point where Amersâl should have been, and still I had not hit the escarpment. The sun was gaining height with every step that I took, but there was no stopping until I obtained water, no matter what. Even the five-minute rests I denied myself. 'Onward' was the name of the game.

Then, near the horizon to my left, I saw movement. I screwed up my eyes and shaded them. Something was moving. I squatted down so that whatever was on the ground would show up in silhouette. It was a herd of camels; not static, scattered and chewing, but in a bunch and moving north. This meant that someone was herding them. People!

I turned east and set a course that would make our paths converge. I tried to quicken my pace, but it didn't work so I just walked on in anticipation. Half an hour or so later I could make out a small, erect figure walking behind the camels; a biped, a human being. I closed in and approached this human. He was a small boy of about eight years. We greeted each other ritually. I tried him on French, but he obviously understood none of it so I resorted to my native Lancastrian and signs.

I asked him for water. He had none. Where was there water? He made signs that the water was beyond a great drop of the land, the escarpment. I gave him a sweet, which he eyed with suspicion, so I indicated its purpose. Into his mouth it went. The taste was unfamiliar to him so he spat it out. He had to go with the camels, he signed, but would return and lead me to water. Then he went north and I collapsed on the ground to await his return.

For half an hour I lay in the sun. Another young boy came from the south, said hello, accepted a sweet, sucked it, spat it out, and vanished after the camels. I could have waited all day. Time is meaningless to a desert dweller. Eventually I decided to backtrack the herd. They had been to water so that was the way to find it. South once more we went, now with conviction; not faith, for is not faith the last refuge of the inadequate? There was light at the end of the tunnel and I was determined to reach that light.

For perhaps an hour I continued in the rising heat, following the footprints of the herd, occasionally losing them but finding them again, eyes constantly on the ground. Then I looked up and there, in front of me, a couple of hundred yards away, were three ragged tents. People were there, looking at me, coming out of their homes and staring at this stranger, looking and waiting to greet. Men, women, children, goats, sheep, camels, I was safe.

Stopping at the first tent I was greeted by a smiling man with enormous, almost Dracula-like teeth. He led me to the headman, obviously a close relative judging from his canines. They brought me a large wooden bowl of camels' milk which I thankfully drained, then the women set about making thin camels' milk yoghourt, sloshing it about in a hard leather churn.

In the tent's shade I explained who I was and what I was about. They were amazed at my journey, readily accepting the truth of my assertions. They were Arabs with a little Touaregh blood, owning virtually nothing but their clothes, their tents and their camels. Having a pet Nazrani in their camp was like winning the pools. They had various ailments for which I prescribed. The head-man asked me for shoes. In my pack were a pair of white plimsolls, new and pristine. These I presented to him with due ceremony. They were a size too small, but since their main purpose was as a status symbol, something to be ritually removed on a rare visit to the mosque, this mattered little.

My main requirement was water. This I explained to them at length and, being of the desert, they understood. They had a little, enough to make tea, which they promptly did. Those three glasses of tea must qualify as the most magnificent drinks I have ever tasted, their sweetness coursing like flood waters through my veins. Two young men were dispatched for water with two drums and a camel. They did not return until evening.

Much revived by the tea I set about ascertaining my position. Where was Oualata, I asked the head-man, expecting his arm to point to the east. His arm shot out, straight and true, to the south. I had learned to trust the desert peoples' sense of direction. If he said that Oualata was south then that was where it was. Sighting along his arm with my compass I drew in a line on my map. I cross-referenced several places and found my true position on the map, confirming it with various questions.

I was thirty miles east of where my calculations had put me, a mere nineteen miles from Oualata itself. For two or three days I had been almost forty degrees off course, an incredible error which could not possibly have happened by sloppy navigation. The explanation had to lie in the abundance of iron ore in the ground. Had I not made that massive intentional error by heading for Amersâl then I should simply have missed the escarpment altogether and stridden on into open desert and almost certain death.

The yoghourt was tangy and cool, and a bringer of life. As the sun reached its majesty we moved into the tent's shade and dozed. Since we were so close to Oualata I tried my radio. Nothing was on the air. This action puzzled the populace greatly for they didn't understand the concept of radio. Cameras, too, were a mystery to them. I showed them photographs and tried to explain that a camera was the machine which made them, but I didn't seem to make any headway. Despite the milk, tea and yoghourt I was still dangerously dehydrated and the hot time of the day saw me lying on the mat, panting through a spittleless mouth, awaiting the arrival of the water. When it did come, at sundown, a bowl of thin mud was rushed to me and I gulped it down, not bothering with the niceties of purifying tablets. I was like a great dry sponge just soaking up the liquid of life. It took about two gallons to satisfy my bone-dry body. Life immediately surged back as if by some miracle. Within minutes I was transformed from a dying man into a reasonably fit, healthy, and very lively creature. The water had intoxicated me. I could smile, and laugh, and be happy, and my happiness became their happiness. These were the most primitive people that I had ever met, but the great gulfs of culture that separated us were as nothing compared to the greater similarities of our needs and joys. We laughed together on the desert, we who shared neither language nor country, race nor creed; only our humanity did we share, and this was enough.

I realised that I was ravenously hungry. For several days I had eaten nothing but boiled sweets, glucose tablets and vitamin C tablets. Now that my body had been rehydrated it demanded more substantial fare. I invited the people of the camp to a feast of spaghetti and onions. There was much pasta in my larder and a large pan was required to cook it. The only cooking pot which they owned was a stout three-legged cauldron which was full of firewood. This was emptied and scoured, and put on to boil. I gave the women instructions on how to prepare this unfamiliar dish and left them to it, for cooking was women's work.

Since cooking was, apparently, such an unusual activity for them, I considered that they must live entirely on milk and yoghourt, except, doubtless, for times of feasting when camel or goat would be eaten. The people owned neither gun nor bow so hunting was not a part of their world. Everything was centred around their livestock which trotted freely around mixed in with children.

They were delighted with the spaghetti's novelty and we

laughed at the experimental techniques for eating it with our fingers, including holding the slippery worms by their ends and lowering them into our mouths. Soon we were full and imbued with a Christmas-like sense of well-being. We talked into the night, and drank glass after glass of Whisky Saharienne. We talked of England, and of the price of camels, and when I slept that night I slept soundly and contentedly. Tomorrow I would be in Oualata. The journey was over bar the shouting, so I thought.

But still that bitch of a desert hadn't finished with me. She even then, at that late stage, had cards up her sleeve.

The eighteenth morning saw me rested and refreshed, and fit to tackle a cavernful of dragons. The people asked me to stay, but my girls were desperate for a drink and Alistair would be getting anxious in Oualata. I loaded the ladies, informing them that upon this very day they would drink water and begin their holidays. Peggy informed me that she'd believe it when she saw the well at Oualata, and Trad just gave a non-committal grunt.

I asked for, and got, a gallon and a half of water. It was more than I thought I would need, and my friends thought it remarkable that the Nazrani should need so much to get him through a morning's stroll, but I was taking no chances. The families in each of the three tents insisted that I drink a bowl of camels' milk as a farewell gesture, and I strode south with about a gallon and a half sloshing around inside me. They told me to look out for vehicle tracks after a couple of hours which would lead me into Oualata. With a wave I was away again beneath the early morning sun.

The terrain became increasingly wooded and within the hour I found myself in a dense forest which, because of its almost magical appearance, I dubbed 'The Forest of Arden'. Iron ore outcrops were everywhere, and great ridges and fields of rocks. The escarpment was at hand and there was joy in the air. I sang songs to the trees and they rustled in approval. Because of the abundance of iron ore, and my recent experience with navigational problems, I imposed a sizeable error on my line of march aiming to hit the escarpment about two and a half miles west of Oualata.

The day heated up, and there, suddenly, was the escarpment.

The trees stopped, there was a rocky apron and the land just dropped away into a great valley some thousand feet below. It was quarter past one.

Here was the escarpment of which I had dreamed for so long, massive, solid and trackless. All I had to do was to find a way down it and turn left. Within the hour I could be in Oualata. I could even hear the sound of an electrical generator whining away, its direction uncertain because of the echoes of the escarpment, but definitely close by.

After a little searching I found a valley, steep-sided and rocky-bottomed, which led downwards. There were tracks of camels, several days old, so it was possible to get the girls down it. They protested as sharp rocks hurt feet used to soft sand, but they followed me down, slowly, painstakingly. Camels are not good mountaineers and I had to pick our route very carefully in order not to overtax their capabilities.

It took us about two hours to reach the valley floor, flat and sandy with large and pleasant trees and much scrub grass, its walls towering darkly all around. We were all exhausted from the climb down during the day's heat, but I was disinclined to rest since we were so close to our goal. We went west for about an hour, the valley becoming shallower as we went on. There were some camels and goats, but no sign of humanity. We came to the end of the valley, with no sign of habitation and seemingly no way out of it up the steep valley sides. It was the wrong valley.

My legs gave up on me at that point. I couched Peggy and mounted. Protesting, she lumbered back the way we had just come. We had to find a way out of this valley somehow, and go around it. The map gave hardly any useful information, being very vague about the general topography. I was not even sure if Oualata was beneath the escarpment or on top of it. I assumed that it was beneath it since it had a well and all the local wells were below it.

I thought that I had found a way out, following a dry water-course. We went higher and higher up a very beautiful rocky valley which looked very much like parts of Snowdonia. Eventually we came to what, when water flowed, would be a waterfall. I dismounted and led the ladies around it. Upwards we went, the valley receding below us. As we neared the top of the escarpment the sound of the generators, unheard in the valley, became audible again.

Within five yards of the top of the escarpment the rocks became just a little steeper. The girls rebelled. They stopped. I pulled and pushed, cursed and swore, stroked and cajoled, and I whipped, but they would not go that last five yards. There was nothing for it but to turn those poor, tired animals around and lead them back down to the valley floor.

It was dusk as we once more reached the sandy bottom, frustration boiling up in me. We would have to spend the night there as to try to leave in the dark over that kind of terrain would have been madness. There was plenty of wood about, great logs of timber awaiting a use. Soon a big, cheerful fire was blazing, partly to cook and partly to attract the attention of anyone who could offer directions. No-one came. I ate something, spaghetti I think, and slept a not too troubled sleep. Surely tomorrow I would escape from this valley and find Oualata. It must be within five miles.

On the nineteenth day I arose quite late. It was eight when I led the little caravan to where we had entered in the first place. It seemed that this was preferable to spending any more time searching out a new route. Wearily at ten o'clock we breasted the rim and heard the generator once more. I turned east and we went along the rock-strewn edge, picking our way through great boulders and around extensive fields of sharp rocks not suitable for the feet of camels.

Soon our way was blocked by another valley, a tributary of the first. This was becoming serious. I had drunk the last of the water for breakfast and the day was heating up again.

To the north I could see a long ridge of rock and sand about a hundred feet high and half an hour distant. Perhaps I would see a way around the valley system from up there. When I topped the ridge I saw just mile after mile of valley after valley. For the first time I felt panic welling up inside me. Was I going to fail at this late stage? After enduring so much must I now fall at the last fence? Was Old Baldie going to win after all?

I tried the radio, but no-one spoke to me. The sensible thing to do seemed to be to go east for an hour which should put me directly north of Oualata, then turn south. I turned that way and dragged the girls after me. We hit the head of another tributary valley which we managed to cross. Then, the hour being up, we went south along its rim. My legs gave up again, weakened by the morning's climb. Poor, sad Peggy staggered to her feet with me on her back and went on. For an hour we followed the rim until we hit a massive valley, several miles across and running east to west. This had to be where Oualata was. It was our last chance for there was no strength left in any of us. We must find a way into that valley. We turned east again, along the new valley's rim. Several times Peggy stopped, couched herself, and gently but firmly pitched me sideways from the saddle. Each time I had to inflict pain upon my friend to get her to do what I had no right to ask, but on which depended all our lives. Eventually even beating no longer worked. She would go no further. It was one-thirty with the appalling sun close to its zenith. I sat in the shade of Peggy and waited, for coolness, for rescue, for death. We had nothing more to give. Peggy, the gallant teenager, was worn beyond all that could be expected, Trad was collapsing at every opportunity, and I was like a wrung-out rag with a body that was hardly my own and a mind that was once again beginning to lose control. We were dying.

I thought that through the constant hum of the unseen generator I heard the sound of a Land Rover, but I dismissed this as fantasy, further evidence of my slipping mind. The day sweltered on. At three-thirty, somehow, in response to my programming of day fifteen, I stood for one last effort. We went on and almost immediately were at the head of a side valley leading into the main strath. It was a tough scramble down to its sandy bottom, especially for my dying girls, but eventually there we were.

There were tracks there, many tracks, tracks of camel, and goat, and donkey. Fresh tracks going up and down the valley, going to water, going to Oualata. My legs wouldn't carry me there. They couldn't. Once more I asked the impossible of Peggy, and once more, moaning the while, she complied. We went down the valley at a crawl, Peggy having obvious difficulty staying erect. It was all I could do to clutch the sides of the saddle to keep myself on board. Down deeper into the ravine we descended until the great main valley was at our feet, trees of all kinds scattered around.

The tracks led to the left, as I knew they must, so that was where we went. There were the tracks of a Land Rover going along the valley bottom. Two people were doing something in a field. I tried to call to them, but nothing happened in my throat. On we went, my head lolling from side to side with the motion of riding. There was a mob of camels in front of me, and people, and a well. One figure detached itself from the crowd and came towards me, smiling.

'*Salaam al laikum,*' he beamed, his great white teeth like piano keys.

'*Al laikum el salaam.*' I croaked.

'Tombouctou?' he enquired.

'Oui, Tombouctou. Oualata?'

He pointed with his hand and there, gleaming whitely in the late afternoon sun, was Oualata. We had arrived. The dragon, not I, was dead.

Postscript

I leaned down and shook hands with the man, who was in charge of drawing water at the well. Couching Peggy I dismounted and led her to the well. The waterman drew water and poured it into a huge metal bucket. The girls made it vanish faster than he could draw it. When they had drunk their fill, their first drink in twenty days, I filled my water-bottle and drank.

There was no sound of a generator in the village. The noise which I had heard must have been the wind in the valleys.

Curiously I felt no emotion. It was like finishing a hard day's work. The job had been done, and that was that. There was no emotion left.

A small crowd had gathered to inspect and congratulate. Alistair and the film crew had left that afternoon on something connected with a rescue mission for me and would return at dusk; so the Land Rover I thought I had heard earlier had been theirs.

People led me towards the house of the Prefect, the local administrative head, a sort of mayor imposed by central government. One little incident I shall not forget. The entire village knew of me and had turned out to view my arrival. A little middle-aged man, sparse of teeth, grinned as I passed, clenched both hands together and shook them about his head in a gesture of triumph. He was just an ordinary man with nothing to gain from my success, just saying, 'Well done, lad!' because he wanted to. That meant more than the official congratulations of the delegation of dignitaries, some uniformed and some not, hastily gathered at the end of the street to make the civic greeting.

They gave me milk to drink and questions to answer.

'Where is your guide?' they wished to know, obviously not having believed Alistair's story of the lone Nazrani.

'This is my guide,' I said, pointing to my Silva compass.

I bathed in a bucket, even managing to remove some of the

muck in my hair, then changed into jeans and tee-shirt. The European dress felt curious, restricting and uncomfortable, but familiar. It spoke of a change in culture. Before, in my filthy robes, I had been of the desert. Now I was once again of Lancashire. It was then I realised at last that this costume drama was over.

A black slave came to my room, in his hand a steaming mug. 'Lip-ton's!' he grinned.

I was half way through a meal of corned beef and rice when I heard the Land Rover arrive. Alistair greeted me like a prodigal and we killed the fatted champagne bottle, knocking it back in two plastic cups, finishing off with gin mixed with water and Alistair's marathon running salts. He introduced me to his new expedition members, for the previous ones had departed for their various homes and he had assembled an entirely new crew.

We exchanged stories of recent happenings into the night. Alistair had spoken to the local military brass about sending out a search plane. Unhappily they had agreed, but considered it a waste of time as no-one could cross the Empty Quarter alone, much less a Nazrani. They would simply be looking for a corpse. Then they had found the well from which the two young nomads had obtained water. Yes, they had been told, there was a lone Nazrani in the area. A guide had led them to the little camp on the plain where they obtained confirmation that I had left the previous morning. To ascertain that it was indeed I that had passed that way Alistair asked various questions.

'Did he have a knife?'

'Yes, he had a knife at his hip.'

'Did he have a bigger knife?'

'Yes, a big curved one. He also had a knife which he talked to.'

This puzzled Alistair until he thought of the walkie-talkie which had a shoulder-strap like the *kukri* and was roughly the same size. He showed them his own, identical one. A miracle. It was absolutely identical. Living in a world where everything was made individually by hand they had probably never before seen two things that were absolutely identical. Further confirmation was obtained by producing his identical compass.

'What was his condition?'

'Very bad.'

'Which way did he go?'

'That way.'

My tracks had been blown away by the wind. Alistair assumed that I would probably be lost in the valley system and wasn't sure what to do about that. There was nothing more that could be done that day, so he returned to Oualata to be told of my arrival.

The next morning we filmed a little at, and near, the well, going through the motions of riding and watering. Then I put two camels up for sale. That was what one did with camels one no longer required. The market was rigged. The Prefect knew that I had to sell quickly as Alistair had to leave that morning for Nouakchott, Mauritania's west coast capital, and I was going with him. I sold Peggy for a fraction of what I paid for her, and Trad I gave to the Prefect at his suggestion. The suggestion of a Prefect in Mauritania carries a little more weight than it would elsewhere.

Then we simply climbed into a Land Rover; the driver, the cameraman, the government fixer, Alistair and myself, and left the dusty town of Oualata, my goal for so long, and two camels with whom I had shared such intensity, without so much as a backward glance. Such was the draining from me of all ability to feel. I had not even bothered to take a photograph.

There is little I remember of that journey of over 600 miles through Mauritania. We stayed the night in a small town and continued down a new metalled road towards Nouakchott, civilisation gradually encroaching and being noted. My mind was not in the banging, roaring Land Rover, but still in the desert with its beauties and its hardships, and its peaceful emptiness across which I had written a thin, brief line. I remember that, from time to time, I would return to the swaying vehicle and speak to Alistair, saying in incredulous tones, 'Alistair . . . I did it!' as a child might seek confirmation and approval.

'Yes, Ted . . . You did it!' Alistair would say, and it was all right.

If we stopped, for fuel or refreshment, he would proudly tell the people what Monsieur Le Professeur had done, whilst I, my ego not having yet caught up with me, would mumble in embarrassment.

In the evening we arrived at the capital, a modern European-style town with one wide, sandy boulevard, and ate superbly for two days. We booked plane tickets, and on the evening before our departure I fell ill. The dragon was having its posthumous revenge. In my weakened state dysentery was a very serious business. All that night I suffered, and most of the following day. When the time came to leave for the airport I was too weak to pack my things and Alistair, steadfast as always, performed the task.

At the airport there were troubles with the authorities, the Edwards Theory of Latitudinal Bureaucracy being much in evidence. I had no entry stamp on my visa, therefore I had not entered Mauritania. How, therefore, could I possibly be granted permission to leave? Our tame fixer tried in vain to explain that at my point of entry there had been no official in evidence. Finally Alistair, resourceful as ever, pointed to my obviously unhealthy state and hinted at some diabolic and virulent plague. I was immediately poured onto the Paris plane mumbling semi-coherently about Bodding-ton's bitter.

By the time our Paris connection arrived at Ringway I was much recovered and we celebrated with fine Manchester beer. The adventure was over. I had wanted it enough.

Our baggage, of course, was lost in Paris. It turned up at the BBC studios a couple of days later and mine was sent home by taxi. As I was heaving Peggy's saddle, my souvenir of the trip, from the back, the taxi-driver asked me, 'What *is* that, mate?'

'It's a Mauritanian camel saddle – innit?'

He viewed it with some doubt, scratched his head, and mused, 'Mauritanian camel saddle eh? . . . Well, I've carried everythin' in this cab now . . . Mauritanian camel saddle . . . Been away then?'

'Just come back from Timbuktu.'

'Oh piss off!' he said, knowingly.

At first friends did not recognise me in the street, so much weight had I lost. I had left these shores an artificially rotund fourteen stone plus and was now little over a skeletal ten. There was public acclaim via the press and media, and it soon became evident that the private life of Ted Edwards was in abeyance. Mine had become a hand to be shaken. My ego having caught up with me this was, for the most part, pleasant, with genuine good will all around. *The Guinness Book of Records* were interested in my journey, it being the longest recorded self-sufficient solo camel journey in history.

In the short two months of my absence relationships had changed, as they always would. Things are inevitably different after a trip, and to set out on one is, in many ways, a minor death; but, always, to return is a small beginning, a birth of new things.

Gradually I came to feel again, and the scars receded, though they would never vanish and, like the old men with their wars, I would always speak of when the adrenalin flowed. But of the real things I could not speak; of the bond between man and beast, and land, which only time and distance could allow into focus. There would be moments in the churn of daily life when I would drift away from those about me and look inwardly outward to the sand, to the Tanezrouft, to Musa, to Ali and Moulaie, to the silent stars, and the roar of the stinging storm, and my eyes would go distant, and damp.

As to my battle, I had not beaten the desert, for the dragon, she-the-desert, and Old Baldie himself, were all inside me.

What of my girls, my bonny lassies? I wonder, often, what became of them. Did they find the easier life they had so richly earned when they set the twenty-day record for camels' waterlessness and ensured their place in camel annals for evermore?

And the thousandth name of Allah? Ah yes! The thousandth name of Allah. It was no mere coincidence that my ladies knew it, for it was 'Peggy' . . . or was it 'Trad?'

Appendix

List of Equipment Taken from England

BASIC

Rope, cord and string (vast quantity)
One gallon container
Two-pint water-bottle, insulated, with strap
Sleeping-bag
Space blanket
Rucksack
Tin-opener
Spare spectacles and case
Pan
Stove } Meta 71
Solid fuel (two packets)
Spoon
Cup
Torch
Two spare torch batteries
One spare bulb
Karrimat
Eight boxes Swan Vestas
Two pounds mixed boiled sweets
Camera with case, strap, haze filter cap and hood (35-mm SLR)
Wide-angle lens and case with lens brush
Six thirty-six exposure Agfa films
16-mm movie camera with tripod and case
16-mm movie film
Lightweight cassette recorder, tapes and batteries
Luggage straps
Ten ballpoint pens
Needle and cotton, etc.
Airmail stationery and paperback books

MEDICAL AND HYGIENE KIT

Veganin and Brufen
Anti-malaria tablets
Halozone tablets
Antibiotics (Ampicillin)
Antiseptic cream
Antacid tablets
Crêpe bandage
Lint
Toilet paper (heavy duty)
Soap
Soap dish
Hand towel
Tissues
Lip salve
Insect-repellant
Toothbrush
Toothpaste
Gentian violet
Anusol
Scissors
Comb
Laxative
Barrier cream
Glucose tablets
Vitamin C tablets
Antihistamine

WEAPONS

Sheath-knife and sheath with carrying strap
Kukri and sheath with carrying strap

NAVIGATION KIT

Maps: Michelin West Africa Sheet 153
      Mali/Mauritania 1:1,000,000 IGS
      Mali 1:200,000 IGS

Optical compass
Wrist compass
Ruler
Protractor
H pencils (two)
Plastic eraser
Log book
Analog-faced mechanical watch; water-, sand- and shock-proof
Quartz digital watch with new battery

CLOTHING

WORN

Tee-shirt
Jeans
Cotton underpants
Woollen socks
Thinsulate jacket
Gore-tex jacket
K-SB-2 lightweight boots
Belt
Woolly hat

CARRIED

Tee-shirt
Cotton underpants
Cotton socks
Burnous
Chèche
Bou-bou

DOCUMENTS

Pouch
Passport
Visa: Mali
Visa: Mauritania
Vaccination Certificates: Cholera
                         Yellow fever
                         Polio

Driving licence
International Driving Permit
Cash
Chequebook
Chequecard
Air ticket: Manchester-London-Algiers
Travellers' cheques
Passport photographs (eight)
French letter

FOOD

Tea-bags
Dried milk
Stock cubes (six)
Salt
Pepper
Tomato Purée (two tubes)
Salt tablets

SCIENTIFIC

Plastic bags
Ties and labels
Instructions

Acquired in Tombouctou

GENERAL

Camels (two)
Mauritanian camel saddle
Baggage saddle
More rope
More cord
Plastic jerricans (four four-gallon)
Pan and lid
Camel-stick
Guerbas très aromatiques

FOOD

Sardines
Beef luncheon meat
Corned beef
More sardines
Pasta
Onions
Jam
Biscuits
More boiled sweets
Peanuts
Lip-ton's
Beer